System Wise

System Wise

Continuous Instructional Improvement at Scale

Adam Parrott-Sheffer

Carmen Williams

David Rease, Jr.

Kathryn Parker Boudett

Harvard Education Press

Cambridge, Massachusetts

Copyright © 2024 by the President and Fellows of Harvard College

Paperback ISBN 9781682538777

Library of Congress Cataloging-in-Publication Data is on file.

Published by Harvard Education Press,
an imprint of the Harvard Education Publishing Group

Harvard Education Press
8 Story Street
Cambridge, MA 02138

Cover Design: Ciano Design
Cover Image: Data Wise Project

The typefaces in this book are Minion Pro, Myriad Pro, Gill Sans MT, and Museo Slab.

CONTENTS

INTRODUCTION

JASMINE, THE ASSISTANT SUPERINTENDENT for the last twelve months at Greenwood School System, reviews her notes for the leadership team strategy retreat scheduled for the following week. Just back from vacation, Jasmine thought she would be energized and ready to rock and roll. But that's not how she's feeling. Yes, she has a vision of what she desires for the system. But if she is honest with herself, she's overwhelmed by the prospect of bringing that vision to life. How is she going to turn this massive ship?

In her previous role in another system, Jasmine experienced success both in leading schools and in engaging with system teams that supported schools through collaborative inquiry processes. While global and national events greatly impacted the normalcy of work during her first year on the job at Greenwood, she knows that the time is right to embark on a systemic change strategy that will require team learning for adults in service of creating more optimal learning environments for students.

Jasmine thinks about what she knows about her new school system and experiences déjà vu. The challenges are so reminiscent of those she faced in her previous job. First, she often hears strong levels of defensiveness when teammates respond to questions about work happening within their divisions. She feels that the culture of the system allows individuals to assign fault to others without implicating themselves—and their actions—in problems. Second, the students, families, and staff members come from a diverse array of religious, ethnic, socioeconomic, language, and racial backgrounds; yet dialogue about the implications of this diversity is nonexistent. Finally, she senses that although the leadership team may appear to work well together because they have few arguments and focus on getting things done, their skill at avoiding conflict means that they are avoiding important conversations about their strongly held opinions.

Jasmine is nevertheless hopeful because she knows that each of her colleagues really cares about students and brings deep skills, knowledge, and commitment to their work. She knows—based on hard experience—that the team will become more skilled at meeting the needs of students only if she and the superintendent create conditions for the group to raise conflict, agree on a shared set of coherent actions, and expand the influence of educators as they engage in improvement work.

1

As Jasmine looks up from her notes, she sees a map of school locations and reflects on how different each school's local context is. How will she and her leadership team ensure results for each student? Families are counting on them. How will they protect the well-being of their staff? Teachers are counting on them. How will they open doors of opportunity and prepare students for jobs that haven't been created yet? The community is counting on them. How will she address the systems that are no longer producing the desired results? Leaders are counting on them. Even as she asks these questions, though, she realizes that a deeper question needs answering: what is *her* role in bringing about change?

In our work supporting educators around the world in collaborative data inquiry, Jasmine's story is quite typical. Our team at the Data Wise Project has encountered many system-level teams composed of smart and kind educators who feel a deep commitment to doing their part so that each student in their care thrives.[1] Some teams effectively align around clear goals and work together for a measured impact. But it seems many more struggle to achieve and sustain their goals. What makes the difference?

We define system-level leaders as "System Wise" when they apply habits of mind and tools of improvement cycles to bring coherence and symmetry to learning across their community of learners. (See figure I.1.) *Coherence* is more than mission alignment; it requires skilled integration of elements, relations, and values.[2] *Symmetry* describes what it looks like when practices in one part of an organization are reflected elsewhere.[3] Nature is filled with examples of these qualities existing together. For example, take the silver fern, a favorite of the Data Wise community since its budding fronds have the same shape as our improvement process. The various parts of this

Figure I.1

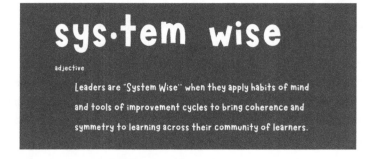

System Wise Definition

sys·tem wise

adjective

Leaders are "System Wise" when they apply habits of mind and tools of improvement cycles to bring coherence and symmetry to learning across their community of learners.

fern are coherent: its roots and stems and leaves all make sense together, working in concert to absorb water, sunlight, and nutrients in service of growth. It also offers a beautiful example of symmetry. As the stems unfold, they reveal a fractal pattern: the shape of an individual stem is repeated in the shape of the leaves that branch off that stem. (See figure I.2.)

Jasmine knows that achieving coherence and symmetry will require her system team to work together differently. Most importantly, she realizes that she is going to have to think critically about how she herself shows up every day. She does not want to be one of those leaders who is so busy performing job duties that they fail to deeply understand how those duties serve children.

There is no such thing as a lone System Wise leader. Instead, they are part of System Wise teams, which have several distinguishing characteristics. First, they recognize that they have a critical role in being the change as they manage

Figure I.2

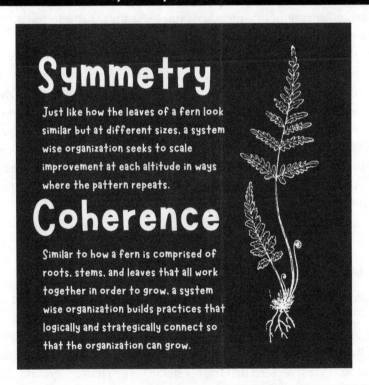

Symmetry and Coherence

Symmetry

Just like how the leaves of a fern look similar but at different sizes, a system wise organization seeks to scale improvement at each altitude in ways where the pattern repeats.

Coherence

Similar to how a fern is comprised of roots, stems, and leaves that all work together in order to grow, a system wise organization builds practices that logically and strategically connect so that the organization can grow.

organization-wide improvement processes. This means that they are willing to adapt how their own teams function even as they seek to influence change in others. Leaders need to do more than model appropriate behaviors: they need to champion the voices and perspectives of those most proximate to the problems. The people who know best what students need are not across the hall from Jasmine's office. They are spread across the map of schools that is hanging on her wall.

Second, System Wise teams support transformation by embracing virtuous cycles of improvement.[4] They are best able to adopt this practice when individual leaders commit and hold one another accountable. Through each cycle, teams build clarity of vision, deepen understanding of their individual and collective identity, increase their capacity to execute strategies, creatively develop methods to assess learning, and create intentional, productive spaces for reflection.

Finally, System Wise teams create conditions where *all people* affected by the organization can participate in transformational practices. With a fern, you see the same pattern whether you are looking through a microscope at a single leaf or through binoculars at a full-grown plant. System Wise teams ensure that whether you are attending a senior leadership team meeting or a brainstorming session for families and other community members, you see familiar patterns too in how people collaborate around evidence to take action for kids.

Does this vision of coherence and symmetry resonate with you? We wrote this book because in working with system-level leaders worldwide, we have gotten to know many leaders like Jasmine who are eager to serve students better. Leaders who hope that as their leadership team grows in its capacity for learning and delivering desired outcomes, the rest of the organization will grow, reproducing wise practices across the many levels or altitudes of the system: divisions, schools, and classrooms. Perhaps, like you, these leaders are inspired by the System Wise vision but are hungry for guidance about how to make the vision a reality. They are looking for insight into the difficult questions: Why? How? What? With this in mind, the next part of this introduction addresses each of these questions in turn.

WHY? SO EACH STUDENT THRIVES

This vision for System Wise leadership can seem simultaneously inspiring and daunting. Surely it is a departure from how most systems currently operate, which can look like lots of people working in silos on more priorities than they can possibly manage. But what could justify taking on the challenge of ushering in a new way of doing business? We have seen that the key lies in system leaders' grounding in a clear statement of *why* they do the work they do. Although the systems we have worked with vary in the exact language they use to describe their purpose, their shared *why* statements always seem to point to meeting the needs of each student. They are also able to

Figure I.3

Equitable Schools

e·qui·ta·ble schools

- Each learner is respected and celebrated for who they are
- Each learner has access to rigorous learning opportunities
- Learner outcomes—whether they be academic, social emotional, or connected to college, career, or community readiness—are not predictable by demographic data

articulate their vision for an equitable school. For many System Wise leaders, their description shares elements of what we at the Data Wise Project use to describe our vision. (See figure I.3.)

HOW? ACE HABITS OF MIND

Clarity on *why* system leaders do their work is essential, but understanding *how* they operate makes it possible to describe the specific behaviors that we see when leaders embrace being the change they hope to see replicated symmetrically across the organization. After several years of studying schools that were engaged in collaborative data inquiry, our team at the Data Wise Project found that there were three habits of mind that distinguished the schools that were able to support real improvements to student learning and those that were not. We call these the ACE Habits of Mind, which include a shared commitment to *action*, *assessment*, and *adjustment*; intentional *collaboration*; and a relentless focus on *evidence*. We have been inspired to see how System Wise teams use their shared values as a North Star and allow the ACE Habits of Mind to guide the organization in everything they do. As figure I.4 shows, each habit fosters equity, offering a compelling alternative to default habits that do just the opposite.

USING THE ACE HABITS OF MIND TO FOSTER EQUITY

A: Shared Commitment to Action, Assessment, and Adjustment

Instead of jumping to action and pressuring educators to get it right the first time, a shared commitment to action, assessment, and adjustment provides System Wise

Figure I.4

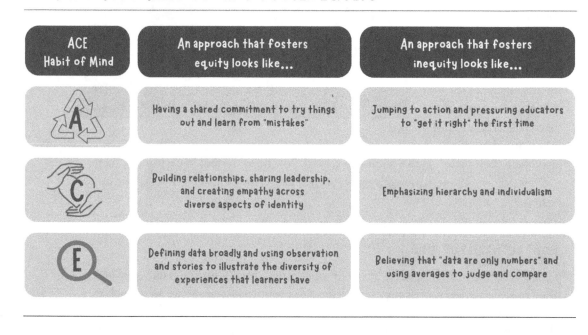

How the ACE Habits of Mind Foster Equity

HOW THE ACE HABITS OF MIND FOSTER EQUITY

ACE Habit of Mind	An approach that fosters equity looks like...	An approach that fosters inequity looks like...
A	Having a shared commitment to try things out and learn from "mistakes"	Jumping to action and pressuring educators to "get it right" the first time
C	Building relationships, sharing leadership, and creating empathy across diverse aspects of identity	Emphasizing hierarchy and individualism
E	Defining data broadly and using observation and stories to illustrate the diversity of experiences that learners have	Believing that "data are only numbers" and using averages to judge and compare

teams with a liberating accountability structure. By practicing this habit of mind, teams enable authentic experiential learning: learning by doing. Teams commonly develop strategic plans and other formal documents that establish multiyear goals with student-focused outcomes. They often cocreate these plans with a group of representative stakeholders. The expectation is that the clarity of the goals and focus on student achievement and well-being will be enough to motivate all members of the organization to do their part. We have seen these good intentions get derailed by changes in personnel, budget, or policy. Systems that adopt a shared commitment to action, assessment, and adjustment are better positioned to stay focused on goals even when a crisis hits. For example, teams with a deep commitment to this habit were better positioned during the global COVID-19 pandemic, when their consistent feedback loops allowed them to monitor progress toward maintaining rigorous academics in an emotionally and physically safe environment.

This habit can prevent acting in knowledge-poor silos and acting with prejudice. System Wise teams use evidence to empower those in the organization with the most relevant knowledge to make decisions. Through this habit of mind, System Wise teams are able to tackle adaptive challenges: those that require people to transform their thinking, being, and believing.[5] System Wise team members commit to individual and collective growth as they embrace learning about the complexity of their context.

C: Intentional Collaboration

Instead of relying on hierarchies and individual efforts, a shared commitment to intentional collaboration entails making deliberate decisions about whom to bring to the table for a conversation. And perhaps most importantly, the conversation is then structured so that the collective wisdom of the assembled group is brought to bear. Many organizations have committed to diversity, equity, inclusion, and belonging efforts to better leverage the strengths that different people bring. These initiatives have included robust employee searches, training on historical context, and community-building exercises. While these serve an important role in developing people and how they work together, cultivating the habit of intentional collaboration means creating conditions that can sustain an authentic culture where *all voices, and especially those at the margins, matter every day.*

Espousing a value for teamwork in an organization is common, but it doesn't always translate to effective teamwork in practice. This habit of mind supports teams in actually enacting values such as inclusion, creativity, and vulnerability. For example, when an organization values inclusion, it moves away from doing work *for* others and toward doing work *with* others. This shift requires teams to be creative in their processes for honoring multiple perspectives to understand the problems, to develop solutions that invite others to share their wisdom, and to experiment in collaborative structures while learning from mistakes with humility. System Wise teams create symmetrical structures that enable intentional collaboration at and between every level of the system in service of coherence.[6]

E: A Relentless Focus on Evidence

Instead of believing that numerical data are all that matters, maintaining a relentless focus on evidence is about defining data broadly and seeing value in observation and stories. In this book, we use "data" and "evidence" interchangeably because both words have been part of the common discourse for many years. But if we had to do it over again, we might have named our first book *Evidence Wise*, as a way to help readers call to mind the broader definition instead of getting caught up in a restrictive definition: one that leaves many teachers feeling like data are something that can get in the way of understanding what their students need.

While "maintaining a relentless focus on evidence" might seem like a straight-forward thing, it can create tension for an experienced leader. Often those with longevity in the field expect and are expected to contribute their wisdom and apply their understanding in leadership roles. A relentless focus on evidence requires leaders to draw on experience and yet be open to new information. We have seen how System Wise leaders develop self-awareness both to understand how their story creates a unique entry point to the work and to learn how to set aside their opinions and biases to focus on evidence. We have appreciated how System Wise teams use this habit of mind to manage complexity: they recognize that individuals are always swimming in a vast sea of data that they interpret through personal experience, and they appreciate that the collective group is needed to see the whole of what these data describe. By exploring multiple forms of evidence, it becomes possible to tell new stories and understand deeply entrenched problems in a new light.

A strong sense of urgency can drive leaders to go with their gut and use previous experiences to make decisions. That same urgency can tempt them to take the easiest route, which may be to use average assessment scores to judge and compare instead of looking more closely at individual student needs. System Wise leaders demonstrate humility by asking questions and resisting the pressure to always have the right answer. Humbly asking questions requires teams to slow the process to gather and analyze evidence, rather than reducing discomfort and jumping to action without due diligence. System Wise teams depend on protocols and other structures to enable consistency in practice until evidence-based inquiry becomes part of the culture or "how we do things."

System Wise leaders use the ACE Habits of Mind as daily touchstones and trusted guardrails when things get hard. When outside events or internal dynamics make leaders feel stuck and frustrated, System Wise teams go back to the ACE Habits of Mind to find their path forward. The repetition of this practice can generate a "causal loop" that strengthens a team's resolve to lean on the ACE Habits the next time things get tough.[7]

WHAT? THE DATA WISE IMPROVEMENT PROCESS

With a clear statement of *why* system leaders do the work they do and the ACE Habits to guide *how* they approach their work, system leaders are well positioned to be effective in *what* they do. In this book, we focus on the aspect of system-level leaders' work that involves continuous improvement of practice, and the framework we use is the Data Wise improvement process. This process was originally designed by educators from Boston Public Schools and researchers from the Harvard Graduate School of Education to capture what equity-minded educators in schools were doing to work collaboratively to improve classroom instruction and student achievement. But leaders using Data Wise across school systems identified the need for a universal Data Wise improvement process that could be used with educators at any level of the organization. A revised version of the universal process is now the process that the Data Wise Project recommends for schools as well.[8]

The goal of this process is to improve what happens in the *learning core*: the critical relationships among learners, facilitators, and content.[9] You may be familiar with how the term "instructional core" has been used to describe relationships in the classroom; in this book we use Elizabeth City and Adonius Lewis's adaptation, since "learning core" more flexibly shows that it is not just students who learn and it is not just teachers who facilitate.[10]

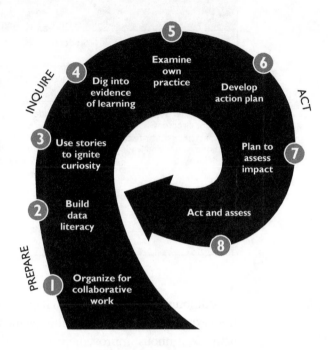

When educators use the Data Wise improvement process, they need to consider who is the "learner" that their team will be supporting in improving outcomes. Table I.1 shows how different teams support different learners and can choose different focus areas, or aspects of the system that the team would like to improve.

In this book, we describe how System Wise leaders answer questions about why, what, and how as they relate to each step of the Data Wise improvement process. Each chapter begins with an essential question and a case study to ground you in the experiences and challenges of real leaders enacting what real conversations at this step can sound like. We then describe the strategic tasks involved at this step, providing guidance where necessary about how tasks might differ if you are using the process to improve the ability of your system-level team to support the adult learners you directly serve or whether you are using it to structure your effort to scale Data Wise across your system. Each chapter concludes with examples of the System Wise approach and a return to the case study.

Table I.I

Different Teams Serve Different Learners		
WHO ON THE TEAM IS ENGAGING IN THE IMPROVEMENT PROCESS?	**WHO MIGHT BE THIS TEAM'S "LEARNERS"?**	**WHAT IS AN EXAMPLE OF A FOCUS AREA FOR THIS TEAM'S DATA WISE CYCLE?**
Teachers, instructional coaches	Students	Literacy
School, instructional leadership team	Teachers	Supporting students in asking generative questions
School leader supervisors, content directors	School leaders, teachers	Providing effective feedback on teacher practice
Senior system-level leaders	System division leaders, school leader supervisors, school leaders, networks of schools, teachers	Developing staff capacity to work together to solve problems
Guiding team	System division leaders, school leader supervisors, school leaders, networks of schools, teachers	Scaling Data Wise across a system

Although we organized our chapters to follow each step in sequence, we know from experience that powerful improvement work can happen without taking a linear path. Continuous improvement cycles at the system level are, by nature, complex and guaranteed to be messy. The steps provide a convenient organizing structure for the book, but you will know best the most effective entry point and pathway for your organization.

Chapter 1 kicks off the prepare phase and explains how System Wise teams *organize for collaborative work* by sharing stories about evidence sources they value as a strategy for uniting teams and coming to a shared purpose grounded in equity. This approach to value-setting centers the humanity of both educators and the students they serve and leads them to consider many sources of evidence, instead of defaulting to overreliance on standardized data sources. Chapter 2 describes how teams then *build data literacy* and assess system capacity to improve instruction at scale. This includes using system readiness criteria to identify a promising point of entry and aligning efforts to a framework that will bring coherence across the system.

The inquire phase begins with chapter 3, where System Wise leaders *use stories to ignite curiosity* and set a vision for wild instructional success. Wild success describes those hopes and dreams we have for our learners and ourselves that we wish for desperately but are afraid to claim in fear that speaking them will make us sound foolish and unrealistic in our ambitions. It is important to ground this vision in the sensual: what will success look like, sound like, and feel like? Chapter 4 describes how teams then *dig into evidence of learning* and develop a symmetric learning-centered problem that captures what needs to happen at all levels of the organization to influence the critical relationships in the learning core. Then in chapter 5, teams *examine their own practice*, turning the mirror on themselves and conducting a candid assessment of how their actions are supporting or hindering the system's vision of wild success.

The act phase opens with chapter 6, where System Wise teams *develop an action plan* that builds coherence across the system. The idea here is to design a strategy that is symmetric from system to school to classroom and directly implicates each leader in influencing what happens in the learning core. In chapter 7, leaders *plan to assess impact,* with a particular emphasis on using program implementation data to sustain the work. Effective program implementation requires gathering information on participants' reactions and learning, organizational support and change, participants' use of new knowledge and skills, and student learning outcomes, with an emphasis on collecting this information in ways that allow for fine-tuned adjustments in implementation.[11] In chapter 8, teams *act and assess*. They use evidence to improve the practice of individuals, their team, the structures and systems of the organization, and the efficacy of school teams. They also use evidence to communicate learning across the organization as well as with students, families, and community members.

In the final chapter, we offer our own story of how our team at the Data Wise Project worked to increase our capacity to serve educators in building equitable schools worldwide. We hope that by sharing candidly our own experience, we can offer some inspiration to tackle the daunting but rewarding work of scaling wisely.

TAKING A SYSTEM WISE APPROACH

There are many unique demands of system-level work, and these require what we call a *System Wise approach.* As System Wise leaders apply habits of mind and tools of improvement cycles to bring coherence and symmetry to learning, they attend to dimensions of scale, expect the unexpected, manage the change process, and practice radical inclusivity. Next, we provide an overview of each of these four practices; in each chapter, we share real stories from a wide variety of contexts that show how twenty-eight System Wise leaders have brought them to life.

Attend to Dimensions of Scale

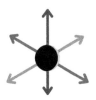

As she prepares for the beginning-of-year retreat, Jasmine is thinking about system teams, school leaders, and classroom teachers focusing and improving their work. Her desire for symmetry across all levels of the organization is fundamentally a challenge of scale.

Too often, scaling is operationalized in practice as simply doing more of something in new places or with new people. Whether the measure is schools served, teachers trained, or revenue earned, the goal is *more*, so success is measured by quantity. This definition of scale leads to several challenges for leaders. First, it often privileges those ideas and actions that are easiest to replicate. These can include aspects of a change effort that are most technical or performative because the focus is on seeing actions occur and not on the impact of those actions. Second, it often prioritizes ideas and actions that can be done *to* other people instead of *with* them. Speed is overvalued and initiatives mandated with little attention to local context and building shared ownership. Finally, focusing on more helps to create the initiative churn that is all too common in our public institutions. When ideas or actions are implemented in new places or with new people without understanding why they worked in one place or which aspects of the change are most important, the initiatives often fail. This leads to abandoning ideas or actions that might have worked if people came together to adjust the ideas to better fit their context.

System Wise leaders work to avoid these pitfalls by understanding the multiple dimensions of scale and being intentional about how and when to focus on each dimension (see figure I.5). Cynthia Coburn and Chris Dede provide a helpful framework that distinguishes between five dimensions of scale: depth, sustainability, spread, shift, and evolution.[12] There are trade-offs and tensions between these dimensions: attending to one may make it harder to achieve the others. But if an improvement is going to take root across an entire system, eventually all will be important.

Let's take an example: suppose you are seeking to scale the Data Wise improvement process at every level of your organization. How might you attend to each dimension?

DEPTH. Depth concerns the nature and quality of implementation. It involves not just changing structures and procedures but changing beliefs and ways of working together. You may find that changes to adult culture and student learning happen in the first year that teams begin integrating the process, habits, and norms into their practice. But we have to be honest here: teams regularly report needing to use the process for two to three years before they see transformational improvements to teaching and learning. Why? It takes some time for educators to experience the difference between *doing* Data Wise and *being* Data Wise. Scaling for depth can feel like digging a well. When you first start digging, you may not see results right away. But if you have planned carefully and aligned with your colleagues' core values, the commitment to going deeper allows you to tap into a generative spring. If you prioritize depth, you may decide to provide intensive support to a smaller number of teams at the outset, with the idea that these teams can be living proof that *yes, collaborative data inquiry can work here.*

SUSTAINABILITY. Sustainability refers to the ability for a change to persist over time despite all the pressures toward entropy in organizations. Scaling for sustainability is like working with the ecosystem that surrounds a pond or lake, which allows water levels to replenish themselves even as seasons change. It involves attending to threats of change in team personnel, leadership, strategic priorities, and resources in order to protect and cultivate what is most critical to the change effort. When scaling Data Wise across your system, you will find that building the capacity of multiple people to lead the work and protecting collaborative time can help ensure that the work can go on even as circumstances change.

SPREAD. Spread is about sharing the process widely with new people; it is the dimension of scale that most people think of first. It is a river that takes the practice from place to place. But as a leader who is working to spread Data Wise practices across your system, you can't just sprinkle seeds and hope for the best. You need to cultivate the soil so that new teams are receptive to change and adjust system-level policies to be coherent with this new approach to working. Depth and sustainability might seem like the most important dimensions to prioritize, but if you wait too long to attend to spread, you may find that those who were not initially included feel left out, or that you have undermined your commitment to

Figure I.5

Types of Scale

Ways to Scale Data Wise

Deepen

Sustain

Spread

Shift

Evolve

Graphic inspired by the work of Cynthia Coburn and Chris Dede

systemwide coherence. For this reason, many leaders begin by engaging everyone in the first couple of Data Wise steps right away, with the understanding that all teams may not progress at the same pace.

SHIFT. Shift in ownership is what happens when teams embrace a change to such a degree that they are doing it because they want to and wouldn't have it any other way. Imagine the power of a waterfall as gravity starts to do the work. You know shift is happening when you hear colleagues using Data Wise language to explain what they are doing and what they need. You *really* know that shift is happening when there is a leadership change and people won't give up their habits of mind and ways of working because *this is how we do things now.*

EVOLUTION. Evolution typically follows shift and is about adapting an approach to respond to new conditions or to solve different problems. Like water goes from liquid to solid or gas depending on conditions, initiatives need to be able to change in new environments. This very book came about because of evolution: system leaders modified and adopted what started as a process for teacher teams in order to solve instructional coherence challenges across their organizations. As you work to scale the Data Wise improvement process across your system, you will discover that the very people who relied on you to learn the process are now your best teachers about where the system needs to go.

Expect the Unexpected

 What can make improvement so difficult is that you do not know with certainty the impact of your actions. Jasmine does not know what will happen if she and her team commit to shifting toward a culture focused on coherence and symmetry. Nor do they know what outside forces they will encounter once they get started. But that's just how the world works. A helpful definition of a system might be that it is *the level of organizational complexity where crisis is a predictable and cyclical feature of the context and where crisis is oftentimes the main driver of change.* In this definition, system leadership is the set of skills required to make positive change within the context of cyclical crises.

When working at scale, we need to expect the unexpected. We are wise to remember Phileas Fogg's confidence, when preparing for his round-the-world journey in Jules Verne's *Around the World in 80 Days,* that "the unforeseen does not exist."[13] We, the *System Wise* authors, *know* that at the very moment you are reading this book, there is a major climate event happening somewhere on this planet. We also know that sometime in the not-too-distant future, your organization will face a threat that will take some (or all) of your focus off instructional improvement. And just as we *don't know* whether the climate event is a fire, an earthquake, a tornado, or something else, we don't know if the next crisis your organization will face will be a leadership scandal, a financial meltdown, a violent act, a global pandemic, or something else. Because the specific details of each crisis are novel and unanticipated, too many systems grow tunnel vision and bounce from crisis to crisis in a never-ending game of organizational whack-a-mole. This creates deep initiative fatigue and the mindset that improvement cannot happen at the system level.

While the maxim *If you can predict it, you can prevent it* might not describe these events, System Wise leaders do subscribe to their own version—*If you can predict it, you can plan for it and respond to it in order to ensure that learning continues as a priority*. There is power in normalizing crisis, as long as we do not minimize it or allow it to reduce our sense of efficacy. System Wise leaders define the continuum of unexpected occurrences and design systems and structures to sustain learning improvement efforts that are resilient to the pressures on the system.

Table I.2 summarizes several events of varying severity that system leaders can envision confronting during their tenure. One of the purposes of slower, more intentional improvement processes is to insulate the core work from the paralysis that tags along with crisis. While we wouldn't argue that there is value in preparing for learning after extremely unlikely but possible species-ending events, we think

Table I.2

A Continuum of Unexpected Events			
LIKELY TO HAPPEN EVERY 1–5 YEARS	**LIKELY TO HAPPEN WITHIN A GENERATION**	**LIKELY TO HAPPEN WITHIN A LIFETIME**	**EXTREMELY UNLIKELY BUT POSSIBLE**
A leadership change	Civil unrest	An organizational takeover	A giant asteroid hits Earth
Recession	Financial crisis	War/multinational violence	Nuclear war
New political priorities	Technology innovation or disruption	Global pandemic	
Organizational restructuring	Significant legal decision delivered by a high court		
Curriculum change			

there is much that leaders can do to support learning through the other types of crises, and many of which became more salient during the COVID-19 pandemic.

System Wise leaders anticipate that a *crisis will put new demands on time and people*. A crisis likely means that fewer people are available and that the people who are available will not always be fully present. System Wise leaders build slack into their plans and adjust timelines as appropriate. Most importantly, they realize that the one part of the learning equation that will always be present is the *learner*. Therefore, they design their work in ways that emphasize the agency and autonomy of learners. They know that the person doing the work is the person doing the learning.

System Wise leaders anticipate that a *crisis will reallocate resources*. All the crises listed in figure I.6 would reduce the resources available for learning or how they can be used. System Wise leaders appreciate that having *fewer* resources does not mean having *no* resources, and that not knowing how you will achieve your goals should not prevent you from taking the steps available to you today. We have seen that places with no contractually available time for collaboration and no additional money to incentivize improvement work will find ways to collaborate. During the pandemic, this ability to adjust resource allocation was most evident in the places where there were creative shifts to virtual and asynchronous instruction. In conflict zones, we have worked with educators who collaborated and taught through WhatsApp when all other infrastructure was destroyed.

System Wise leaders anticipate that a *crisis will create a shift in values*. A crisis causes us to see the world differently. We might view things with a mindset of scarcity. We might see life as more precious and reevaluate what is important to us. We might try to prepare for imagined threats or live each day as our last. System Wise leaders know that crises are liminal moments where who we are as individuals and who we are collectively are no longer who we will be. Lots of people and organizations experienced the winnowing effects of a crisis during the pandemic as it became clearer what mattered most.

Attending to a crisis while continuing the core learning work of a system requires leaders to know what is most important to learning. System Wise leaders anchor their leadership to the ACE Habits of Mind and use these habits to weather inevitable storms. As they confront crises, they reimagine what collaboration looks like in the new context. They redefine what evidence should ground their efforts.

Figure I.6

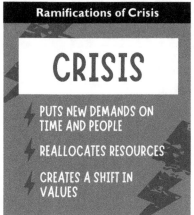

They assess, act, and adjust at a different level of intensity or speed. Ultimately, System Wise leaders view each crisis through the learning core. With learning simplified to the relationships between learners, facilitators, and content, they can build a path to improvement through the assets available, informed by the ACE Habits of Mind.

Manage the Change Process

 Jasmine is stuck; she does not know where to begin. She desires change but is not clear on what needs to happen to manage the process or define her role within the change effort. System change literacy requires an understanding of what System Wise leaders must do regardless of the specific details of the particular change effort. This is the literacy of managing the change process in a way that advances equity.[14]

- System Wise leaders are *responsive to relationships*. These leaders recognize that change will bring differing feelings and reactions, so they create space to engage and attend to these impacts. They hold space for individual and collective processing and for developing connectedness among all members of the community.

- System Wise leaders *champion change*. Inclusive leaders inspire and call stakeholders to action through their communication about the change. This includes the frequency of communication, formats for communication, and the inclusion of diverse stakeholders in development and dissemination of the communication. As a result of this attention to communication, all members of the organization can embody the why, how, and what of the change.

- System Wise leaders *map the movement*. Inclusive leaders consistently check and refine change efforts based on the impact on key stakeholders to ensure change is leading to more equitable opportunities for students.

- System Wise leaders *attend to power*. Inclusive leaders attend to power dynamics and leverage "power *with*" instead of "power *over*" as they structure and implement change efforts.

These actions facilitate an equitable approach to change and help ensure that leaders do not misuse their roles to replicate the inequities currently baked into their organization or their leadership. (See figure I.7.)

Figure I.7

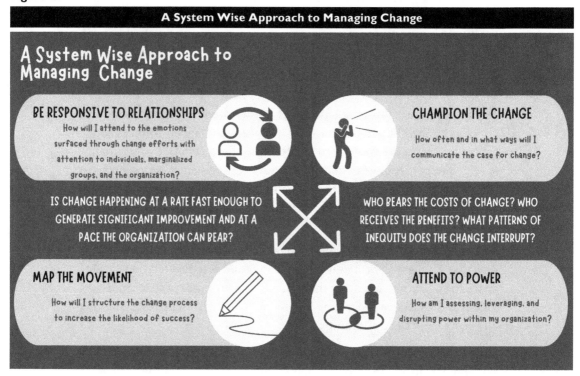

A System Wise Approach to Managing Change

Practice Radical Inclusivity

 Jasmine feels the weight of having so many people counting on her and her team: students, families, teachers, leaders, and the broader community. She has a really important choice to make. She can shoulder this weight and use her best judgment to make decisions, or she can foster a culture that values collaboration and develop structures that support inclusive practices. She feels an immense amount of pressure to do what is best *for* the organization, but is there an opportunity to do what is best *with* the organization?

System leaders are uniquely positioned within their organizations to both build and dismantle structures in service of the vision and mission of the organization. System Wise teams are charged with recognizing oppressive structures that yield inequitable outcomes and working collaboratively to remove these barriers. This collaboration requires *radical inclusivity*, which ensures that voices across all levels of the system are heard and that the perspectives of students and the community—especially the most marginalized members—are taken into account.

Data inquiry cycles provide system leaders with a common language and experience for seeing and understanding the systems they intend to impact.[15] The individual perspectives, assets, and wisdom of leaders are important, but system change management is a collective effort. When you commit to the ACE Habits of Mind and an equity lens, you are committing to transforming your culture. As stated earlier, the Data Wise Project describes an equitable school as one where each learner is respected and celebrated for who they are, each learner has access to rigorous learning opportunities, and learner outcomes—whether they be academic, social-emotional, or connected to college, career, and community readiness—are not predictable by demographic data. If this is the goal for an equitable *school*, then an equitable *system* is one that creates the conditions where educators have aligned beliefs, values, strategy, capacity, and resources to build and sustain equitable schools.

While system leaders need to develop a lens for equity and identify structures that perpetuate inequity, the "how" of this work requires teams to practice radical inclusivity. Traditionally, leadership teams have held the responsibility and privilege of identifying problems, solutions, and criteria for success. And historically, top leaders of organizations have disproportionately been white (in the United States) and male, demographics that do not typically represent the organization as a whole. Radical inclusivity involves significant and purposeful engagement with all community members to share leadership throughout the continuous improvement process. Radical inclusivity is the connective tissue that aligns the organization's values, beliefs, and actions to shift the culture in favor of equity.

Figure I.8 offers a series of questions to prompt System Wise teams as they reconstruct systems to create radically inclusive organizations. These questions are set against a backdrop of an iceberg to indicate that, although system actions are visible to all, the beliefs and values that lie beneath the surface are equally important to acknowledge and address.[16] The questions are grouped along a developmental continuum that starts with *awareness* of the need to include others and progresses to *engagement* of multiple voices before getting to *radical inclusivity* as a sustained approach. While it is a progression, most leaders will be addressing awareness, engagement, and radical inclusivity at the same time in different parts of the organization.

Returning to these prompts regularly supports system teams in practicing radical inclusivity. When your team commits to enacting your value for equity, you give permission, provide the structures, and develop an organizational culture that is conditioned to deliver equitable outcomes for students.

Figure I.8

A Developmental Path to Radical Inclusivity

A System's Developmental Path to
Radical Inclusivity

	AWARENESS	ENGAGEMENT	RADICAL INCLUSIVITY
SYSTEM ACTIONS	TO WHAT DEGREE HAVE WE ALLOWED OUR VALUE FOR TRADITION, PRECEDENT, PRACTICES, AND DOMINANT CULTURE TO GUIDE OUR DATA COLLECTION AND ANALYSIS PRACTICES?	HOW MIGHT WE PROVIDE ADEQUATE REPRESENTATION OF IDENTITY, EXPERIENCE, AND EXPERTISE ON OUR TEAM?	HOW CAN WE AUTOMATE FEEDBACK LOOPS AND ACTION STEPS THAT EXPRESS OUR VALUE FOR DIVERSE VOICES AND WORKING STYLES?
SYSTEM BELIEFS	WHAT ASSUMPTIONS ARE WE HOLDING AND WHAT FACTORS ARE INFLUENCING OUR THINKING?	HOW HAVE WE DEVELOPED AND COMMUNICATED OUR SHARED VISION FOR AN EQUITABLE SYSTEM?	HOW IS OUR VISION OF EQUITY REFLECTED ACROSS ALL LEVELS OF THE ORGANIZATION?
SYSTEM VALUES	HOW HAVE WE PRIORITIZED DATA SOURCES?	HOW DO WE RECOGNIZE THE STRENGTHS AND ASSETS OF OUR TEAM AND COMMUNITY?	WHAT STRUCTURES BEST SUPPORT OUR ABILITY TO REMAIN CURIOUS?

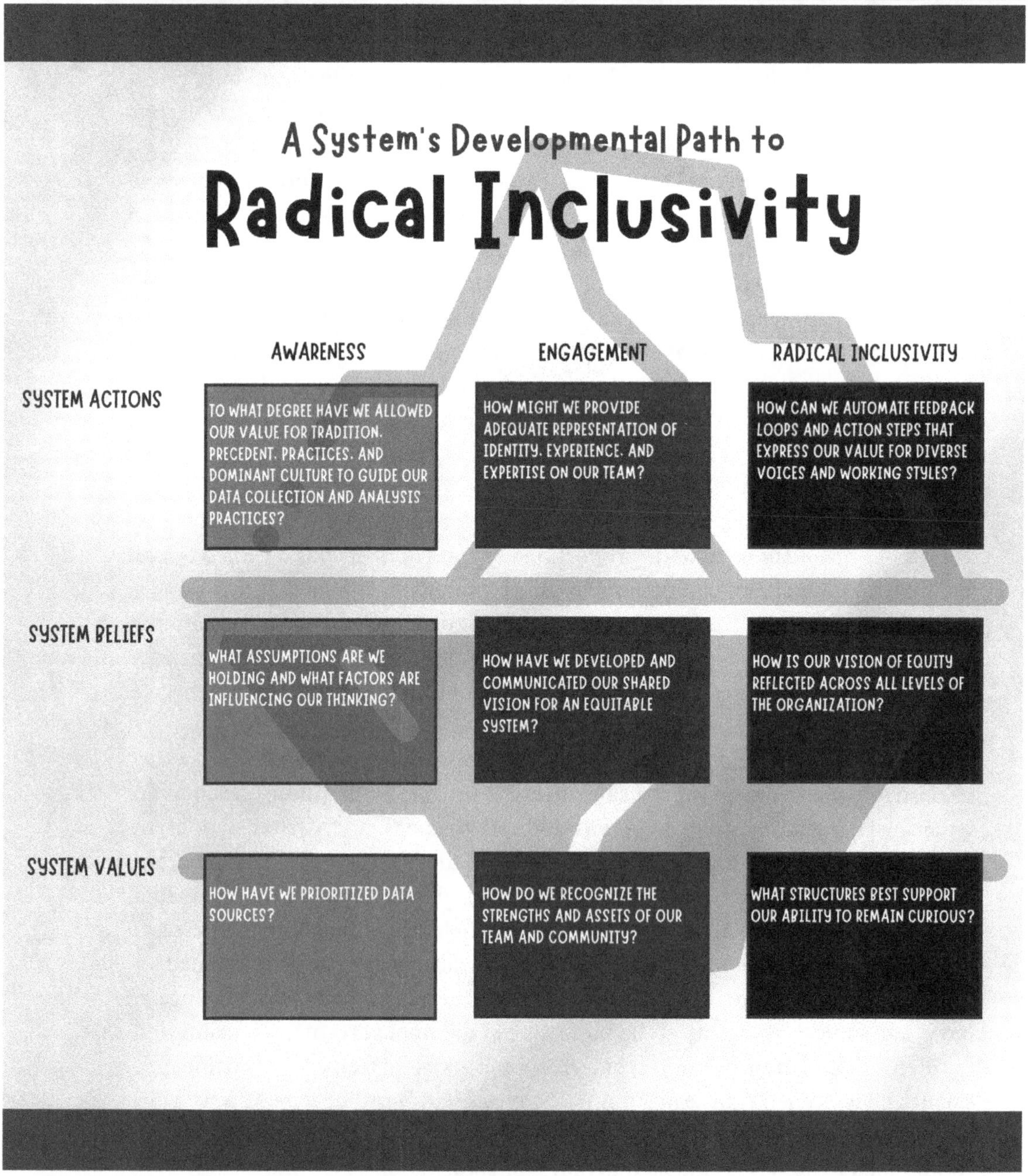

INTEGRATING THE SYSTEM WISE APPROACH INTO THE DATA WISE FRAMEWORK

Figure I.9 offers a visual representation of how System Wise leaders address the three questions that we explored at the beginning of this chapter. "Why?" is the most important question, so it is only fitting that the halo of equity questions surrounding

Figure I.9

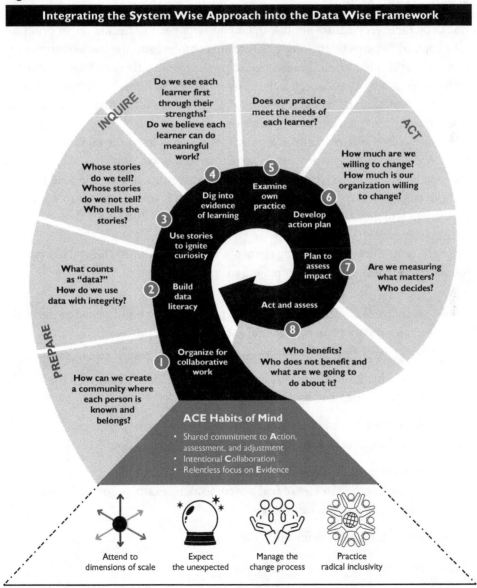

Integrating the System Wise Approach into the Data Wise Framework

the work take up the most space. "How?" is foundational, which is why the ACE Habits of Mind are the sturdy base holding up the eight-step process, which answers the question "What?" Beneath the Data Wise framework are the four icons that symbolize what is involved in taking a System Wise approach to this work.

HOW TO USE THIS BOOK

Books by their very nature are linear, and authors need to decide on an order for the chapters. Systems by their very nature are complex, and the work of improving them is *anything but* linear. Books also elevate the perspective and judgment of the authors, yet in our experience, it is the perspective and judgment of the practitioners closest to the problem (you, our readers!) that matters most. The pages that follow represent our effort to resolve these tensions.

As described earlier in this introduction, we have used the eight steps of the Data Wise improvement process to structure this book. But that doesn't mean that you need to engage with these ideas in a linear way. You can be System Wise without engaging in formal inquiry cycles, and even if you do choose to do formal cycles, you will quickly realize that, in practice, improvement doesn't happen in a step-by-step way.

Each chapter has the following elements, and you may find it helpful to first read the elements that seem most compelling to you:

- A stylized *case study* that threads throughout the book, showing the challenges system teams can face at each step of the process

- An analysis of how the *ACE Habits of Mind* do or do not show up in the case, which includes an exploration of how leaders' actions are informed by their values, beliefs, and mindsets

- A detailed description of the *strategic tasks* associated with each step, with examples, checklists, and templates for implementation

- A discussion of what a *System Wise approach* looks like at each step, featuring multiple stories of real system leaders, examples of work products, and a return to the case study

- *Reflection questions* for discussion

We've also included a System Wise tools section in the appendix at the end of the book, which includes:

- *Two sample throughlines*, tracing how Jasmine's *leadership team* used the Data Wise improvement process to improve their support of learners they directly serve (school leaders) and another showing how the system's *guiding team* used the process to scale Data Wise across Greenwood School System

- *Big ideas of data literacy*, a high-level summary of concepts that support responsible data use

- *Templates* that you can use in your improvement work

- *Protocols* for structuring focused discussions that practice radical inclusivity

Reader, the choice is yours. Turn the page and explore how you might organize your team for collaborative work. Jump to the chapter that most closely resembles where you are stuck in your improvement journey. Skim the chapter specifics on the ACE Habits of Mind or taking a System Wise approach. This book is *our* vision of wild success for what System Wise leadership could look like, but you need to paint your own. Although the book is grounded in evidence and written collaboratively, we expect that you will act, assess, and adjust its ideas to take into account your context and collective wisdom. As you embark on this journey, we invite you to join our community of learners and share your story.

We give you permission to hack this book. However, we hope that by the time you are done reading it, you realize you never needed permission in the first place. If you hack it based on evidence gathered and analyzed with a team in order to assess and adjust your actions to serve kids better, then you have plenty to teach others (including us!) about being System Wise.

1

ORGANIZING FOR COLLABORATIVE WORK

> How can we create a community where each person is known and belongs?

SEVEN MINUTES AFTER THE 8:00 A.M. start time of the meeting to plan the beginning-of-year retreat for the leadership team, a team member enters the room and silently mouths an apology. Jasmine, the assistant superintendent, clears her throat and announces, "Now that everyone is here, we should get started. As you know, literacy is a priority this year given how many students were not proficient on the state language arts assessment. We need teachers to work together to use data more consistently to meet the needs of all learners."

A few team members shift in their seats. "Of course, having data is important; I'm all for teachers using helpful data to make decisions," responds one person. "But this is a contract negotiation year, and I can't spend political capital on mandating common planning time when we likely will need to adjust salary schedules. Anyway, those assessments do not tell us anything useful about *why* some students are struggling. We need to deal with a leaner budget and consider more teacher autonomy before—"

"Are we already giving up on improving teaching?" interrupts another. "The mayor just announced their priority for investing in early childhood. We need a systemwide focus on universal preschool and family engagement."

The person next to Jasmine nods in agreement and whispers, "Our most vulnerable students—especially those from racially, culturally, and socially marginalized groups—are not served well. We need to focus on our state audit of special education services."

As the conversation goes on, Jasmine can feel the swirl of emotions in the room. Jasmine wonders how people who work together every day and care deeply about their work can see the organization and their priorities so differently. She came to this school system committed to sharing leadership and empowering her team to make decisions, but that doesn't seem to be working. Before she opens her mouth to respond, she wonders whether she just needs to lead in a more directive manner—at least for the next couple of years.

ACE HABITS OF MIND IN STEP 1

In Step 1, System Wise teams combine a shared purpose with the ACE Habits of Mind to ground their actions in shared values. Let's consider this case through these three habits (see figure 1.1).

Figure 1.1

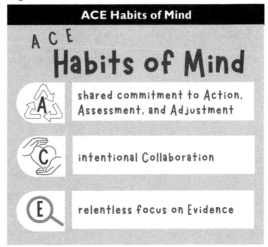

A: Shared Commitment to Action, Assessment, and Adjustment

Jasmine is wavering, unsure what to do. The question, "Where do we begin?" is one many teams have. The work of continuous improvement sometimes feels too large and unwieldy. When she accepted the role of assistant superintendent, she envisioned that she would practice distributed leadership to address the many adaptive challenges facing the system. A sense of urgency combined with a fear of inadequacy can make it tempting to just do something. But adaptive challenges by their very nature require people to co-construct solutions to problems. Deep down, Jasmine knows that if she tries to force the system to do things her way, she will fail. Part of the commitment to *action* is knowing when it is not yet time to act.

Jasmine opens the meeting with *her* priorities. She states her priority of focusing on literacy and expresses her value of using data to inform instruction and her concern that the system lacks the capacity to use data well. Before she can make the case for what she thinks should happen, another member of the team questions the validity of the inferences that can be drawn from assessment data, and others advocate for alternative priorities. These leaders are clearly not on the same page, yet they are engaged and willing to bring their perspectives to the table. If Jasmine had made room to surface the many perspectives in the room, she would have had the opportunity to *assess* where her team is and to make *adjustments*.

C: Intentional Collaboration

System leaders have the opportunity to create intentional spaces where team members with differing opinions can authentically listen to one another and commit to working collaboratively. In the Greenwood case, there are several instances of actions that are not collaborative. A late entrant holds up the meeting start time for everyone, which could send a signal to colleagues that she thinks whatever she was doing was more important than respecting the time of her waiting colleagues. One team member interrupts another mid-sentence. Is everyone allowed to interrupt, or just the people with the most power or loudest voices? Jasmine is still relatively new to the Greenwood School System. She is continuing to learn the historical and relational context that informs team members' mental models and interpersonal dynamics. She is learning that there is a continuum of stakeholder perspectives from "we don't have a problem" to "we have a deep-seated systemic problem." Supporting the team in cultivating the habit of mind of *intentional collaboration* will require setting norms and using strategies that draw out the collective wisdom and purpose of the group.

The process of creating a shared purpose, which we call a shared *why* statement, allows the team members to see what they have in common. When this statement is developed by first having team members share about who they are, what they believe about equity, and how that impacts how they approach their work, team members begin to know that each person on the team will be heard, seen, and valued. This conversation shows that each member has unique assets and can inspire the team to leverage those assets so that together they can achieve more than they could as individuals.

But for a shared *why* to be useful, the team needs to commit to norms of collaboration, sometimes called community agreements, that clarify how they will treat one another as they work toward bringing their shared *why* to life. This is the next level of work for Jasmine and her team.

E: Relentless Focus on Evidence

Contemplating where to begin in a change effort is a significant effort on its own. There are so many priorities to consider, and each person's rationale for their stated priority may differ. This is when cultivating the habit of mind of maintaining a *relentless focus on evidence* is essential. Jasmine tries to direct the group's attention to performance on the state test, another team member points to data from a state audit of services, and others draw on their observation of political realities. Each person is confident about the power of the data they know well, but the team members are not yet in the habit of providing specific and descriptive evidence to support their arguments. On the surface, they are using inferences made from these data sources to argue for opposing priorities. But if they had a shared *why* and the discipline to look closely at evidence together, they might see that they need multiple sources of evidence to serve their shared purpose.

Even before collecting evidence connected to their shared *why*, System Wise leaders need to think about what evidence they have that their team is ready to meaningfully engage in continuous improvement. It is important that teams create safe, brave spaces to authentically share not just who they are and what they *know* but also where they are on their professional journey and what they *don't know*. Sometimes the leader herself needs to model using evidence. After all, when Jasmine asserts that the system needs "teachers to use data more consistently to meet the needs of all learners," what evidence does she offer to show that she knows what teachers' data practices actually look like?

STRATEGIC TASKS FOR STEP 1

So how do you get started using a continuous improvement approach? The goal of Step 1 is to launch a collaborative and aligned team that is well prepared to engage in improvement work. (See figure 1.2.) The Data Wise "swoosh" is especially wide at this part of the process because it has to be: the remaining steps of the process need a broad base of support on which to rest. Your team's ability to collaborate effectively depends on intentional design of both the team itself and the structures it will use.

The strategic tasks for Step 1 include establishing the structures of inquiry, preparing to team effectively, and taking stock to inform scope. As you read this book, begin thinking about why you are learning about the Data Wise improvement process. Is it because your system leadership team plans to use this process to improve your ability to build the capacity of the adults you directly serve? Or are you planning to scale the Data Wise improvement process to schools across your system? Perhaps your intuition (or your Data Wise coach) is telling you that you will eventually be using it for both purposes? If so, your intuition or coach is onto something. But on your first time through this book, you may find it helpful to keep one or the other purpose in mind.

Next, we describe the strategic tasks for Step 1, clarifying the situations where this task looks different depending on whether you are using Data Wise to improve your own practice or if you are scaling Data Wise.

Figure 1.2

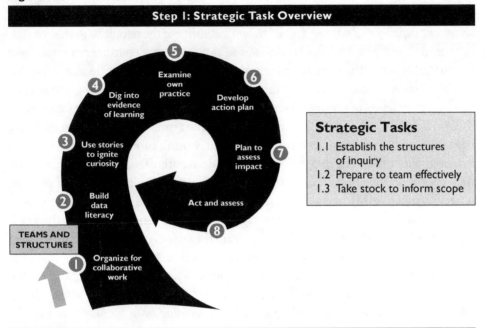

Step 1: Strategic Task Overview

⑤ Examine own practice

④ Dig into evidence of learning

⑥ Develop action plan

③ Use stories to ignite curiosity

⑦ Plan to assess impact

② Build data literacy

Act and assess

TEAMS AND STRUCTURES

① Organize for collaborative work

⑧

Strategic Tasks

1.1 Establish the structures of inquiry
1.2 Prepare to team effectively
1.3 Take stock to inform scope

Strategic Task 1.1: Establish the Structures of Inquiry

Your first task is to *adopt an improvement process*. If you are reading this book, we imagine that this task might be complete: you've chosen Data Wise. Another task is to *make time for collaborative inquiry*, which often means adjusting or expanding the amount of time when educators can work together. Time tends to be one of the biggest barriers to staying the course on continuous improvement; consistent meeting time of significant duration helps people focus and it makes the work between meetings more likely to happen. We have found that teams make the most progress when they commit to meeting at least seventy-five to ninety minutes every other week, which amounts to less than 2 percent of a typical employee's work time. It is a small investment that can pay dividends when protected. That said, teams that can commit to sixty minutes once a month still get enough traction to make an impact.

Finally, you need to *build a strong system of teams*, which involves planning carefully who should be engaged and how the work of your team will interconnect with other teams. This should be enough structure to get started if you plan to use Data Wise practices on your own work, but you need to consider several more actions if you are scaling Data Wise practices across your system.

The goal of inquiry is to create positive change, but institutions by nature are designed to resist change.[1] So when scaling Data Wise across a system, you'll need to *secure the support and engagement of system authorizers*: the people who sign checks, cut through red tape, and have the power to sanction any departure from the "way we do things here." The system leader and school board members are always on this list. The list can also include community leaders, union leaders, elders, and trusted advisers at all levels of the organization. System Wise leaders know that authorizers must engage and champion the improvement effort or it will be abandoned in the next budget cut or shift of political winds, so they think carefully about the level of involvement in the work that makes sense for each authorizer. In your context, you may choose to invite some authorizers to participate fully in the inquiry process, others to join meetings as guests, and still others to respond to consistent communication and updates on progress. However you engage your authorizers, the key is that authorizers see how having all educators in the system use a shared improvement process will help advance *their* priorities for the system too.

Authorizers are essential, but so are the people who will roll up their sleeves and do the work of integrating the Data Wise process into people's daily work. That is why this strategic task also involves *launching a guiding team that is responsible for scaling Data Wise* and *building a foundation for symmetrical teams across the system*. The guiding team is composed of people who are responsible for steering the work of implementation, but this team is only one piece of the puzzle. There will be additional teams within system-level divisions and within schools, and System Wise leaders plan how these teams will coordinate and communicate. There is extraordinary power in having these teams be symmetrical along key dimensions: how they are structured, their approach to collaborative work, and the language they use to talk about the work.[2] System Wise leaders can leverage these commonalities in candid conversations where people identify points of connection between teams and clarify the responsibilities and autonomies of each. In each of these conversations, System Wise leaders begin by establishing how each team prefers to give and receive communication and feedback.

Improvement cannot happen without allocating time, people, and stuff. That is why System Wise leaders recognize and deliver on their critical role to *allocate structures and resources for scaling Data Wise*.[3] Finding time for the guiding team and other teams enacting Data Wise can be difficult. We have seen many creative solutions to this challenge over the years, including staggered starts for staff, collaborative Wednesdays where all work time is teamwork, and compensated time beyond the workday. In our experience, "not having the time" could be an explanation that masks other fears and mental barriers to the change process. If you can't find the time, you are prioritizing competing interests over collaborative work and not all of those interests are serving you, your educators, or your students well. While this may not fit with your perception of yourself, if you wanted to make time, you would. So make the time for yourself and for others. Your future self will thank you.

With time sanctioned and protected and teams established, the stage is set for collaboration. Strategic task 1.2 helps you think about what to do once you have everyone in the same room.

Strategic Task 1.2: Prepare to Team Effectively

Effective teaming requires preparation and intentional design, and this task looks very similar when a system leadership team uses collaborative inquiry to improve its own practice and when a guiding team is scaling Data Wise across a system. As we discussed in the ACE Habits of Mind section of this chapter, two important things to do early on are *setting norms for collaborative work* and *developing a shared why*.[4] We mention the importance of a shared *why* frequently throughout this book. You can find instructions for the Shared *Why* Protocol in the appendix.

We use this icon to help you quickly find the sections that leverage your shared *why* to advance the work of your team. The shared *why* is a way to collaboratively enact the principles from Simon Sinek's *Start with Why: How Great Leaders Inspire Everyone to Take Action*.[5] As we attempted to model in the introduction, there is power in beginning with *why*, then explaining *how* you approach your work, and ending with *what* you actually do. If you see this icon, spend some time thinking about how you could leverage your shared *why*.

With a shared why in place, the next step is to take some time to deeply consider and *agree on a vision for an equitable school*. It is possible that your individual why is rooted in a goal for equity. The Data Wise Project's vision is designed to center "each learner" in all instructional conversations. While the term "equity" is common, it is often conflated with justice, fairness, and even equality. Having a dialogue about team members' individual understanding and experience with working toward equity provides a foundation for co-constructing a common vision and shared understanding.

In addition, it is helpful to *set expectations for effective meetings*, which you can do by adapting some of the practices in *Meeting Wise: Making the Most of Collaborative Time for Educators*, including agreeing on a meeting template that ensures you pay attention to purpose, process, preparation, and pacing and addressing common dilemmas that meeting facilitators and participants can face.[6]

Finally, take some time to *discuss workstyle preferences.* A few minutes spent early on to understand how people instinctively orient when working with a group can provide helpful insights that you can use to address interpersonal conflicts in the future.[7] This can lead to a conversation about the diversity of your *collective team identity*. For example, which work styles are well represented on the team and which styles might you need to deliberately cultivate? As a whole, do members reflect the different identities of the system, including the students you serve, with particular attention to identities that historically have less power and influence? Does the team intentionally make space for members who may be skeptical of change or who represent other interests? If you have inherited an existing team, you may have little room to adjust membership and will therefore need to think about creative ways to increase diversity, perhaps by providing more active roles for the system authorizers you identified in strategic task 1.1. If you are building a team from scratch, your goal is to have a team big enough to capture a mostly complete picture of competing perspectives without being so large that the team is unmanageable. In our experience, teams of four to eight members can be especially effective, but with intentional design around participation and strong facilitation, teams of twelve to fifteen can work well.

Preparing to team effectively for the purpose of scaling Data Wise also entails *clarifying roles on the guiding team*. Guiding teams are typically cross-functional, with each member having different responsibilities, perspectives, and priorities. How these cross-functional teams identify their individual roles is described in detail in the Attend to Dimensions of Scale section of this chapter.

Strategic Task 1.3: Take Stock to Inform Scope

Before your team engages in improvement or scales improvement, take stock of where you are *now*. Just as effective teachers begin by figuring out their students' strengths, background knowledge, and learning edges, System Wise leaders recognize that they are never starting from scratch with adult learners. In strategic task 1.3, teams go through different, but parallel processes depending on whether their goal is to use Data Wise to improve their own work or to scale Data Wise.

If you are engaging in Data Wise to impact the adult learners you directly support, we recommend you *assess current improvement efforts* by completing the Stoplight protocol available on the Data Wise website.[8] If you are scaling Data Wise, at this point your guiding team's work is to *evaluate system readiness for change.* We recommend that you gather evidence around the criteria summarized in the Readiness Guidelines for Systemwide Instructional Improvement Efforts, which you can find in the appendix. With either tool, teams discuss what strengths, weaknesses, opportunities, and threats they see in how prepared they are to collaborate.

Successful teams take the learning from their respective tools to paint a realistic picture of where they are now. Then they *identify collaboration priorities*: what are a few things they are going to do to improve how they work together? For example, when evaluating against the criteria, you may find that you have significant strengths, including a clear vision for improvement and protected time for collaboration. But you may also find that your system lacks robust norms of collaboration and that the coherence between the work of individual divisions is low. One mistake teams often make is thinking that they need to have all of the readiness criteria in place in order to begin. There are some criteria that you may want to address right out of the gate; you'll need collaborative norms in place before you can tackle anything else. But for other criteria, like coherence of activities, it is best to just dive in and learn the work by doing the work. The improvement process itself will provide a strong container for the coherence-building work.

With a shared understanding of the current state of the organization and a narrow set of collaboration priorities, you are ready to *identify which teams will engage in inquiry* and *set a pacing goal for the cycle* (if using Data Wise on your own practice) or *set a pacing goal for scaling* (if you are working to foster Data Wise practices across your system). Setting a goal for the cycle involves deciding where in the process you are starting and how long you expect your team to spend on your next improvement cycle. Experienced teams aim to go through two to three improvement cycles a year. New teams often start midyear and use the months they have to acclimate to the process and perhaps test-drive it on a modest goal. Others have to address complex issues of organizational culture and will rightfully plan to spend significant time on Steps 1 and 2, which could mean that the first cycle takes an academic year. We have found that teams benefit from revisiting Steps 1 and 2 in every cycle, and some even call them the "forever steps." Your context informs how long your cycles will be, and that is why it is important your team drives the pace of change.

Setting a goal for scaling involves deciding where you will start and how deep, locally owned, and differentiated you expect implementation to be for the next one to five years. To make these decisions, you may consider culture, current context, resource availability, competing priorities, and external mandates. You will balance these factors against the urgency and importance of your shared *why*. For most teams, setting a pacing goal involves a pragmatic conversation where teams ask, How big a bite of the apple does it make sense for us to take right now? If your schools are already using an improvement process, you can focus on integrating the System Wise practices that will allow you to support school-level cycles more effectively. If using a shared improvement process is new to educators at both the school and system levels, you may consider starting the work in a few schools and then bringing along others when there is proof that "this can work here." We trust teams to select the pacing that is best for them and focus on ensuring that the team can use evidence to explain its choice.

Table 1.1 summarizes the strategic tasks for Step 1, depending on purpose. You may find this level of detail for tasks useful, or you may be ready to zoom out to a

Table 1.1

Strategic Tasks for Step 1, Depending on Purpose		
Step 1: Strategic tasks	**What this task looks like when:**	
	A SYSTEM TEAM IS SUPPORTING LEARNERS IT DIRECTLY SERVES	**A GUIDING TEAM IS SCALING DATA WISE ACROSS A SYSTEM**
1.1: Establish the structures of inquiry	• Adopt an improvement process • Make time for collaborative inquiry • Build a strong system of teams	• Adopt an improvement process • Make time for collaborative inquiry • Secure support and engagement of system authorizers • Launch a guiding team that is responsible for scaling Data Wise • Build foundation for symmetrical teams across the system • Allocate structures and resources for scaling Data Wise
1.2: Prepare to team effectively	• Set norms for collaborative work • Develop a shared why for our team • Agree on our vision for an equitable school • Set expectations for effective meetings • Discuss workstyle preferences and collective team identity	• Set norms for collaborative work • Develop a shared why for our team • Clarify roles on the guiding team • Agree on our vision for an equitable school • Set expectations for effective meetings • Discuss workstyle preferences and collective team identity
1.3: Take stock to inform scope	• Assess current improvement efforts • Identify which teams will engage in inquiry • Set a pacing goal for the cycle	• Evaluate system readiness for change • Identify collaboration priorities • Set a pacing goal for scaling

bigger picture of what System Wise approach looks and feels like in Step 1, which we offer in the following section.

TAKING A SYSTEM WISE APPROACH

Attend to Dimensions of Scale

In the introduction, we introduced Coburn's and Dede's five dimensions of scale: depth, sustainability, spread, shift, and evolution. In Step 1, System Wise leaders often start by considering *depth* and *sustainability,* knowing that if the team championing Data Wise does not have deep skill in and knowledge of the work of improvement, there will be little chance that the process will successfully spread, *shift,* and *evolve.* To make progress with depth and sustainability, clarifying and assigning the roles on the guiding team (part of strategic task 1.2) is key.

Scaling for depth is possible when team members collectively have both the technical skills to lead the work and the interpersonal skills needed to address the adaptive challenges that are sure to arise. Technical skills might include content knowledge relevant to Data Wise, historical knowledge of the organization and key stakeholders, expertise in facilitation, or proficiency in management or continuous improvement practices. Interpersonal skills could include conflict management, decision-making, political mapping (identifying champions and detractors), coalition-building (creating shared ownership), and communication.[9] In initial meetings, we recommend that you have team members share the technical and interpersonal skills they bring to the group. This will help all team members know the teams' collective assets—and it will also reveal gaps. The goal is to identify and confirm that all needed skills exist on the team with some overlap to ensure sustainability of the team when membership inevitably shifts over time.[10] This skill-set balance then becomes part of your collective team identity. (See figure 1.3.)

To lay a foundation for eventual ownership of the work beyond the members of the guiding team (known as *spread* and *shift* in scaling terms), your team needs to be a cross-functional group that includes folks from different altitudes of the system, including system authorizers, those ultimately responsible for doing the work, and those in direct support roles of those doing the work.

The guiding team has several responsibilities that rely on its cross-functional composition: coordinating information and activity across the organization, incentivizing cooperation across organization boundaries, building capacity across the

Figure 1.3

A Guiding Team's Needed Roles and Skills

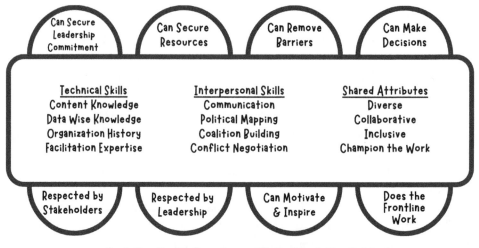

organization to do the required work, and connecting both internal and external partners to the Data Wise work and each other.[11]

Discussing the following questions as a guiding team can ensure you are planning for scale from the very beginning:

1. What processes are in place to help harmonize information and activities across divisions?

2. What processes, power allocation, and cultural norms are in place to encourage working together?

3. What processes are in place to ensure team members and those they support have the skills to do the work required of them?

4. What processes are in place to develop relationships with internal and external stakeholders beyond the team?

A powerful strategy for supporting collaboration across the system is to have guiding team members serve on multiple teams where they can serve as ambassadors for the work. An assistant superintendent who is a member of the guiding team can build bridges to the other teams they serve on, for example, the system leadership team and the office of curriculum. Getting the right people and talents at the table will not guarantee success, however. That is why System Wise leaders expect the unexpected.

Expect the Unexpected

 Building a new team or reestablishing a current team in light of a new goal offers an opportunity to reset expectations for how teams engage together or with other teams in the organization. But change is difficult, because—whether we realize it or not—change is associated with loss.[12] Even when we are excited about our shared goals and believe that continuous improvement will lead to a better tomorrow, we need to understand that there is a process of letting go and a process of embracing the new, and both can be difficult. When you share your vision for scaling Data Wise beyond your guiding team, people may tell you that they are "all in" for the adventure. As a System Wise leader, though, you need to expect that things *will* get hard. Researchers have shown that as people process change, their emotions follow a "change curve" informed by Elisabeth Kübler-Ross's stages of grief.[13] The stages include shock, denial, frustration, depression, experimentation, decision, and (hopefully) integration. Individuals may experience the stages in a different order or even skip a few along the way. When we develop awareness of where others are in the change process, we can lean into empathy and show understanding. We can learn to see a team member's display of frustration as neither a personal attack nor a reason to abandon the improvement effort. It may just be an early stage in a process that we can teach ourselves to expect.

Or there may be a real conflict that needs to be resolved. And conflicts are to be expected! System Wise leaders anticipate that the various stages of change will lead to both internal and external conflict. We may tend to avoid conflict because we have so many images and experiences where conflict created winners and losers, or because we want to avoid loss. Scaling Data Wise will likely require compromise but doesn't need to require conceding. These four principles of negotiation support teams with attending to conflict before, during, and after it surfaces:[14]

PEOPLE ARE NOT THE PROBLEM. An individual living their truth and experiencing human emotions is not a problem to solve. As a System Wise leader, you resist the urge to conflate a person with a problem and remain curious about the person. You choose to see each individual beyond their title, role, or résumé and practice empathy. You understand that change is a process.

THE SHARED INTEREST IS THE SHARED *WHY*. Focusing on isolated opposing views or actions is a distraction that can drag out the change process. Negotiation experts often talk of the power of uncovering shared interests. As a System Wise leader, you have already laid the groundwork for this. Whenever you return the team to your shared *why*, you provide an opportunity for each team member to untether themselves from an "I" position and reconnect with the collective purpose.

FIND THE DOORS, WINDOWS, AND ESCAPE ROUTES. Traditional conflict resolution typically leads to either/or thinking. System Wise leaders tap the wisdom of the team to cocreate options and alternatives that are mutually beneficial and in service of the shared *why*. Identifying a variety of possible paths forward empowers your team to make sound decisions.

COAUTHOR THE CRITERIA. Power dynamics can undermine your goals for negotiation and your progress through the change process. It may feel disingenuous to say that everyone on your team has equal power within your organization. But if you truly believe in collective wisdom, you can invite everyone on the team to be part of the process of creating the guardrails within which potential options can be evaluated. Coauthored criteria are not strict rules, but guidelines that increase the likelihood of agreeing on a path forward. (See figure 1.4.)

These negotiation principles can support System Wise leaders in taking a skillful approach to expected conflict. Khaleel's story shows what it looks like to approach conflict with the idea that "people are not the problem." (See "Khaleel's Story" on p. 40.)

We've learned time and again that a degree of psychological safety—the shared belief that it is OK to take risks, share concerns, and admit mistakes—is absolutely foundational for individuals and teams to lay the groundwork for looking at their own practice. Feeling this safety makes it possible for teams to consider how their own decisions may have created, or at least complicated, the very problems the system faces.[15] We can't tell you what types of conflicts will arise, but we can assure you there will be conflict. Engaging in developing a shared *why* and adhering to norms or agreements about how team members will treat each other will support

Figure 1.4

What to Remember When Conflict Arises

What to remember when conflict predictably arises

People are not the problem

The shared interest is the shared Why

Find the doors, windows, and escape routes

Coauthor the criteria

your teams in addressing and managing that conflict. Failing to do these things can result in conflict-avoidant teams that are unable to resolve the issues that matter most.

Manage the Change Process

As we mentioned in the introduction, System Wise teams manage change by being responsive to relationships, championing change, mapping the movement, and paying attention to power. In Step 1, managing the change process is often focused on laying the groundwork that allows a System Wise leader to be responsive to relationships. Penny's story offers a window into what this can look like. (See "Penny's Story" on p. 41.)

KHALEEL'S STORY

I've had the opportunity to lead two different schools, work for a state department of education, and work with a network of schools within a charter school organization. In one setting, we knew that it would be important to have a consistent improvement process across our system, and we chose the Data Wise improvement process.

When we initiated the work, some people were hungry for the learning, feeling that it was long overdue and what we needed. But there were those who expressed doubt because of our stops and starts with so many other initiatives in the past. I realized that we had an opportunity to bring people together in a constructive way, but I knew that we had to confront some deeper philosophical beliefs to make that happen. We gave people space to name their hopes and fears and identify ways in which we might mitigate their fears so we could break free from our past.[16]

For example, there was a narrative that our system's curriculum was aligned with state standards. I realized that the improvement process could shine light on the extent to which that was actually the case. Data Wise required that the data drive the narrative and helped us go beyond individual personalities.

Also, I got the sense that, given the high levels of staff transitions for some schools, those in leadership believed that we could bring change through personnel change management. Sure, you might get some artificial bumps in results that way: terminate someone here, reassign them there, change a reporting structure over there, but that's just a patch-up job with no long-term sustainability. And this type of change management meant we never got too far because we always had to restart for new people. I needed to help people see that we had the right people—we just needed to trust them.

My goal with Data Wise was to allow us to understand that we needed to let people with instructional expertise lead instructional decisions across our schools. This required negotiation between people who held decision-making power and those who were doing the work of teaching and learning. Finding non-instructional things for non-instructional team members to lead to help mitigate their experience of loss was an important part of this effort.

—**KHALEEL DESAQUE**
Pennsylvania, United States

PENNY'S STORY

In many years of leading improvement work, I've seen the essential role of school leaders in modeling and supporting teachers to successfully manage change. Leaders need to lead from the front, but also create the preconditions of trust and psychological safety needed to bring their people along. Because it can be so hard for leaders to shift habitual ways of leading, I make a point of creating opportunities for school leaders to build relationships with one another. Leading a school can be so lonely. So, when I bring leaders together, it is powerful to see them share their hopes and fears about leading in a different way and realize that they are not alone in their desire to do so. I model how to provide the preconditions needed to candidly share ideas about how they can support collaborative inquiry, which often involves stepping back to let teachers do the work themselves.

One way I do this is by asking school leaders to describe what it felt like to share their personal *why* story with staff. One leader explained that he had intended to share a "cleaned-up" version with those at his school. Then at the last minute, he found himself telling the real story, which revealed how he would have dropped out of school if it hadn't been for a teacher who asked him each day, "How have you been successful today?" The vulnerability he modeled in telling his "true" story caused a dramatic change in the way staff "saw" him, not just as their boss but as the young man who may have fallen through the cracks. Indeed, other school leaders who heard this leader share his experience later described how they were inspired to do the same, with similar impact.

—**PENNY JAYNE**
Victoria, Australia

As Penny's story shows, one way of being responsive to relationships is by creating opportunities for empathy. We have found that building empathy around data can be especially important as you begin improvement work, in a large part because data have a legacy of being used by those in power as a weapon. You are likely to find that your colleagues may seem to hold a range of beliefs about the role of data in education, but when you probe deeper, that is because they have very different definitions of what they mean by "data." (See figure 1.5.)

Teams can build relationships rooted in empathy by telling the stories of the data they value.[17] These stories give each person an opportunity to share an artifact—a report, a chart, a tool, observation notes, student work—that they use to do their job well. The key is that the artifact must be a source of evidence they truly value, so much so that they feel they could not do their job without using it. One way we ask teams to select artifacts is to request they bring something that they would create or use, *even if their organization did not provide it*. Each team member then addresses a set of prompts that tells the story of how they learned about this data source. You can find instructions for the Data We Value Protocol in the appendix.

Figure 1.5

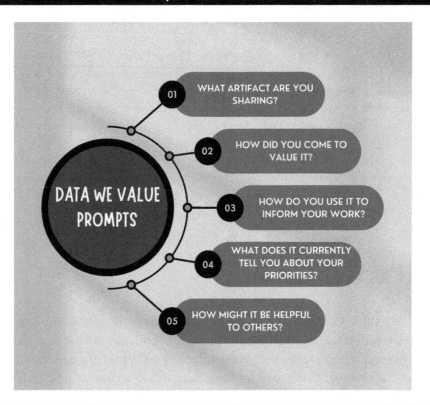

With this foundational relationship building, teams are well positioned to leverage radical inclusivity to mitigate bias and ensure that they truly welcome multiple perspectives.

Practice Radical Inclusivity

You are likely attempting to use Data Wise in a system that was not designed to work well for all learners. Exclusivity and exceptionalism rooted in bias are belief systems that have dominated societies worldwide. All nations have an education origin story that begins with the education of *some* citizens, but not *all*. Education was originally designed to support the development of those with wealth, power, or religious affiliation in order to maintain the family lineage and superior status. Colorism (discrimination based on skin color) has also played a significant role in determining who is educated in South Africa, India, South America, and the United States. In many places, it used to be unlawful to educate girls or people of lower classes because of fear that they might rise from their subdued social status and compete for positions and resources.

As a result of protests, civil wars, and court battles, many countries now espouse the value of educating all citizens. Education is a right and privilege that affords our communities greater understanding, creativity, and advancements. Over the last hundred years, we have witnessed a global movement toward equity in education for students and citizens vowing to continue to strive for this until it is clear that *demography doesn't equal destiny*.[18]

With this charge and the daunting gap between it and our current reality, System Wise teams ask themselves: *What structures best support our ability to remain curious?* With this question, you embrace the idea that someone else's perspective could be just as insightful as your own, and you begin to let go of the "knowing" that is so incentivized in educational settings. You resist maintaining the status quo and consider your own role in working toward a more just future.

Team members must be ready to determine the degree to which they believe that governments and institutions, *including their own,* continue to perpetuate a system that values the leadership of *some*, but not *all*. Recognizing this pattern is an important first step in creating the conditions for your system to practice radical inclusion. Given the legacy of exclusion, tinkering toward improvement while maintaining current practices may not be enough to achieve your team's shared *why*.

Beverly Daniel Tatum uses the analogy of the moving walkway at the airport to describe how to break cycles of injustice.[19] She explains that simply standing still on the moving walkway does not change your direction, only your speed. Even if you turned to *face* the other direction, you would still be dragged along. Tatum exhorts us to turn around and *run* in the opposite direction, to actually move counter to the momentum. The work of System Wise teams is to first identify the exclusive walkways, then move against unjust, inequitable, and biased practices at all levels of the organization. They actively pursue inclusivity through systemwide infrastructure, guidelines, practices, and performance assessments.[20] For example, many organizations have committed to shifting their recruitment, hiring, and retention efforts to establish a more diverse workforce. Yet the procedures and expectations for promotion within these organizations have changed very little, if at all, which results in leadership teams that do not reflect this diversity. System Wise teams appreciate the need to reimagine selection procedures for those teams.

Step 1 offers leaders an invitation to deeply think about team composition, with considerations of team skill and roles as described in the Attend to Dimensions of Scale section of this chapter. Donna's story shows what practicing radical inclusivity can look like when considering team composition. (See "Donna's Story.")

DONNA'S STORY

Having a shared improvement process allowed our system to work and learn in ways that I had never seen before. We literally became a learning organization, in part because we used a common process and used common language and protocols, and this developed common knowledge.

I was a member of the Improvement Office. I coordinated support from various system instructional offices to several school leadership teams. Once, during a debrief of an instructional learning walk attended by system-level leaders, someone noticed that paraprofessionals (classroom personnel without a teaching license who support teachers with instruction) were actively engaged in teaching small groups of students. But paraprofessionals were not invited to the debrief, which left their perspectives about how students were engaging with them and the content out of the analysis. During our debrief, we committed to changing this.

After several drafts and many conversations, we landed on a schedule that allowed everyone to be at the table. Paraprofessionals had to have computers to access our rolling agendas and data during meetings, so we provided them with devices that students weren't using. During the meetings, they saw themselves as being on the same level as the team of teachers. They were no longer "just the paraprofessional." This work allowed us to see the value of every person in the stakeholder group.

As I shared this story across schools, more school-based leadership teams across the system began including their paraprofessionals in meetings. All of a sudden, everybody understood that anyone who was in an instructional capacity had an impact on a child's learning. We were doing equity work and weren't even calling it that.

—**DONNA DRAKEFORD**
Washington, DC, United States

System Wise teams pursue radical inclusivity by recognizing and mitigating bias as often as necessary. If you study how the eyes of any living being work, there are light-sensitive cells that send information to the brain through the optic nerve. Where the optic nerve attaches to the eye, there are no light-sensitive cells, so this part of the eye cannot see and creates a blind spot. This biological reality is a helpful metaphor when we think about how no individual can see the whole picture without the help of others. Engaging in the completion and analysis of the Readiness Guidelines with community members beyond the guiding team, especially families and students, provides teams with additional data points, illuminates blind spots, and reduces bias.

CASE STUDY REVISITED

That afternoon, Jasmine is participating in the guiding team that meets biweekly with their coach Charlie to prepare to scale Data Wise across the Greenwood School System. She reflects on her morning meeting with the leadership team, saying, "I'm realizing that when I think about the work from each person's perspective, I would come to the same conclusions that they do—even though those conclusions are so different."

Charlie encourages Jasmine: "It isn't your job to have the answers; the answers will come from everyone bringing their best thinking. How might you communicate that to your leaders?"

A guiding team member nods and shares, "As we prepare to integrate the Data Wise improvement process at all levels of our system, it would actually be really comforting to know that you and the leadership team are test-driving the process in your own work." He looks at Jasmine with encouragement. "I strongly believe that changing how both the leadership team and this guiding team function as teams is the first step. Perhaps in this meeting we can talk about what this group can do to really organize for the collaborative work that lies ahead and figure out how we can pilot some practices here that could be useful on the leadership team as well."

Charlie supports the guiding team with setting norms, developing a shared *why* for their team, and setting themselves up for their next meeting, where they will hear everyone's perspectives on how different sources of evidence can support their purpose. Jasmine leaves the meeting confident that many of these same activities will serve the leadership team well at next week's retreat.

REFLECTION QUESTIONS

1. How can we create a community where each person is known and belongs?

2. How do our identities, beliefs, actions, and values interact with and influence each other?

3. How do our individual *whys* connect to a shared *why* for our team?

4. How representative is our team of the learners we serve? What does this mean for our work?

2

BUILDING DATA LITERACY

> What counts as "data"?
> How do we use data with integrity?

THE GREENWOOD SCHOOL SYSTEM leadership team spends the first morning of the beginning-of-year retreat building a shared *why* and learning about the evidence sources each team member values most. As they enjoy lunch together outside in the sun, Jasmine notices that she feels closer to her colleagues than she has before. Hearing stories about why and how each person does their work is helping her see them in a new light.

When the team members come back inside, they work together to list the evidence and initiatives related to their focus area, which is literacy (specifically, school leader support of teacher teams' use of evidence to improve literacy instruction).

They go around the table, having each person share something they notice when they step back and look at the two lists they have created. Then each person shares a "wondering":

> "I wonder what half of these evidence sources even are . . . what they could tell me, or how to access them. I mean, what is QSST anyway?"

> "I wonder how everyone manages to keep all these balls in the air. I'm exhausted just looking at this list."

> "I wonder about our school leaders. How do they make sense of all these different initiatives? This is a lot more than I had to deal with back when I was leading my school."

"I wonder if I need new glasses. I just can't get my mind to focus on all this information."

"I wonder how we could ask anyone to take on one more thing when there is already more to do than we can do successfully."

"There is so much that needs to be better. How do we even begin?"

ACE HABITS OF MIND IN STEP 2

The ACE Habits of Mind help System Wise teams develop their culture. Intentional practice in data inquiry cycles is similar to a medical practice or law practice: the more you engage, the deeper the learning and the more expansive the practice. We build individual and collective capacity when we cultivate these habits of mind and embrace learning and growth. In the Greenwood case, we can see the development of the team's culture as they begin to build data literacy in Step 2.

A: Shared Commitment to Action, Assessment, and Adjustment

Let's be honest, you are unlikely to hear a lot of cheering from your team if you announce that you are about to dive into building their data literacy. Instead, some people might be stifling yawns and others quietly panicking, worrying that they will say something that reveals them to be not just "bad at math" but bad at their jobs, too. The Greenwood case illustrates the frustration that team members experience when there are initiatives and data sources that have not been clearly communicated and there is uncertainty about whether the team is up for the job. Many members feel overwhelmed; one experiences such a complete disconnect from the work and can't even focus on what is on the list. Jasmine herself may be going into the new school year feeling solid in her commitment to action, assessment, and adjustment, but at this point it is a stretch to assume that the commitment is *shared*.

The person who expresses exasperation at adding "one more thing" is managing risk. This is a common and understandable response of leaders juggling competing priorities. Before committing to action, this person will need to know the why, who, what, when, and how related to what they are considering taking on. System Wise teams recognize the value of building understanding so that members can make a genuine commitment to the continuous improvement process. Building understanding is an equity exercise. System Wise teams create a learning environment that honors the learning style and needs of everyone on the team and choose asset-based framing to design supports. When your team experiences deeper learning through shared understanding and practice, you will find you are better positioned to *act* strategically, *assess* ethically, and *adjust* responsibly.

C: Intentional Collaboration

The Greenwood team is beginning to embrace intentional collaboration. The members spent a morning getting to know more about how each person approaches their work. They took a break to share a meal together. When looking at their inventories of initiatives and data, they took turns sharing noticings and wonderings, ensuring all voices would be heard.

But they will need time to continue to get to know one another better. Are the people who say they are exhausted or in need of new glasses trying to be funny, or are they truly discouraged? Depending on the depth of individual relationships, different team members may make different assumptions about what is behind these statements. Another member of the team expresses frustration about not understanding an acronym. Many of us have experienced this or something similar and have spoken up. Or perhaps unlike the person in the case, we didn't say anything and just continued on as if we knew what everyone else was talking about. This lack of understanding results in the team member having reduced access to what the organization believes to be a priority. Additionally, they may feel minimal connection, community, or empathy for those deeply engaged in that particular initiative. Truly *intentional* collaboration becomes possible when people share a language and are able to use this language to communicate meaning and value in a way that everyone can access.

E: Relentless Focus on Evidence

On this sunny afternoon before students come back to school, Jasmine's team is engaged in an activity that will serve them well throughout the year. They are taking the time to review and reflect on the evidence and initiatives related to their focus area of literacy. In the case at the beginning of chapter 1, each person made an argument about system priorities that was driven by the particular data sources most relevant to their own work. In this chapter, they take a step back—together—and consider a wide range of information across the system. This data inventory will help them avoid relying on one source of data or a single story to get the pulse of what is really happening in the system.[1] And to have a holistic picture of system health, they will need to continue to investigate how this changes over time.

One way System Wise teams have a *relentless focus on evidence* is to develop data inventories that they can draw on in Step 3 when they use stories to focus and motivate the need for improvement. For centuries, when sailors were trying to determine the location of a desired destination, they would chart a course by creating triangles that included multiple points whose locations were known. In the same way, as a system leader, you can triangulate using both qualitative and quantitative data to get a more accurate sense of where you are and how to get to your destination. It is OK to place value on analyzing proficiency level and growth percentiles, as long as you also value exploring human experiences. Engaging with multiple media will support the team's ability to resist the urge to make general statements and assumptions or offer judgments that are not supported by evidence.

STRATEGIC TASKS FOR STEP 2

In Step 2, your team builds data literacy to ensure that everyone can participate with confidence in conversations about what each source of evidence can—and cannot—tell you. The strategic tasks for this step include choosing a focus area, creating an inventory of existing and desired evidence related to that focus area, and understanding the strengths and limitations of each evidence source. (See figure 2.1.) In the following descriptions, we explain how these tasks look similar or different depending on whether your system team is using Data Wise to improve your own practice or you are scaling Data Wise across your system.

Strategic Task 2.1: Choose a Focus Area

We are still waiting for the day when we partner with a system and our advice is to "do more." With system leaders, one of the first mindset shifts requires openness to reducing the number of initiatives and being comfortable saying no or "not yet" to some important work. Our work begins with helping system teams choose a focus area. Busy-ness can work against building an inclusive culture and can enable individuals and groups to avoid holding themselves accountable for results. After all, it is reasonable to not deliver what you said you would when everyone agrees that the demands are unrealistic in the first place. This leads to a system-level version of the bargain between students and teachers that Theodore Sizer describes in *Horace's Compromise*, which we paraphrase as *"We all agree that we are working as hard as we can, and if you don't point out the places I fall short, I will do the same for you."*[2]

System Wise leaders reject busy-ness and embrace accountability for their results. The first step is narrowing the focus of the organization to what it has the capacity to do well. This narrowing makes it easier to ensure that the right people are on

Figure 2.1

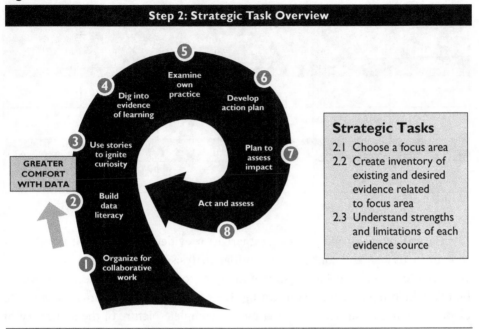

the team and your list of evidence sources is manageable. For system teams using Data Wise to support learners they directly serve, the goal of selecting a focus area is to identify the aspect of the system you want to improve. Examples could include social-emotional learning or leadership feedback practices. When scaling Data Wise, the focus area is just that: scaling Data Wise. As the process unfolds, you will decide whether you will go deep on a particular step or in a particular set of places or work on spreading the work more broadly. Making this choice at the system level will in turn allow you to narrow and focus at each level of the system.

Strategic Task 2.2: Create Inventory of Existing and Desired Evidence Related to Focus Area

An evidence inventory can be an effective way to capture the information you need. This inventory lists each evidence source, how frequently you collect it, what information you can gather from it, who can access it, and how you currently use it.

The inventory also provides space for your team to identify more effective uses for each evidence source and capture a wish list of evidence your team feels it needs in order to better understand the focus area. Table 2.1 shows how the columns of an evidence inventory could be labeled.

Table 2.1

Evidence Inventory Template					
EVIDENCE SOURCE	COLLECTION FREQUENCY	WHAT DOES IT TELL US?	WHO CAN ACCESS AND HOW EASILY?	CURRENT USE	MORE EFFECTIVE USE
EVIDENCE WISH LIST					

The goal of the inventory is to summarize the evidence sources that are relevant to your focus area and conduct some initial analysis of their use. Do not feel as if you need to list every evidence source that you could possibly collect; that would be overwhelming and time consuming. Instead, have the inventory capture the evidence sources that would paint a mostly complete picture of the focus area of the initiative. For example, if your focus area is literacy, your inventory would likely include curricular-based assessments, writing samples, early literacy screeners, student interviews, teacher unit plans, gradebooks, parent surveys, literacy budgets, and rosters. An initiative to scale Data Wise might include each school's readiness assessment, grade-level meeting agendas, teacher observation notes, professional learning presentation decks, spreadsheets of school-level focus areas and the evidence sources identified by teams, teacher/leader culture, and climate surveys. Notice that our examples include sources that have been most consistently prioritized as evidence in recent decades, including assessment scores or survey results, and also data that Shane Safir and Jamila Dugan would call "street data," which includes detailed information about how students and adults experience the system.[3]

One aspect of the evidence inventory that is particularly important for system leaders is the accessibility column. Most systems are swimming in data. The challenge tends to be that the barriers to accessing that evidence can be close to insurmountable for those who need access. System leaders have a unique role in removing barriers to access. The maxim for the system leader is that "evidence *access* should be easy, evidence *analysis* should be rigorous." If people spend all their time gathering and organizing evidence, they won't have time to make sense of it. We have found that the surest way to test who can easily access a particular data source is to invite people who you *think* have access to "pull it up" on their computers. This simple task will teach you a lot about where there may be unexpected barriers to accessing important information. (See "How to Make Access to Evidence Easy" for some best practices for ensuring teams have the evidence they need.) In addition to access, system leaders must be strategic about the formatting and organizing of evidence. We will discuss this in chapter 3.

HOW TO MAKE ACCESS TO EVIDENCE EASY

Keep evidence in one place.
- Use a single sign-on for digital assets where possible.

Be as transparent as legally possible.
- Everyone connected to a student should be able to access information. Typically, homeroom, elective, and special educators have different permissions.
- Grade teams and school teams benefit from universal access.
- Make your work public. Provide open access to system-level evidence.

Remove gatekeepers.
- Allow people to access evidence directly instead of requesting it from administrators.
- Consider proactive models of sharing evidence where updates are sent to people instead of requiring them to seek out the information.

Consider default data-sharing agreements for vendors and families.

When scaling Data Wise, you need to make sure you have enough bandwidth for the work, so one of your most important sources of evidence will be an initiative inventory. Conventional wisdom says that two to five priorities tend to be the sweet spot for most organizations. What can be difficult for the people closest to students is that this rule of thumb is usually enacted as follows: the system leader has five priorities, the chief academic officer has five priorities, each school leader has five priorities, and the grade-level leader or division chair has five priorities. This results in teachers having to sift through up to twenty priorities before they even begin to consider their particular class needs. System Wise leaders bring cross-functional teams together to look closely at the initiatives they already have in place and decide which initiatives they are going to prioritize (see the Attend to Dimensions of Scale section of this chapter for a suggestion on how to do this). The goal of this prioritizing is to bring coherence to the system so that examining the work of the levels closest to students will reveal thoughtful adaptations of the system priorities, not a grab bag of unrelated approaches.

When collecting evidence about your focus area, how will you know when you have enough information to paint a complete picture of what is happening with learning? As we mentioned in the introduction, for many years, our favorite framework to describe learning has been the "instructional core." First described in 1999 by David Cohen and Deborah Loewenberg Ball, this framework shows that learning happens in the interrelationships between students, teachers, and content around an instructional task.[4] More recently, City and Lewis offered an adaptation they call the "learning core," which uses the term "learner" instead of "student" and "facilitator" instead of "teacher." These same terms are also used to name the vertices in work that Michelle Forman and colleagues have done on supporting systems focused on coherent professional learning.[5] Since this more general language may make it easier for system-level leaders to think of their learners (who include many adults), we'll be using the term "learning core" throughout this book.

We recommend that you analyze your evidence inventory through the lens of the learning core. Does it include sources that will reveal what is going on between each of the relationships? If you are missing insights into any of the relationships in the learning core, well, that is what the wish list on your evidence inventory is for. At this stage, it is wise to plan for how you will collect that additional evidence. (See figure 2.2.)

Strategic Task 2.3: Understand Strengths and Limitations of Each Evidence Source

Like school teams using the Data Wise improvement process to improve student outcomes, system teams need to *understand what is being measured*, *study how results are reported*, and *learn and apply the principles of responsible data use*. Chapter 2 of *Data Wise* provides guidelines for how to build assessment literacy in these ways, and there is a high-level summary of the big ideas of data literacy in the appendix.[6]

System Wise leaders have the additional responsibility to ensure that they use evidence for *learning* purposes, resisting the temptation to use it for *political* purposes. Many of the evidence sources people think of first when engaged in collaborative data inquiry have political origins. Reporting scores on national and state tests or college entrance exams, assigning letter grades to whole schools, and calculating value-added

Figure 2.2

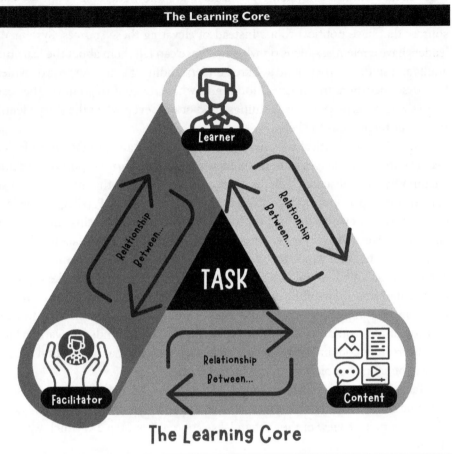

The Learning Core

scores for teachers are often done to categorize and sort systems, schools, teachers, and students. This evidence is often used to tell a simple story about schools that has little to do with learning and everything to do with who has power and how healthy our institutions are.

Depending on the perspectives and political persuasion of the group sharing it, evidence can be designed, collected, and reported in ways that either provide legitimacy for systems or attempt to discredit them. It is common to see systems herald improvements in test scores or graduation rates that are not reflected in other sources of evidence. Achievement results are often used to argue for dismantling public institutions without any attention to the context of historic disinvestment in these same institutions. System Wise leaders are knowledgeable about the origin stories of their evidence sources. They are especially discerning regarding evidence sources that have political roots. Instead of elevating these sources, System Wise leaders have a relentless focus on what evidence can tell them about the learning of adults and students. They build a shared understanding that the purpose of evidence is to describe where the organization is and where it needs to go next. They reject stories whose purpose is to label things good or bad, even when the story identifies the leader themself as the hero.

Rejecting the political purposes of evidence is not an easy task in today's climate. Doing so challenges leaders to resist selecting only bright spots or formatting data in ways that obscure challenges. Leaders need to trust that people can absorb hard truths, especially when coupled with hope and vision. Privileging the learning purposes of evidence over political purposes means surfacing more complex and qualitative evidence. For example, a learning purpose might acknowledge the graduation rate, but it would focus on sources of evidence that explain why students persist through high school and what experiences made them most likely to pursue college. It means reimagining our evidence and assessment infrastructure. It means telling more complicated stories and being comfortable with admitting to people that sometimes you do not know the answer. A learning mindset toward evidence means creating containers for people to engage in sensemaking around evidence instead of telling people what the evidence says.

Table 2.2 summarizes the strategic tasks for Step 1, depending on purpose. You may find this level of detail for tasks useful, or you may be ready to zoom back out to a bigger picture view of the System Wise approach in Step 2w, which we offer in the following section.

TAKING A SYSTEM WISE APPROACH

Attend to Dimensions of Scale

 It is difficult to scale instructional improvement with depth when there are too many priorities. Scale requires organizations to systematically narrow their work to what they can do well. But to make wise decisions about *how* to narrow your work, you will need evidence. That is why, when scaling Data Wise, it is important to create an initiative inventory. An initiative inventory lists all current initiatives, who is involved, the evidence for depth of implementation, the time commitment, and the impact on learning. With everything captured in one place, your

Table 2.2

Strategic Tasks for Step 2, Depending on Purpose		
Step 2: **Strategic tasks**	**What this task looks like when:**	
	A SYSTEM TEAM IS SUPPORTING LEARNERS IT DIRECTLY SERVES	**A GUIDING TEAM IS SCALING DATA WISE ACROSS A SYSTEM**
2.1: Choose a focus area	• Choose a focus area for inquiry: the aspect of the system to improve	• Confirm that the focus area for inquiry is scaling Data Wise
2.2: Create inventory of existing and desired evidence related to focus area	• Create an inventory of existing and desired evidence related to the focus area	• Create an inventory of existing and desired evidence related to the focus area • Build an initiative inventory to focus improvement efforts • Examine quantity and quality of evidence for all relationships within the learning core to identify any additional evidence needed
2.3: Understand strengths and limitations of each evidence source	• Understand what is being measured • Study how results are reported • Learn and apply the principles of responsible data use	• Understand what is being measured • Study how results are reported • Learn and apply the principles of responsible data use • Prioritize data for learning over other uses

team can decide what to prioritize and what to abandon or postpone. Increasingly, we hear both system- and school-level educators talk about suffering from "initiative overload." If you hear this in your setting, making an initiative inventory may help you understand why.

In the Greenwood case, a guiding team was established to support scaling Data Wise across the system. When the guiding team members created the initiative inventory shown in table 2.3, they realized that they had too many priorities, so they crossed out the grammar scope and sequence and student information system to revisit later. To help with coherence, they decided that they would encourage each school to use Data Wise as a framework for making progress on either their standards-based grading or Universal Design for Learning efforts.

Table 2.3

Initiative Inventory for Greenwood School System					
NAME OF INSTRUCTIONAL INITIATIVE*	INTENDED TO BE IMPLEMENTED BY	EXTENT OF CURRENT IMPLEMENTATION AMONG STAFF MEMBERS	EVIDENCE OF IMPLEMENTATION	TIME COMMITMENT	IMPACT ON LEARNING
Data Wise	All educators in system	1	Meeting agendas Department minutes Assessments	1	1
Standards-based grading and formative assessment	All teachers; priority is language arts and math	1	Completed rubrics Digital gradebook	1	2
Universal Design for Learning	All teachers; priority is primary grade teachers	2	Observations Professional learning agendas	2	2
Diversity, equity, inclusion, and belonging initiative	All educators in system	1	Staff, student and family culture survey	2	1
Curriculum review	All language arts teachers; priority is grade and department leads	1	Meeting agendas Student data Curriculum review handbook	2	2

*The complete initial inventory had twenty-five items on it.

Limiting the focus of an organization is not easy to do. Law or policy requires that certain things must be done. There are political projects and pet projects. There are urgent needs and crises that cannot wait. Limiting initiatives so that you can have enough bandwidth to scale Data Wise does not mean ignoring these realities. It means you have decided that collaborative inquiry is where you will invest the most time and resources, and you are going to support schools in thinking about how other initiatives may be enhanced by having this collaborative process in place.

Some teams conduct a time audit in conjunction with the initiative inventory. This practice identifies the time available during the year by stakeholder. How much time is allocated to grade-level meetings that school leaders direct? How many hours of professional learning are there across the system? How much time will this require in classrooms? How much time and what resources can system divisions allocate to the effort? The guiding team then adds up the time commitments for the items on the initiative inventory by stakeholder and makes sure the initiative time commitment number is less than the time available. Whom does it serve if we hold people accountable for managing more things than humanly possible? For an initiative to be successfully scaled for spread across a system, it needs to be *possible* for it to be done in sufficient depth in each location.

Expect the Unexpected

 You can expect a level of anxiety, hesitancy, and even resistance when you introduce a new way of working. Many educators who have had long careers manage the anxiety by referring to the pendulum swinging back and forth, saying, "We've seen the new thing before." When teams engage in identifying a focus area, they create space for clarity, depth, and reprioritization. However, the System Wise approach intentionally defines a culture that invites teams to distance themselves from "the way we've always done things" and embrace an appreciation for possibility.

You can predict some tension within and among team members when attempting to shift the culture. Many organizations attempt to capture culture in their mission and vision statements and develop core values and commitments to excellence, citizenship, and engagement. Strategic plans, improvement plans, and action plans are then written with these core values in mind. The Data Wise process and habits are centered on strong values for equity, collaboration, and inclusion. Figure 2.3 illustrates the subtle but important differences between these two sets of values; the shift to System Wise core values represents a shift in what Zaretta Hammond calls deep culture.[7]

We recommend that teams assess their current culture, appreciating that written statements may be aspirational and not necessarily reflected in the lived experiences of all community members. Looking for evidence of enacted values will help your team assess what is currently true about your culture. What is your team's readiness to shift to an evidence-rich culture where people are able to speak truthfully and directly about what they see? It is wise to anticipate a learning process as members grapple with their understanding of how the culture is shifting.

The Evidence Culture Assessment tool in the appendix is designed to support your team in unpacking the current state of your culture and understanding the

Figure 2.3

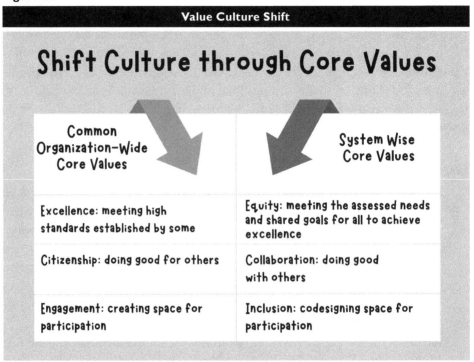

shift that will occur as you embrace System Wise practices. Kris's story shares a way in which leaders can help their teams begin these cultural shifts. (See "Kris's Story.")

 An evidence-rich culture is less about the numbers in a spreadsheet and more about how we make meaning together. Our values are not rooted in averages or growth models but in relationships and shared accountability for our shared *why*. Shifting the data culture will require System Wise teams to change the narrative about data collection and analysis. Unfortunately, there is still a fear that data will be weaponized to attack, blame, and shame those closest to the work. System Wise teams predict those possibilities and act to empower, providing strategies for evidence-based decision-making, grounded in humanizing core values. When teams are clear about the values that ground their work, they can increase that clarity even more by situating their scaling effort within a shared framework.

KRIS'S STORY

As a coach of system teams, I have found that building data literacy collaboratively can be a series of minefields that surface negative aspects of an organization's culture. Bringing teachers, school leaders, district leaders, and the assistant superintendent to the same table can be awkward at first. The very task oftentimes challenges the system's culture by elevating the voices of people who didn't have a seat at the table.

For example, on my team, it became clear that team members had very different understandings of what data mattered, and these understandings reflected competing values and purpose. Part of my role was to help the team uncover their shared values. This step for us was about identifying a shared purpose beyond our shared *why* and then getting clear about how we were going to prove it with convincing use of evidence. My team tapped into their frustration about being perceived as less important than the "flagship" programs of English and math and unified with a focus on evidence that would raise their status as a team and shift the culture of the organization. Data literacy went from boring to a way to talk about our passions. If we talk about data and success as a test score and narrowly define it, *what does that say about our values*? Instead, my team leveraged their passion to expand the data that mattered and therefore what the organization valued about learning. This led to our greatest culture shift.

Data literacy principles provided our team the courage to see that the rules that limit us are fake: we make them up. Each individual claiming that courage took time and the support of their team. As a team, we did not need authorization to do the work if we found that what we wanted to do passed our bar for legitimacy. Legitimacy was based on whether we felt the evidence was enough to support our inferences and actions.

—**KRIS COMEFORO**
Washington, United States

Manage the Change Process

Engaging in Step 2 allows teams to reduce some uncertainty by focusing their work and defining the boundaries of the evidence they will and will not collect. The other way that teams combat uncertainty and anxiety at this step is to align their improvement work to one or more shared frameworks and make sure that everyone understands how to use any assessment tools associated with them. An effective framework helps teams to map the movement by providing a common perspective and definition of what they are trying to achieve and a shared data for talking about it.[8] Frameworks are important to consider when building data literacy because they can serve as a primary source of evidence about what is working and where there are opportunities for growth. (See figure 2.4.) With Data Wise, team members independently evaluate the extent to which they believe that the strategic tasks for each step of the process are happening in their setting. When team members disagree in their ratings and then ask one another for the evidence underlying their assessment, the

Figure 2.4

Quality Indicators for an Anchor Framework

ensuing conversations build shared understanding of what doing each task well looks like. Once this is established, it is easier to identify which steps and strategic tasks would benefit from intentional efforts to improve practice.

Many teams use multiple frameworks that reinforce each other in order to scale improvement. Systems commonly use the Data Wise improvement process (the swoosh) to support implementation of a Multi-Tiered System of Supports framework for intervention.[9] Other teams connect the Data Wise swoosh to a school quality rubric such as the New Teacher Center's Effective Schools Framework or a system-level tool like the PELP Coherence Framework.[10] While we naturally have a bias toward the Data Wise process, habits, and norms as an anchor framework for improvement, we are by and large framework agnostic about which ones a team might pair with Data Wise. There are many useful frameworks for data-informed continuous improvement, content areas, and instructional or leadership practices. What matters is that the guiding team selects frameworks and sticks with them. In our experience, the best frameworks are organized around a few (three to five) domains with a limited number of subcategories, rooted in essential questions that center equity priorities, and describe levels of performance with specific measurable language from initial efforts to fully integrated and transformative practice. (See "Vy's Story.")

VY'S STORY

A little over five years ago, we began to talk about a persistent challenge facing our district. There were achievement gaps that were replicated year after year. We would see incremental progress on some indicators, but there were always groups of students whose achievement was not as high. We asked ourselves, "Given the high socioeconomic status of our community, our access to resources, and the high involvement of families, *why do we keep seeing gaps?*"

Our first approach was to adjust the curriculum to be more rigorous and inclusive. Then, we started to look at instruction. We organized our work around several frameworks including personalized learning, Universal Design for Learning, trauma sensitivity, and restorative justice. We aligned our evidence priorities to these frameworks and focused on gathering evidence of student and equity outcomes—college and career

(continues)

VY'S STORY *(continued)*

readiness, enrollment in college, Advanced Placement course achievement and access, state test performance, and staff diversity and hiring goals, and so on. This helped bring a common language to our work.

By engaging in the Data Wise process, we have begun to narrow our focus on common district questions. We have been more intentional about asking leaders what they need from the district, and we have become clearer about what we need from them.[11] We hope to provide teachers with more opportunities to choose their learning pathway. It is still a work in progress, but we now have a consistent data-based approach. We try something, collect data, and if it doesn't work, we try the next thing.

As director of data and analytics, I think a lot about organization and what makes sense structurally. What are the processes, procedures, and tools we can set up to get the results we want? However, what I have realized is that structures and time are not enough to ensure people engage. You also have to manage trust and relationship building as the key part of the change process.

—**VY VU**
Massachusetts, United States

Practice Radical Inclusivity

 In Step 2, your team defines the universe in which you will work. The danger is that ideas outside the experience of team members will not even surface as part of conversation. One way to think about this challenge is through the Johari Window.[12] This tool breaks knowledge into four quadrants organized by what we know and do not know and what others know and do not know. (See figure 2.5.)

In Step 2, be on the lookout for confirmation bias: the tendency to seek out information that supports familiar ways of knowing and being. This bias is often rooted in social identities, including race/ethnicity, gender, class, education, ability status, and work history, or by the social and cultural rules of the organization. It limits the evidence you consider because your team's thinking is constrained by the ways in which things are always done or by the social and cultural rules of the organization.

System Wise leaders address confirmation bias through the practice of radical inclusivity. They build structures that allow them to remain curious. Instead of

Figure 2.5

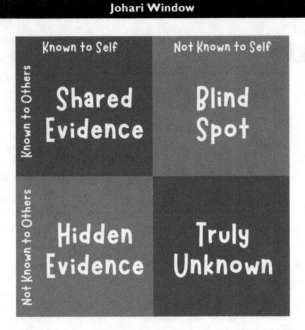

Johari Window

Source: Mindtools Content Team, "The Johari Window," https://www.mindtools.com/au7v7ld/the -johari-window.

collecting evidence "the way we have always done it," they compose teams that include multiple perspectives, listening especially carefully to those closest to students. They design structures for feedback and inquiry that surface new understandings. Ultimately, they seek to create a culture that increases the amount of shared evidence and minimizes the truly unknown.

Radically inclusive teams start with the premise that there are things others know that they do not, there are things no one knows yet, and there are things they have not trusted the team enough to share. Teams make a commitment to radical inclusivity because they accept that there will always be blind spots, hidden evidence, and unknowns. Understanding the strengths and limitations of evidence involves approaching an improvement cycle with a healthy dose of humility. Jorge's story shows the importance of creating learning experiences for adults that allow them to move beyond their current knowledge. (See "Jorge's Story.")

JORGE'S STORY

We knew that we were getting better, addressing deeper cultural problems in two key ways.

First, the regional directors who supervised principals in our network of two hundred private religious schools realized that the operational work was most urgent for our principals. Most of their focus was on operations: budgets, logistics, collecting tuition, dealing with upset parents, and working with the pastor. There was much less focus on academic concerns. After experiencing our modeling the use of protocols to build data literacy, where principals were the learners and we were the facilitators, principals felt better able to in turn serve as facilitators at their schools. This adjustment to our practice was an improvement—a necessary improvement but insufficient to get us to more critical work.

Second, we had several new families in the suburbs who identified as Mexican or Mexican American. Once we began discussing instruction and looked at assessment data with increased knowledge, further questions emerged like "What can we do to support the literacy levels of students who speak more than one language—or when English is not their first language—while maintaining high expectations?"

We got information from schools serving these families indicating that the expectations were not as high for students from these backgrounds. While we took pride in having students from multilingual and Mexican backgrounds in our system, we were not proud to learn that our expectations were lower for people who were making a choice, and sometimes a financial sacrifice, to attend our schools. Because of the sensitivity and newness of talking about race, ethnicity, and expectations, we chose to have targeted, private conversations with the regional directors and principals to support them in leading discussions around the identities of teachers and students.

—JORGE PEÑA,
Illinois, United States

GREENWOOD CASE REVISITED

"How did it go?" Charlie asks Jasmine about day one of the leadership team retreat.

"We had some really important conversations in the morning, but when the afternoon started, we were all over the place," Jasmine replies. "I think we were overwhelmed by how much we ask of ourselves and our schools. But when we looked at our initiative inventory, it was clear we were taking on too much. We were able to make some important decisions. We also talked about the implication of choosing to do our own Data Wise cycle focused on how as a leadership team we build the capacity of school leaders to support their teacher teams' in using evidence to improve literacy instruction. We're seeing firsthand how the inquiry process itself takes time to learn. It was good to hear the superintendent making the case that you and other members of the guiding team pointed out when we first talked about scaling Data Wise across our system: we'll need to build in time for people at all levels to do that learning."

"Will you be transparent with the guiding team about your team's struggles with using inquiry to improve your own practice?" Charlie asks. "They need to see you as co-learners in this work, not experts."

"I know, I know . . ." Jasmine says, closing her eyes. "But I'm hoping you as a coach will offer ideas about how I can do that in a way that doesn't make us look like we are just novices stumbling through something we've never done before."

Charlie smiles. "What do you have to lose if you let them in on your secret? What do you have to gain?"

REFLECTION QUESTIONS

1. What counts as "data"? How do we use data with integrity?

2. How has our historical context shaped what kinds of evidence we do and do not collect?

3. How can we build knowledge about sources of evidence we don't typically use?

4. How confident are we with the validity of the inferences that we make about learners or groups of learners?

5. Who suffers when we make inferences that are not supported by data?

3

USING STORIES
TO IGNITE CURIOSITY

Whose story do we tell? Whose story do we not tell?
Who tells the stories?

THE GREENWOOD GUIDING TEAM MEMBERS are reviewing their slide deck as they prepare to make a presentation to the school board about why improvement is necessary and how integrating a shared improvement process across the system will help. After four slides showing correlations between student success and race, gender, and economic status, the next slide shows quotes from students and teachers about how learning suffers when students do not see themselves in the curriculum.

"Our effort to tell our story through data has helped me to feel urgency about the need to change some of our practices," says one team member. "But this is a stark picture we are showing. Can we trust our school board to see this as an opportunity to learn and grow or will we find ourselves blamed for challenges that started long before we got here?"

"I'm worried too," responded another team member. "Within our team, we have set norms and built relationships that allow us to talk openly about places where we fall short. What will happen when we share this outside of the team that has engaged in that hard work? I know our vision as a system includes being 'lifelong learners' and 'compassionate community members,' but in practice that is just lip service. We churn through people as we look to place the blame."

A third member adds, "Who we are is how we actually treat people and what we accomplish. The words on our website don't mean too much to me. They are so bland and generic that they could work for any system anywhere. What do they say about us?"

The team sits reflecting in silence for a minute. "Let's run through the deck one more time and think about our balance between data displays that offer hope and those that clarify our call to action. I am not yet sure how we will start to live our vision."

ACE HABITS OF MIND IN STEP 3

When System Wise teams address the complexity of building a coalition, persisting through difficult conversations, and galvanizing others to act, the ACE Habits of Mind guide their thinking. Let's analyze the Greenwood case and consider possibilities through an equity-focused lens.

A: Shared Commitment to Action, Assessment, and Adjustment

Our case opens with the guiding team preparing to present data to the school board. Most school systems have a reporting cycle that holds them accountable for results. Expectations for what success at Greenwood should look like are driven by vision statements and performance goals but are also set by historical trends. The team members are dissatisfied with the data they plan to show, but they do not express surprise at the gaps in performance between different student groups. They are beginning to realize that if they fail to act, assess, and adjust their practice across the system, past results will be predictive. This team feels implicated in the problem, but not hopeless.

One member of the team is concerned about lip service, the act of making promises without genuine follow-through. System Wise teams value honest communication and action. Overpromising is a trap that deteriorates trust and creates barriers between leaders and the communities they serve. At the same time, under-promising creates a sense of hopelessness and devalues those who have made a commitment to the mission. That team member points to how people are treated as evidence of a gap between Greenwood's lofty vision and what actually happens in practice: the system vision includes a commitment to being compassionate community members, yet the system itself churns through employees. Courageously assessing these systems will be important if Greenwood is to live its core value of community and increase student academic outcomes. Employee satisfaction and engagement is likely an area for data collection and analysis.

C: Intentional Collaboration

We often see leaders struggle to tell their story. Branding and public relations is an industry of its own, and school systems can lean on these experts to craft messages designed to connect and inspire. Unfortunately, at times these messages feel transactional in nature, and it seems the goal is compelling consumers to buy in to goods or services being sold. The Greenwood team desires authentic communication that is not transactional but transformational. The desire to offer hope and call people to action is about hoping to influence not just their colleagues' thinking but how they choose to show up in their work.

Transformational leaders develop communication practices that invite members of the community to deeply reflect on how they are currently collaborating. A member of the case team acknowledges uncertainty about how the system will start to live its vision. System Wise teams do this by using a story to illustrate what the journey of achieving a shared vision could look like. There is an opportunity for the team to share its data story with the school board in a way that invites board members to see themselves *as part of the story* rather than as audience members or consumers. Perhaps they can write the board into the story with a stronger partnership role in which the level of collaboration can begin to transform the dialogue.

E: Relentless Focus on Evidence

A relentless focus on evidence often requires courage. For the Greenwood guiding team, finding the courage to see the current landscape, believe in possibilities, and act on new strategies may feel like no small feat. Knowing that the trends predate their tenure, they have named the fear of being blamed for the current reality. But *taking responsibility* for creating solutions is not the same as *taking the blame*, and System Wise teams understand that the weight of taking responsibility requires courage.

The question the team is grappling with centers on how to best communicate the data. They recognize the importance of transparency and hope to build trust by focusing on evidence and not excuses. When teams share a relentless focus on evidence, they model their value for truth. Within their own team, they have begun to create a culture where people experience psychological safety. Psychologically safe organizations accept failure as an opportunity to learn. Problem *posing* is as important as problem *solving*, and individuals are both encouraged to identify areas of concern and empowered to be a part of the solution. Additionally, success is defined not only by outcomes but by perseverance in the growth journey. The team does not feel psychological safety with the board yet. However, their relentless focus on evidence could be part of a strategy that begins to shift the culture and build trust.

STRATEGIC TASKS FOR STEP 3

Step 3 is about igniting curiosity. The strategic tasks for this step include analyzing evidence related to the focus area you identified in Step 2, identifying stories that compel action, deciding how to communicate the evidence, and engaging stakeholders in making sense of the evidence and identifying a priority question. (See figure 3.1.) When assembling evidence in a way that makes it easy for people to see trends and comparisons, the goal is not to lead others to a conclusion we have already drawn, but to authentically invite colleagues into conversation.

Strategic Task 3.1: Analyze Evidence Related to Focus Area

This task involves making a series of decisions. First, you need to determine which of your sources to look at (teams typically narrow to the three to five most relevant sources from the evidence inventory). The goal is to eventually create a data overview, and most inventories have so many sources of evidence that it can be overwhelming to look at them all at once. If you are hesitant to leave a data source out of the

Figure 3.1

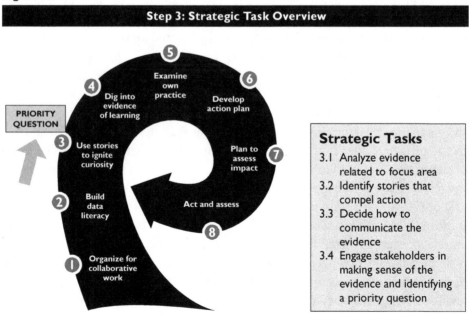

Step 3: Strategic Task Overview

⑤ Examine own practice

④ Dig into evidence of learning

⑥ Develop action plan

PRIORITY QUESTION

③ Use stories to ignite curiosity

⑦ Plan to assess impact

② Build data literacy

Act and assess

① Organize for collaborative work

⑧

Strategic Tasks

3.1 Analyze evidence related to focus area

3.2 Identify stories that compel action

3.3 Decide how to communicate the evidence

3.4 Engage stakeholders in making sense of the evidence and identifying a priority question

overview, don't worry: as your inquiry becomes increasingly specific in later steps, you will have opportunities to examine additional sources of evidence. For example, the Greenwood guiding team members might have chosen these data sources to explore their focus area of scaling Data Wise: data about teaching and learning (including literacy benchmark assessment results, teacher observation ratings, and student survey results), data about existing improvement practices across the system, and data about what educators' aspirations are for students.

Next, you need to decide which questions you want to explore with each data source. For example, when looking at data about teaching and learning, the guiding team might have asked:

- How does literacy performance differ across grades?

- Are there any disparities in literacy performance for students in different racial groups?

- On which aspects of teaching practice are observation ratings highest? Lowest?

- How do student perceptions of the classroom environment differ across grades?

- How do student perceptions of the classroom environment differ by race/ethnicity of students and teachers?

Then you need to determine who will do the technical work of compiling the data and creating data displays that provide answers to these questions. Making evidence accessible is a big job that requires a level of expertise. This is true whether the evidence is quantitative, such as thousands of proficiency scores, or qualitative, such as open-ended survey responses. While it is admirable to build these data skills across senior leadership, it is rarely practical. Our recommendation is that system-level leaders designate or develop some internal data experts who complete the initial compiling of evidence. This allows leaders to focus their cognitive energy on making sense of what the data mean and deciding how to best share the evidence with others. In the Greenwood example, the data and accountability office may have been responsible for making charts that shed light on the guiding team's questions, and that office may have created a whole stack of charts, including those shown in figure 3.2.

Figure 3.2

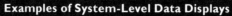

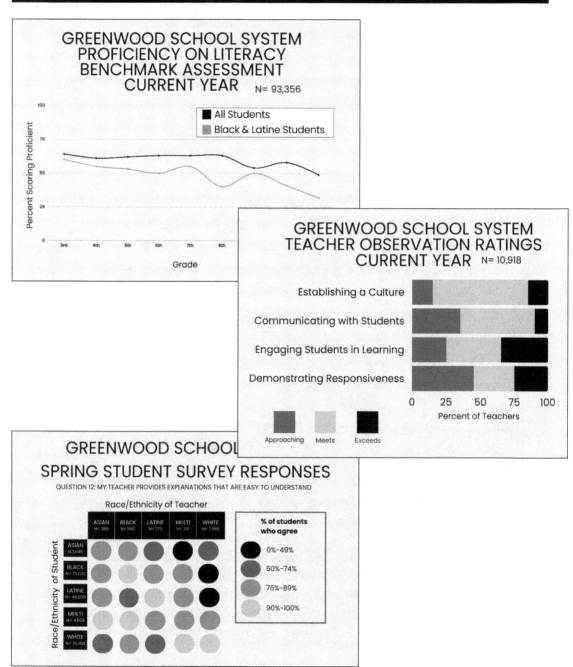

SYSTEM-LEVEL DATA DISPLAYS

Your team needs to look at the compiled evidence together with the purpose of being collectively curious about what you can learn. Resist the urge to draw conclusions, suggest solutions, or name problems. Instead, build a collection of low-inference statements and questions about each evidence source. Our go-to tool for this is the I Notice/I Wonder Protocol, in which teams go around a circle sharing factual statements about what they see ("noticings") and questions they are curious about ("wonderings"). In this protocol, the facilitator invites each person to share in turn, which ensures all voices are heard.

At first, team members may find it hard to make strictly factual statements about what they see, and instead go straight to making judgments or drawing conclusions. To deal with this, we recommend that you point people to the "ladder of inference" mental model shown in figure 3.3.[1] The ladder of inference is a way of describing the thinking process people typically go through unconsciously as they move from

Figure 3.3

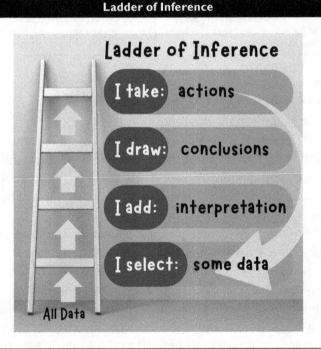

Ladder of Inference

Ladder of Inference

I take: actions

I draw: conclusions

I add: interpretation

I select: some data

All Data

Source: Adapted from Peter M. Senge et al., *Schools That Learn (Updated and Revised): A Fifth Discipline Fieldbook for Educators, Parents, and Everyone Who Cares about Education* (New York: Doubleday/Currency, 2012), 102.

recognizing facts to taking action. When you ask team members to begin on the first rung of the ladder, you support them in developing a shared understanding of the facts before making meaning together.

When doing the I Notice/I Wonder protocol it is is helpful to have having a notetaker capture responses in a chart like the example rows from the Greenwood case shown in table 3.1.

Table 3.1

Example Rows from Noticings and Wonderings Table Used by the Greenwood Guiding Team	
I NOTICE...	**I WONDER...**
I notice that eighth-grade proficiency data show the largest gap between Black/Latine students and white/Asian students.	I wonder how placement rates in basic and advanced reading classes differ by race and ethnicity.
I notice that, generally, our percent of students scoring proficient is less than 60% at each grade level.	I wonder how we are celebrating the brilliance that each student brings to class, regardless of their proficiency levels.
I know that the standards for eighth grade ask for students to do a lot: comprehend literary nonfiction, understand the role of a sentence in refining a key concept, and comparing using analogies.	I wonder if teachers were able to teach the standards well in that year given what was going on in the world. I also wonder how the classes are organized thematically to support students.

Strategic Task 3.2: Identify Stories That Compel Action

As you look for patterns in the data, stories begin to emerge. If your system allows you to disaggregate outcomes by student race, socioeconomic status, special education, and multilingual learner designations, you may be able to identify growth and performance gaps that illuminate historic patterns of inequity. Stories that compel action couple a hard truth with the realization that addressing that hard truth is our collective responsibility.

When identifying stories, your purpose is not to find some innovative insight that will revolutionize the way you see your system. Instead, the purpose is to define the boundaries of something you will no longer tolerate and to surface an inequity within your system that is so clear that you have no choice but to act. Teams can get bogged down thinking they need to find something new. Oftentimes these stories are not the surprise twist when Luke Skywalker figures out Darth Vader is his father, but the familiar fairy tale of the three little pigs where we are reminded to build our houses of strong materials before we need them. Your story can succinctly capture something you have known for years (boys are twice as likely to be suspended from school compared to girls) or it can provide a jaw-dropping revelation (15 percent of freshman read at a first-grade level); what matters is that the truth reveals something you know must change in order to move toward your team's shared *why*.

We recommend teams identify two to four stories in their evidence. As you consider potential stories, your team can discuss the merits of each one and the degree to which it may be compelling to different audiences. You may decide to merge a couple of stories into a composite story. For example, table 3.2 shows stories that the Greenwood guiding team felt would compel action.

Table 3.2

Stories That Compel Action Identified by the Greenwood Guiding Team
Story 1: At every grade level, the percentage of Black or Latine students who are proficient in literacy is lower than the percentage of all students.
Story 2: Nearly half of all teachers do not meet expectations around responsiveness to students.
Story 3: Students experience teachers who share their racial/ethnic identity as being more effective in providing explanations that they can understand.
Composite story: There is variation along race and ethnicity lines in student performance and student experience of teacher practice.

Strategic Task 3.3: Decide How to Communicate the Evidence

We have all looked at displays of data that cause our eyes to blur and our brains to turn off. Imagine the reports with never-ending tables or the chart with so many words that you do not know where to begin. System Wise leaders understand that their portrayal of evidence will only be as effective as their audience's willingness to make meaning from it. There is a delicate balance between being simple and clear enough that the stories you hope to communicate show through and providing enough complexity to allow the audience to draw its own conclusions.

System Wise leaders use data overviews to share evidence. A data overview is a curated collection of two to four charts or easy-to-read tables related to the focus area. Effective data overviews can contain displays of both quantitative and qualitative data evidence. Figure 3.4 provides criteria for effective data displays.[2]

Figure 3.4

Effective Data Display Criteria

Data Display Criteria

Each display provides a complete title including:

- ☐ Name of data source
- ☐ Who data source refers to
- ☐ Date data source collected
- ☐ Number of people included (n=_)
- ☐ Any other important information needed for readers to interpret the information (e.g., groups compared)

Each display is simple and easy to read:

- ☐ Choice of chart style is appropriate
- ☐ Space and color are used effectively
- ☐ Fonts are large enough that the audience can read them
- ☐ X- and Y-axes are clearly labeled
- ☐ Y-axis has an appropriate scale
- ☐ Legend is included (if needed)

Considerations when displaying qualitative evidence:

- ☐ We provide captioning or a transcript for any audio or video content
- ☐ We provide direct quotes without editorializing them
- ☐ We share quotes that highlight recurring themes as well as quotes that offer alternative perspectives
- ☐ We limit how much content we put on a single display so that it is easy to read
- ☐ Our displays are simple and easy to read (see above)

If the people who help you compile your evidence keep these criteria in mind from the beginning, your main task will not be to revise charts but to decide which of the well-designed displays to include and in what order. Expect that you will not end up sharing all the displays that were created. Your goal is to share evidence that inspires action; when did a never-ending slide deck ever lead to action? So, as you curate your data displays, share only those that will lead to the richest conversation and generate the most interesting questions.

Strategic Task 3.4: Engage Stakeholders in Making Sense of Evidence and Identifying a Priority Question

The purpose of the data overview is to create a shared text that a group of people can look at together and use to develop a priority question that will narrow the scope of inquiry. This initial data analysis does not lend itself to identifying answers. This is true because the data are typically drawn from what Shane Safir and Jamila Dugan would call "satellite" data, which shows us our world from a distance.[3] Satellite data include test scores, graduation rates, staff attrition reports, and other annual markers of performance, giving us an overview that summarizes performance within a domain.

At this point your goal is to authentically engage others in looking at the data. Do they see what you see? Do they illuminate your team's blind spots? When identifying stories, a common trap that teams fall into is privileging the experiences of those at the table and the perspectives of those with positional power. Examples include using high-stakes academic data or prioritizing aggregated evidence over evidence that centers the perspectives of a particular population. That is why it is important to share your data overview with those at the margins of the system who may see the organization and its impact very differently from how your team sees it. Inviting people with a variety of positions and perspectives to engage with the data overview can help you increase the chances that the priority question driving your inquiry cycle will be a generative one.

Our guidance about how to identify a priority question differs based on your purpose for using the Data Wise improvement process. When you are using the process to scale Data Wise across the system, your priority question is simply, *What is helping and hindering realizing our vision of wild success*? (We describe how to set this vision, which is essential preliminary data, in the Attend to Dimensions of Scale section later in this chapter.) When you are using the process to improve how you support people whose learning you directly support, we recommend that you generate a list of questions using the criteria for an effective priority question summarized in figure 3.5.

Figure 3.5

When you have a list of three to five questions that meet the criteria, use a transparent decision-making process (such as voting with sticky dots) to have the group decide how to select one. Here is where some teams find themselves paralyzed. The good news is that there are many priority questions, and all the options would lead to interesting and important work. Selecting one priority now does not preclude you from saving the others for a future inquiry cycle. In the Greenwood case, Jasmine's leadership team committed to "doing Data Wise on themselves," even as the guiding team was working to scale Data Wise across the system. Table 3.3 shows the focus area and the priority question the team agreed on after collaboratively analyzing a data overview that included these sources: school improvement plans, observations of school leaders, and surveys of students and teachers.

One pitfall educators can face when engaging in this strategic task is developing questions that cannot be answered with the readily available evidence. While it is true that groups may not have a current way of knowing, a System Wise leader can use these questions to build a more robust data infrastructure so that the needed evidence is available in the future. System Wise teams often find it helpful to work with a data coach to generate questions that support their thinking and progress toward goals. Seeking feedback from a coach improves your work and models for

Table 3.3

Example Focus Area and Question Developed by Greenwood Team	
Focus area	Building capacity of school leaders to support their teacher teams' use of evidence to improve literacy instruction
Priority question	Why do we see so much variation in student performance across schools with so many of the same schools at the bottom levels of performance year after year?

others in your organization that embracing the support of a coach is a valued professional development practice.

Table 3.4 summarizes the strategic tasks for Step 3 depending on purpose. If you are not yet sure about which column best describes your team's purpose, your data analysis in this step should support you in deciding whether you are using a data inquiry cycle to support your leadership team in improving its practice or working to scale continuous improvement across your system.

Table 3.4

Strategic Tasks for Step 3, Depending on Purpose		
Step 3: Strategic tasks	**What this task looks like when:**	
	A SYSTEM TEAM IS SUPPORTING LEARNERS IT DIRECTLY SERVES	**A GUIDING TEAM IS SCALING DATA WISE ACROSS A SYSTEM**
3.1: Analyze evidence related to focus area	• Leverage an internal data expert to compile and organize evidence related to the focus area so the team can analyze	• Leverage an internal data expert to compile and organize evidence related to the focus area so the team can analyze
3.2: Identify stories that compel action	• Identify stories that compel the team to act	• Identify stories that compel the team to act
3.3: Decide how to communicate the evidence	• Decide how to communicate the evidence	• Decide how to communicate the evidence
3.4: Engage stakeholders in making sense of the evidence and identifying a priority question	• Engage stakeholders in making sense of the evidence and identifying a priority question	• Engage stakeholders in making sense of the evidence and rallying around the priority question: *What is helping and hindering realizing our vision of wild success?*

TAKING A SYSTEM WISE APPROACH TO STEP 3

Attend to Dimensions of Scale

A challenge for System Wise teams seeking to scale an instructional improvement process is that they are not directly responsible for making the change they seek to enact. Therefore, in order to spread a change effort across the organization, System Wise teams must facilitate alignment on what successful enactment will look like based on their efforts. The need to communicate a clear vision of how practices need to change and evolve to yield improved outcomes is especially important when you are working to scale

Data Wise across your system. We call this a *vision of wild success*. The vision of success allows teams to scale by deepening everyone's understanding of the change effort and beginning to create the conditions for spread to happen.

When crafting a vision of wild success, your team starts by reviewing your shared *why*. Then you imagine that you have been transported several years into the future and that your change effort has been successful beyond what you could have ever imagined. You then describe what you would see and experience as you walk into school buildings, down hallways, and into classrooms. What are students doing? What are teachers doing? Who is talking and to whom? What emotions are experienced? As you do this, visualize explicit details of teaching and learning, centering the learning core that defines the relationship between learners, facilitators, and the content.

While more descriptive and detailed than a typical vision statement for a school system, the vision for wild success does not need to be very long. Most teams find that a few paragraphs are sufficient. Figure 3.6 offers criteria for this vision.[4] The sidebar "Example of Vision of Wild Success" is the vision of wild success created by the guiding team charged with scaling Data Wise across Greenwood School System.

When teams struggle with developing a vision of wild success, it is usually for one of two reasons. One is that members of the team may have *differing visions* for what quality teaching and learning look, sound, and feel like. The other is that the members of the team have *limited knowledge* of these things. It cannot be assumed that all system-level leaders have seen effective learning environments, much less experienced them. The process of developing a vision of wild success allows the team to unpack individual understanding, address gaps, and cocreate a statement that the team members can return to as they work through the remaining steps in the improvement process.

Figure 3.6

Quality indicators for a Vision of Wild Success

Quality Indicators for...
Vision of Wild Success

✓ The vision is specific and attends to what learning and change will look like, sound like, and feel like when success is attained.

✓ The vision describes learning and attends to all aspects of the learning core.

✓ The vision provides sufficient clarity to guide the work of diverse stakeholders towards rigorous, equitable learning outcomes.

✓ The vision is futuristic, compelling, desirable, feasible, and appeals to people's emotions.

EXAMPLE OF VISION OF WILD SUCCESS

Developed by Greenwood Guiding Team

Three years from now . . .

We walk into a board meeting hearing applause as the superintendent announces that our most recent data show there is no longer a relationship between students' racial/ethnic identities and their perception of how teachers from different racial and ethnic categories explain things to them. The group erupts like a volcano of joy when the next slide shows that all kids are reading at grade level or meeting their annual growth targets. What is surprising to outsiders but unremarked on by those within the system is that students, teachers, and school leaders all had roles in presenting the progress report to the community. A realtor in attendance remarks that it has gotten easier to sell houses to families within the community because of the school system's reputation.

In classrooms we see students participating in collaborative tasks that exceed grade-level standards. A student confidently shares that they are confused, and both another student and the teacher support them with questions until they confidently explain the content of the lesson. A community member volunteer says that they find that they have to read the latest news in order to keep up with the students' conversations. A parent proudly shares that you can walk anywhere in the building and not be able to tell which students are labeled advanced and which are students with disabilities because everyone has what they need to be successful.

In the faculty rooms, we notice only positive conversations about students and their potential. Staff members directly talk about race and gender and the impact it has on students and their own learning edges on the topic. You overhear an insensitive comment, and another staff member invites the person into restorative dialogue. Wherever you go the conversations are about learning.

At the system office, few people are at their desks because so many are directly supporting schools and collaborating with teachers and leaders. You feel a sense of calm that seems to stem from how well everyone knows what everyone else is doing. It is like entering a meditation center. Email inboxes are full of requests for support because teachers truly value the ways in which system leaders engage them. Unfortunately for job seekers, the human resource division has tripled the number of rejection letters it sends to candidates because so many educators see the system as a top employer.

Returning to the school board meeting, the board thanks the superintendent for creating spaces for system leaders to speak more candidly about why disparities in success connected to race, gender, and economic status existed. The board remarks on how the three-year journey of having candid conversations where everyone could value various perspectives was a game changer for improvement efforts.

Expect the Unexpected

 It is often difficult to predict how others will perceive well-intended communication. Creating a vision for wild success does not begin with crafting *your* message. Galvanizing the community around a compelling purpose comes only after members of the team have taken the time to understand. Shane Safir recommends that leaders take a listening stance, which she describes as "mature empathy."[5] Mature empathy is achieved through mirroring a person's verbal and nonverbal cues. This practice can be especially

Figure 3.7

Tips for Addressing SCARF Threats	
SCARF THREAT ●	**SYSTEM WISE COMMUNICATION TIPS**
STATUS	**THE LOOK BACK:** Recall a time in which the organization and individuals demonstrated shared values and commitment in the face of hardship or something unexpected.
CERTAINTY	**STRONG VISUALS** Use visual representation to illustrate the end goal as well as the benchmarks, land posts, and guardrails that indicate the boundaries of the work. Send the message that we won't do too little and waste energy nor will we go beyond our capacity to do excellent work.
AUTONOMY	**AGENCY AVENUES** Detail the ways in which self-expression benefits the organization, then provide strategies, procedures, and practices for members of the organization to assume leadership within their roles.
RELATEDNESS	**MIRROR AND DOORS*** Reflect back on what you have seen and heard from your community, demonstrating mature empathy. Establish the importance of personal and organizational well-being as a priority in the process.
FAIRNESS	**EXPLICIT EQUITY** Create transparency by sharing your Why and demonstrating how decisions are made to address identified needs or shared goals.

*Rudine Sims Bishop originated the concept of mirrors and doors as a decision tool; see "Mirrors, Windows, and Sliding Glass Doors," *Perspectives: Choosing and Using Books for the Classroom* 6, no. 3 (1990).

valuable as you attempt to understand people with different and intersecting identities along dimensions including race, culture, gender, and age. Mature empathy and mirroring provide you with valuable information and send messages of deep regard and respect to the person to whom you are listening. This can be particularly important when enlisting authorizers in the work of improvement. By taking a listening stance, you can build relational trust, the foundation of a shared vision.

As we stated in chapter 1, the change process can be likened to a grieving process because we are experiencing loss. System Wise leaders commit to a listening stance with an awareness of SCARF threats.[6] SCARF is an acronym that captures five social needs that neuroscientists have demonstrated can activate a reward or threat response in humans: status, certainty, autonomy, relatedness, and fairness. When leaders have an awareness of SCARF threats, they can craft a vision of wild success that mitigates these threats. Figure 3.7, on the preceding page, offers tips for addressing SCARF threats when communicating a vision of wild success.

System Wise teams demonstrate their commitment to equity when they first listen with mature empathy and then develop a vision of wild success that acknowledges their community and shows how their very human needs for status, certainty, autonomy, relatedness, and fairness can be met even as deep change happens. Rafael's story shows what it can look and sound like to inspire autonomy, provide more certainty, and create conditions that strengthen relatedness. (See "Rafael's Story.")

RAFAEL'S STORY

In all my work with systems, I keep coming back to the same realization: I can't underestimate how afraid people are of data. Teachers think data are for controlling, that they are about making rankings of the bad schools and the good schools. Instead, I tell teachers and school leaders that the data are for them. I say, "I'm not going to tell you what to do. It is your choice, your school. . . . You know your strengths and your problems better than anyone else. You are going to build your own destiny; I am just here to help."

This is not what they are used to doing. So, they actually have to learn how to be autonomous. I see them thinking, "OK? We are the ones making the decisions? We can build our own priority question?" It is like the old mindset is hard to get out of their heads. As they experience

(continues)

RAFAEL'S STORY (continued)

for the first time that *they* are choosing, I say, "You are your own research group. You are do-ing an investigation together. No one is spying. Just do your work and see what happens."

As we start building the mindset that educators need to be their own investigation group, it is so helpful to show examples of real schools doing this work. "Do you want math? I have it, sixth grade. Portuguese learning for little kids? I have that here." When educators see other schools doing this work, they feel more certainty about what the end goal looks like and believe "we can do it too."

When I lead a system of schools, I now expect that people will be scared. And I real-ize that my most important job is to help educators build the mindset that "we can do this." I do this by having people from different settings work together. When people work with people they know well, it can make them more relaxed, but it will also be less like they will get out of their comfort zone and say what they really think, especially when they are in the presence of a leader they may not want to disappoint.

When there is a chance to mix people in the most heterogeneous groups (sex, gen-der, school level, number of years working at the school, role, etc.), then I take it. The richness of this process is to allow people to say what they really think and lose the fear of data. People need to realize that the benefit of the work is bigger than one classroom or one school and understand it is about helping the whole community.

—RAFAEL KORMAN
Rio Grande do Sul, Brasil

Manage the Change Process

 A data story is a powerful tool designed to deepen understanding and connection among speakers and listeners. It is a critical way to champion the change effort by showing where the organization is on the path to realizing its vision of wild success. Storytelling is a practice that began nearly fifty thousand years ago. Whether oral, written, or picto-rial, stories are how we share our human experiences and have traditionally been used to inspire hope and teach important lessons.

Stories are powerful because they are so common. There is a cadence to stories, a beat that we have all tapped our feet to. Stories transcend generations, cultures, and languages. For example, the familiar tale of Cinderella, a teen mistreated by her family and forced to do an unreasonable number of chores before a prince selected her to be his bride, reportedly has over five hundred versions and has been told since the year 850.[7]

While the practice is common, telling a powerful story that is capable of igniting change and transformation requires strategy. Skilled storytellers are honored with both literary and humanitarian awards for their ability to invoke change in our society. Malala Yousafzai, the youngest Nobel Peace Prize winner, shared her story, detailing her life in a country where her pursuit of education for young girls like herself led to an assassination attempt. Malala used her story to advocate for change in education in her home country and has informed educational policy around the globe.[8] This story of an unassuming hero, a seventeen-year-old girl, has inspired so many to speak out against injustice for women and children. Yet, this is a familiar plot line. We love to hear stories about the underdog being victorious, the powerful and mighty being humbled, or the everyday Joe finally catching a break. Powerful stories act as gateways from where we are to where we could be.

System Wise teams are encouraged to strategically select story framing that can deliver the vision of wild success in the most compelling manner. Whether you are sharing your team's journey or attempting to galvanize the community and build a coalition to rally around a vision of wild success, storytelling is a skill that requires intention and practice. After taking a listening stance and committing to an equity lens, selecting a frame for a compelling story will support your team in conveying your message of change through a familiar medium. There are many ways to tell a story. The following examples explain how patterns of storytelling can support System Wise teams to inspire change. (See figure 3.8 here and "Dan's Story" on p. 89.)

ANALOGIES AND METAPHORS. We use this type of storytelling to create openness and inspire inquiry. By likening two objects or ideas that are not at all alike, we give members of the organization space to use their imagination and focus on what is common or what establishes a connection between objects. Our human nature tends to default to categorization and definitions that divide, so creating space for even abstract connections supports a System Wise team's mission of unification. For example, you might compare using Universal Design for Learning in classrooms to the environmental justice movement, which provides

Figure 3.8

citizens with many options for accessing and engaging in environmental justice, including conserving water, recycling, and tree planting. Just because a person can't bike to work doesn't mean they are not working to protect the earth.

PERSONIFICATION. We use this type of storytelling to humanize ideas that are typically lifeless, cold, or negative. Personification gives human characteristics to animals and inanimate objects and can be used to shift a traditional understanding. For example, you may have heard people refer to data as a "four-letter word." This statement associates data with profanity and inappropriate language. Instead, we could refer to data as mysterious. Personas in stories that are characterized as mysterious often have layers that need to be uncovered, and there is often a process of learning or *getting to know* that takes you on a journey. Personifying our ideals helps establish a way of talking about them that makes the brain feel safe by changing our orientation to concepts that may originally have felt abstract and threatening.

THE PLOT TWIST. We use this type of storytelling to revive hope and renew faith. If you have worked within a particular field for a long time, you can begin to predict what is likely to happen. Just as we can predict how the air will feel when springtime comes, we can predict what will happen when a new CEO takes office or how a board of trustees will react to budget requests during contract negotiations. Though we find comfort in the predictable nature of our work, a favorable plot twist is always a welcome surprise. System Wise teams are not expected to foretell the future, but they can revive hope by offering the possibility that things can be different this time around. Using what-if statements is a powerful way to help members of the organization consider alternatives to the status quo. Planting these seeds and demonstrating faith should not be confused with making false promises, however, so you will want to do this with intention and within a clear story arc. When you can identify plot twists easily, lean into using them. However, not everything can be easily framed as a plot twist. Do not let the desire for this innovation and element of surprise distract you from telling stories that really matter—even if the story seems a little obvious.

THE UNASSUMING HERO. We use this type of storytelling to signal our faith in the members of the organization. It provides an opportunity to highlight the assets and contributions of community members who don't hold official titles. Additionally, we can illuminate how seemingly small, run-of-the-mill activities have yielded significant benefits and can inspire others to reflect on their role as change agents. Unassuming heroes in the stories we are familiar with are not seeking glory but are

DAN'S STORY

Our system-level leaders and school teams found challenges in creating data overviews. Because of how we had used data historically, many felt that the data overview had to be this perfect quantitative display that led people to some sort of right action.

We overcame that hurdle by embracing learning from our study of *Street Data* and using the concept of Google Earth. This was critically important for us in helping schools understand the purpose of the data displays: we only needed to use the overview to inspire wonder and curiosity. Anybody who has used Google Earth could connect with what it meant to start broadly in the clouds and then narrow to the street level or what the student was doing in the classroom. Once we started talking about "street data," leaders felt that they had *permission* to bring in qualitative data. They let go of the pressure they felt to rely solely on quantitative data overviews to tell the entire story of learning, knowing that we'd eventually get to discussions about students' experiences. This metaphor helped release the anxiety that leaders felt because they knew that the goal would be for teacher teams to get focused on what their students were doing every day.

In my role as executive director of school innovation, I knew that we needed facilitative support to move the process at each school. We asked each school to appoint a person to be the improvement specialist for the school. This person could have any role (e.g., teacher, data coach) but would be responsible for facilitating the meeting alongside the school leader. Our system leaders and external coaches built their capacity in understanding how to plan and lead meetings. We shared the stories and experiences of the early adopters who had strong collaboration between the school leader and improvement specialist to help other school teams see that this work was possible. Sharing stories of success was powerful for helping other schools decide to commit to getting more involved.

—**DAN HURLEY**
New York, United States

very committed to the goal. Think about how you can create value for this type of hero in hierarchical organizations that have typically privileged those with positional power and longevity. Take the time to listen to individuals' stories and highlight someone who models the ACE Habits of Mind: the ways of thinking that you want to permeate your organization.

Practice Radical Inclusivity

 System Wise teams utilize data inquiry cycles as a foundational step in pursuing a vision for equity. john a. powell developed the concept of targeted universalism to support system leaders in developing outcome-focused policies and practices.[9] Targeted universalism begins by establishing a universal, shared community goal and ends with the development and implementation of targeted strategies to ensure each group or individual reaches the universal goal. This approach doesn't place the expectation on the individual to adapt to meet the organization; rather it places the expectations on the organization to adapt to better meet the needs of the individual. System Wise teams use data inquiry cycles to recenter policies and practices, ensuring all can achieve the universal goal.

We have witnessed organizations improve their data collection practices by collecting multiple points of data and disaggregating data by subgroups. Summary data often hide the reality that some students are consistently underperforming. In the Greenwood case, leaders are considering strategies to close both achievement and opportunity gaps. While these leaders see themselves as change agents and accept the responsibility of focusing on the needs of marginalized populations, radical inclusivity takes this practice a step further by asking,: *How can we express our value for diverse voices and working styles?*

Embracing targeted universalism through radical inclusivity requires your team to lean into Strategic Task 3.4: engage stakeholders in making sense of the evidence and identifying a priority question. Your team is likely composed of individuals with expertise in certain *professional* areas. How can your team create space for members to bring their *personal* experiences to the conversation and provide an alternative point of view? For example, a team member who has children could wear the hat of a parent during a data discussion. It is important to create space for team members to bring all aspects of themselves to a productive conversation. At the same time, your team likely does not fully represent the community you serve. You will want to invite others outside the team to offer their voices and share how they make sense of the data. Here is an opportunity for your team to practice listening deeply and taking a learning stance.

Teams need to include the voices of students as they analyze and make sense of a data overview. Students can often share perspectives through their lived experiences that teachers and leaders do not have. Including students' responses to the interview questions on how they feel about the assessments you featured in your data overview will provide insights that could help you focus your inquiry on what matters most. (See figure 3.9.)

You can adjust these sample questions to be developmentally appropriate for different students, and you can also offer variations to families, community members, and fellow educators. Radical inclusivity at the earliest steps of the improvement process will enable members of your community to not just deeply understand and connect with shared goals but to also share responsibility for designing and implementing improvement strategies. (See "Eva's Story.")

Figure 3.9

Student Interview Questions

Four Student Assessment Interview Questions

? How prepared did you feel for the test?

? What did you think or feel about the testing experience and the format of the test?

? Do you believe your scores represent what you have learned and are able to now do? Why or why not?

? Which learning experiences were most and/or least helpful to you?

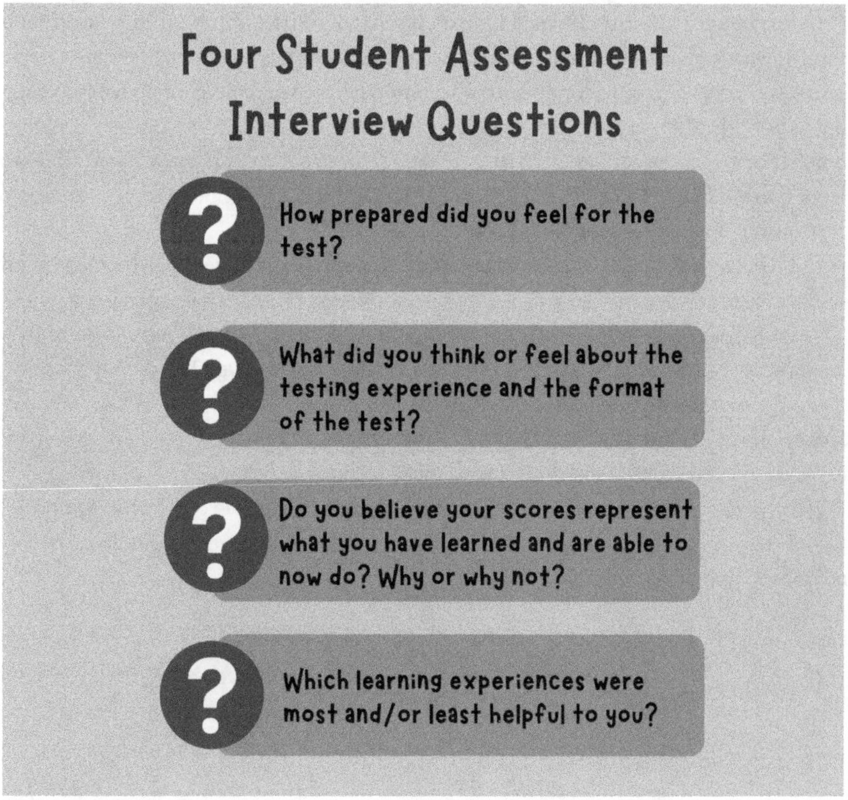

EVA'S STORY

I have found that systems are wisest when they push past status and hierarchy to allow for a variety of perspectives at the decision-making table. In my work with both K–12 education-adjacent organizations and school systems, it's still far too common to see decision-making power rest with those who have the most seniority, formal education, or status afforded them based on identity markers they can't control. It's those very characteristics that influence how they see the problems that systems face, which is often very different from how those closest to the problems experience them.

A teacher, school-based testing or assessment coordinator, student, or school leader will always bring a different lens and rationale for their interpretation of the data than the person who leads a box on the organization chart. The ladder of inference is a great tool to get their thinking into the dialogue. The ladder of inference is a powerful thinking tool that helps you decouple "expertise" (which is often a proxy for power and not really about knowledge) or hierarchy to push past bias-based beliefs about a topic or problem long enough to hear different interpretations.

It's awkward at first to hear someone say, "What assumptions are you making about what the data say or what did you see that makes you say that?" It's less awkward when those with power use protocols to invite everyone at the table to use questions like this and direct them toward everyone at the table. When used this way, I've seen the ladder of inference encourage people to think about their beliefs and perspectives in ways that deepen the discourse quickly. With more understanding of what people think and why, teams have more collective knowledge to make smarter decisions.

I'd encourage anyone reading this to consider what they have gained by inviting dialogue from a variety of perspectives, and what they might have lost out on by choosing not to bring others into the work.

—EVA MEJIA
California, United States

CASE STUDY REVISITED

The Greenwood guiding team members adjust their presentation to their school board. Before sharing their data displays, the team members share their vision for what student success would look like, sound like, and feel like in every classroom once they had transformed the system's culture to focus on learning at all levels. By starting with a specific description of what they want for all students and then offering clear charts describing the most up-to-date academic data, they reveal the gap between their aspirations and their current reality. The team then invites the board to ask questions and offer feedback on both the vision and the evidence.

When the guiding team members meet the following morning to debrief, their coach Charlie asks how the board meeting went. "I nearly hugged the board member who said, 'This is the most I've understood about what is happening in the system and why it matters,'" says Jasmine.

"Look how powerful it is when ownership and belief in this work start to shift to the board," responds Charlie.

"Ownership is shifting in lots of ways," says a guiding team member who has been in his role for many years. "This is a puzzle that will take all of us to solve, and this is the first time I've felt included in doing the work."

The Greenwood team members smile at each other, proud of their progress. Then one of the school leaders on the team takes a deep breath and says, "Creating our vision of wild success and benchmarking are initial steps. The real work is understanding *why* we are where we are and figuring out a path forward."

REFLECTION QUESTIONS
1. Whose story do we tell? Whose story do we not tell? Who tells the stories?
2. What biases or assumptions should we be aware of as we look at learner evidence?
3. How do the data we collect connect to our shared *why*?

4

DIGGING INTO
EVIDENCE OF LEARNING

Do we see each learner first through their strengths?
Do we believe each learner can do meaningful work?

WHEN THE GUIDING TEAM leading Greenwood's efforts to scale Data Wise across the system meets to discuss the school walkthroughs it has done over the past few weeks, there is an animated discussion.

"I found myself wondering why there is so much variation in student experiences and outcomes across classrooms and schools. As a team, we seem to be on the same page about our vision for what good instruction looks like, but something happens between our conversations and the school door. What is going on?"

"It feels like we are playing that old telephone game. We start with one message, and by the end of the chain there are all sorts of messages that have nothing to do with the original."

"It's not that people are lazy or aren't trying. I'd take our teachers and leaders over any other system's. It's just that their actions do not seem to build on each other."

The team looks back at the descriptive vision of wild success posted on chart paper. "We've got the right people who want to do the right things, but for some reason it isn't all coming together. For us to get better, we need to understand what is happening at each connection point across our system."

"I don't know where that will go, but I know where we need to start—with what is happening in classrooms."

ACE HABITS OF MIND IN STEP 4

The ACE Habits of Mind support System Wise teams in understanding the thinking and belief systems that are at play when they dig into evidence of learning. To create a data-rich culture that fosters authentic understanding and problem identification, teams rely on these habits to help them acknowledge assumptions and mitigate bias.

A: Shared Commitment to Action, Assessment, and Adjustment

The Greenwood team members are grappling with a common puzzle: what to do when early efforts are not producing results. Their vision of wild success was supposed to inspire the community and unite their group of competent, passionate educators. But transformation takes time, and the vision statement itself is not magical. This is because each educator interprets the vision according to their unique context and acts according to their capacity and access to resources. As in so many systems, it could well be that most Greenwood educators are doing the best that they can and, as one member says, "it's not that people are lazy or aren't trying." But when viewed from the system level, it is clear that these positive intentions are not guaranteeing a positive impact on students. The team members are realizing that it is up to them to assess the conditions they have created and understand what is happening at each connection point.

The members have committed to further investigate and collect evidence that will allow them to better understand where things stand. To adjust their data collection and analysis practices, they will need to commit to a growth mindset for both themselves and the educators they serve. A growth mindset, or belief that learning is both possible and probable for everyone with appropriate support, is an orientation to leadership and learning essential to developing an inclusive data culture. The team members are demonstrating that they are beginning to approach improvement work as a journey. Their beliefs and thoughts about evidence collection are shifting as they see value in thinking more creatively about the sources of evidence needed to act, assess, and adjust.

C: Intentional Collaboration

The Greenwood guiding team members have worked to get on the same page. They have a shared *why* and have collaboratively developed a vision for wild success. They invested time and energy in reviewing multiple forms of data, and they are actively communicating their vision to the broader community. However, what they have established so far is a one-way line of communication. One member likens the experience to a game where a person starts by whispering a message to the person seated next to them, who in turn whispers what they thought they heard to their neighbor. Each whisperer assumes that what they heard was correct and that what they passed along was interpreted correctly, but *there are no checks for understanding*. Adopting intentional collaboration as a habit of mind will move your team from relying on this simple messaging to engaging in two-way communication that yields collaborative work not just within but *across* teams as well.

E: Relentless Focus on Evidence

The team expresses concern about the lack of alignment between its intentions to deliver a message for change and the impact of its message. It has committed to maintaining a relentless focus on evidence, so it decides to dig deeper into more granular evidence that will really shed light on "what is happening in classrooms." It is important to stay low on the ladder of inference when examining evidence, especially when in exchanges with colleagues. We see a member of the guiding team make a positive assumption about educators when they say, "We've got the right people who want to do the right things . . ." This may seem harmless, but the practice of making sweeping generalizations about the intentions of others hinders the team in its quest for understanding. Remaining curious about others' actions and intentions is not about questioning colleagues' value as human beings. It is about understanding what "doing our best" looks like in practice and appreciating that each individual's personal best shifts with understanding and wisdom. The award-winning author, poet, and activist Maya Angelou said, "Do the best you can until you know better. Then, when you know better, do better." A relentless focus on evidence is a journey toward individual and collective betterment. The guiding team's decision to better understand what is happening at the classroom level and other connection points is a first step to *doing better*.

STRATEGIC TASKS FOR STEP 4

In Step 4, you dig into learner evidence with the goal of forming a testable hypothesis about what learners can do well and where they struggle. (See figure 4.1.) This knowledge will allow you to move into Step 5 with enough understanding about your learners that you and your team can turn the mirror on yourselves and examine your own practice as leaders. The strategic tasks for this step include examining a wide range of evidence about learning, coming to a shared understanding of what evidence shows, and identifying a learning-centered problem.

Figure 4.1

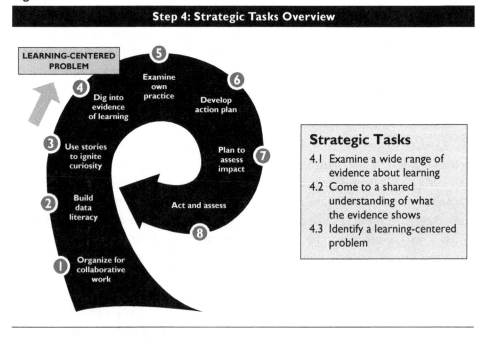

Step 4: Strategic Tasks Overview

LEARNING-CENTERED PROBLEM

⑤ Examine own practice

④ Dig into evidence of learning

⑥ Develop action plan

③ Use stories to ignite curiosity

⑦ Plan to assess impact

② Build data literacy

Act and assess

⑧

① Organize for collaborative work

Strategic Tasks

4.1 Examine a wide range of evidence about learning

4.2 Come to a shared understanding of what the evidence shows

4.3 Identify a learning-centered problem

Strategic Task 4.1: Examine a Wide Range of Evidence About Learning

Knowing where you desire to go is only helpful if you have a clear sense of where you are now. When a system team is using Data Wise to improve its own leadership practice, Step 4 is when it examines evidence to shed light on the priority question it identified from looking at overview data about its focus area. When a guiding team is scaling Data Wise across a system, the priority question is simple: *what is helping and hindering realizing our vision of wild success?* Guiding teams must use multiple sources of evidence to help one another see the system at work and understand the complex relationships, patterns, and influences that impact outcomes.[1] But what types of evidence should you consider and how many sources of evidence should you dig into?

When teacher teams use the Data Wise improvement process, their learner is clear: the students in their classrooms. If a leadership team uses the process to improve how to support the people immediately below them on the org chart, those are the learners to focus on. Teams that are guiding the work of scaling Data Wise across a system have a more complex charge, which is to understand learners at multiple levels or altitudes of the organization. As our mountain image shows in figure 4.2, the landscape in a guiding team's purview can seem vast. It needs to think

Figure 4.2

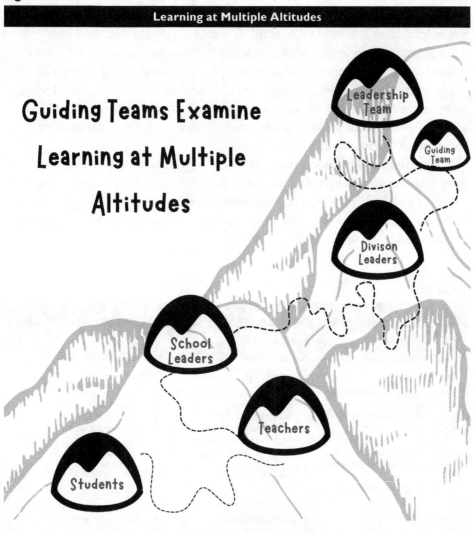

Learning at Multiple Altitudes

Guiding Teams Examine
Learning at Multiple
Altitudes

Leadership
Team

Guiding
Team

Divison
Leaders

School
Leaders

Teachers

Students

about the many learners who will be needed to make the scaling effort successful: students, teachers, school leaders, division leaders, the leadership team, and perhaps many others in between.

For whatever learner you focus on, ideally you should examine a *variety* of data sources. At the student level, examining four nationally normed multiple choice exams in literacy is less helpful than looking at one nationally normed exam plus results from a student survey about how they experience learning at school. At the division leader level, looking at notes from all division meetings across the year is less helpful than looking at a handful of meeting agendas and then interviewing a sample of division leaders about their work. Consider evidence that is collected through a variety of means, including interviews, surveys, observation, collection of work products, and formal assessments. These evidence sources should focus on different aspects of learning, such as knowledge mastery, feelings about learning, and the culture of the learning environment. Table 4.1 gives examples of evidence sources at different altitudes of the system.

Once you have selected sources of evidence, you take the same approach you used when looking at overview data in Step 3: you start at the bottom rung of the ladder of inference, noticing and wondering about what you see. This prepares you to move to the next strategic task, where you and your colleagues add interpretation as you begin to climb the ladder together.

Table 4.1

Examples of Learning Evidence That System Teams Examine		
SYSTEM LEADER DATA	**SCHOOL AND SCHOOL LEADER DATA**	**CLASSROOM DATA**
Performance • Meeting agendas and notes • Attendance • Formal evaluations • Complaint log summary • Peer/supervisor feedback • Workflow/process analysis • Key performance Indicators (KPIs) • Awards and recognitions	**Performance** • Meeting agendas and notes • School ratings • Standardized test performance • Peer/supervisor feedback • Professional learning surveys	**Performance** • Student writing • Curriculum-based assessments • Standardized tests • Student work • Attendance • Behavior referrals
User experience • Surveys • Focus groups • Exit interviews • Shadowing protocol	**User experience** • Surveys • Focus groups • Shadowing protocol	**User experience** • Student writing/art • Surveys • Focus groups • Shadowing protocol
Environment • Office floor plan • Calendars • Professional development	**Environment** • Physical space management • Master schedule • Calendar events	**Environment** • Classroom observations • Time on task audit • Routines • Lesson plans

Strategic Task 4.2: Come to Shared Understanding of What the Evidence Shows

The goal of this task is to develop a shared understanding of what learners know and are able to do related to the priority question. One approach to doing this is to use a modified Affinity Protocol, which has the three steps shown in figure 4.3.[2] Depending on the size of your team and its levels of expertise, you may create subgroups to look at different sources or you may look at all sources together. In this protocol, each team member begins by writing four to ten low-inference statements from the evidence on separate sticky notes.

Shared sensemaking begins when each person reads aloud a statement from a sticky note and places it on chart paper. Team members who have other related

Figure 4.3

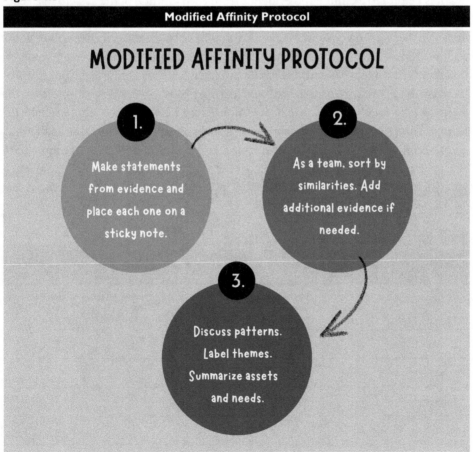

Modified Affinity Protocol

MODIFIED AFFINITY PROTOCOL

1.
Make statements from evidence and place each one on a sticky note.

2.
As a team, sort by similarities. Add additional evidence if needed.

3.
Discuss patterns. Label themes. Summarize assets and needs.

notes then read and place them near the original note. The process continues with other team members reading their evidence until they have placed all sticky notes.

The next step is for your team to describe the patterns that characterize each grouping of notes. The discussion here is the "secret sauce" of this protocol: the back-and-forth of team members explaining what the evidence means to them builds shared understanding. Once your team feels it has had a robust discussion (we recommend setting a timer for ten to fifteen minutes to encourage focus), you are ready to draw some conclusions about what you see. If you are on a guiding team that is scaling Data Wise, for each level of the system, you start by listing the assets that could be leveraged to realize your vision of wild success. Then you describe the learning gaps that, if addressed, would bring you closer to your vision. We find that a table, like that shown in table 4.2, is an easy way to gather these ideas.

It is helpful to examine the evidence from each altitude of the system in a separate round of the protocol, beginning with *students*. As you list the assets and gaps, consider the learning core and make sure you have collected evidence about all the relationships within it, which at this level are the relationships between students, teachers, and content. When you have completed analysis at this level, use the protocol again to develop a list of assets and learning gaps for *teachers*. At this level, the learning core relationships to pay attention to are between teachers (who are the learners), the coaches or others who guide teacher learning (who are the facilitators), and the content that is the focus of the teacher learning experience. Continue until you have examined all relevant aspects of the system. As a system leader, know that you will explore your own practice deeply in Step 5, but in Step 4 you may find that

Table 4.2

Assets and Learning Gaps Template for a Guiding Team That Is Scaling Data Wise		
	Evidence-based **assets** relevant to realizing vision of wild success	Evidence-based **learning gaps** relevant to realizing vision of wild success
Division leaders		
School leaders		
Teachers		
Students		

this activity begins to surface important information about what system leaders are doing or not doing to support the vision of wild success.

Collectively analyzing data can lead to riveting conversations. It is common to rely on memories or previous experiences to make sense of the data and important to guard against allowing bias to influence your assessment about what constitutes an asset and where the gaps are. It can be helpful to include a team role of "inference monitor" who has the job of listening for claims that are not supported by evidence. This person's role is to ask questions like "What evidence supports your claim?" or "How could we make the case for that claim if a visitor joined our group?"

Strategic Task 4.3: Identify a Learning-Centered Problem

When looking closely at evidence, your team may have experienced a range of emotions including pride, shame, and fear of the unknown. These emotions are to be expected, but it is wise not to allow them to drive your decision about which learning-centered problem to select. Acting only on these emotions could lead you down a path to perfectionism, where you are determined to find the "right" response to what you have learned. The trick is to engage in productive struggle and not get stuck. To avoid analysis paralysis, agree to a modest amount of time to craft a learning-centered problem that satisfies the quality indicators shown in figure 4.4. The goal is to select a good option and not to struggle to find the best one. You can always revise your learning-centered problem when you know more.

The sentence stem in figure 4.5 can help ensure that teams include all aspects of an effective learning-centered problem.

Each component of this sentence stem serves an important purpose. First, by starting with evidence, you ensure that your statement is grounded in the current reality. Then, by stating learner strengths, you ensure that learners will be able to leverage their existing assets as they grow.

Figure 4.4

Quality Indicators for a Learning-Centered Problem

Quality Indicators for a...
Learning-Centered Problem

- ✓ Directly related to priority question.
- ✓ Based upon multiple sources and different kinds of evidence.
- ✓ Composed of learner assets and a meaningful and connected learning gap.
- ✓ Within our control.
- ✓ Specific and small enough to be actionable.
- ✓ A statement, not a question.

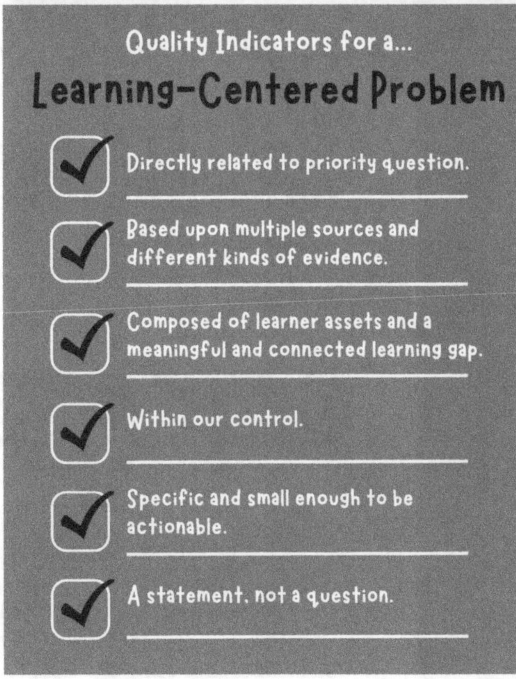

Figure 4.5

Sentence Stem

Learning-Centered Problem Sentence Stem

Based upon <list evidence used to arrive at the learning-centered problem>
our learners are good at <insert the strengths your team identified that are relevant
to the priority question>
and experience a learning gap with <insert one thing your learners are challenged by
or struggle to achieve that acts as a barrier to realizing the vision of wild success>.

Learners are never blank slates. Building on their talents, passions, and experiences is essential if they are to be able to construct new knowledge. Finally, by stating a learning gap, you clarify the priority of the team. Table 4.3 shows an example of a learning-centered problem that the leadership team for Greenwood School System identified as it worked its way through Step 4 of its improvement cycle focused on its learners, who are school leaders.

If you are on a guiding team that is scaling Data Wise across your system, your task is actually to craft a *symmetric learning-centered problem* that situates multiple assets and learning gaps within the ecosystem of your organization. We explain how to do this and give an example in the Attend to Dimensions of Scale section, which is just after the summary of what the strategic tasks for Step 4 look like depending on purpose. (See table 4.4.)

Table 4.3

	Example Learning-Centered Problem Developed by the Greenwood Leadership Team
Focus area	School leader support of teacher teams' use of evidence to improve literacy instruction.
Priority question	Why do we see so much variation in student performance across schools with so many of the same schools at the bottom levels of performance year after year?
Learning-centered problem	Based on our review of school improvement plans, observations of school leaders, and student and teacher surveys, our school leaders are effective at consistently observing teachers and providing initial feedback, and the learning gap is in following up with teachers to support them in integrating feedback into their practice.

Table 4.4

Strategic Tasks for Step 4, Depending on Purpose		
Step 4: Strategic tasks	**What this task looks like when:**	
	A SYSTEM TEAM IS SUPPORTING LEARNERS IT DIRECTLY SERVES	**A GUIDING TEAM IS SCALING DATA WISE ACROSS A SYSTEM**
4.1: Examine a wide range of evidence about learning	• Examine evidence of *learning outcomes* • Examine evidence of *learner experience*	• Examine evidence of *learning outcomes* • Examine evidence of *learner experience* • Describe the gap between current reality and vision
4.2: Come to a shared understanding of what the evidence shows	• Notice and wonder about the evidence collected • Identify patterns and themes	• Notice and wonder about the evidence collected • Identify patterns and themes • Map assets of all learners to the learning core
4.3: Identify a learning-centered problem	• List the sources of evidence used • State learner strengths and identify learning gap	• List the sources of evidence used • State learner strengths and identify learning gap • Develop a *symmetric* learning-centered problem that situates multiple learning gaps within the ecosystem of the organization

TAKING A SYSTEM WISE APPROACH TO STEP 4

Attend to Dimensions of Scale

 Foundational to addressing the depth dimension of scale is creating a *symmetric learning-centered problem* that distills the evidence collected in multiple assets and gaps charts. The symmetric learning-centered problem is a connected story that shows the relationship between practices and outcomes at each altitude of the organization.[3] The arrows in the template in figure 4.6 show how to work back from the vision of wild success to describe learning needs at multiple levels.

When completing the template, your team starts by writing a concise statement in the box on the far right that describes what you expect students to be doing. Then you keep moving one box to the left and asking yourselves: "What is it that the actors at this altitude are doing or not doing related to this vision?" To show what this process looks like, let's walk through the example in table 4.5.

In this example, the team members began by placing the key ideas from their vision into the student actions box, which were about students engaging in peer feedback. Then they then asked themselves, What are teachers already doing that is in service of this vision, and where do teachers have learning gaps? With that answer

Figure 4.6

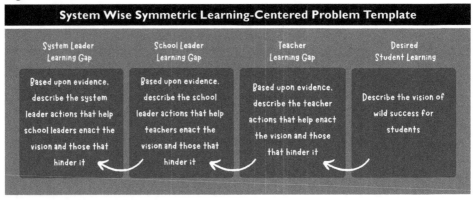

Table 4.5

Example of Symmetric Learning-Centered Problem for the Greenwood Guiding Team			
Based upon evidence, describe the system leader actions that help enact the vision for school leaders and those that hinder it	Based upon evidence, describe the school leader actions that help teachers enact the vision and those that hinder it	Based upon evidence, describe the teacher actions that help enact the vision for students and those that hinder it	Describe the vision of wild success for students
Based on school leader surveys, our system leaders are effective at communicating priorities around collaborative learning, and the learning gap is allowing school leaders an opportunity to experience it for themselves.	Based on school visits, our school leaders are effective at monitoring the pacing of curriculum, and the learning gap is adjusting support based on differing needs of teachers.	Based on classroom observations, our teachers are effective at communicating what high-quality work looks like, and the learning gap is providing collaborative peer learning experiences to practice giving feedback.	Students work collaboratively with peers and help each other master grade-level content.

captured as a learning-centered problem in the teacher box, the team then asked a similar question about school leaders. This pattern of inquiry continued when considering system leaders. Each level is implicated in the problem, so each level will be essential to engage in action planning later in the cycle.

If this team had stopped after identifying teacher actions and learning, it would be blaming teachers for student outcomes. But when a guiding team works to identify learning needs throughout the organization, it both builds empathy for those it supports and agency for making the vision become reality. For many guiding teams, the process of developing this symmetric problem leads to a sobering realization: when the teams read their work from left to right, they see that the current system has been perfectly designed to get the results they are currently seeing. Those results are unlikely to change unless the system changes too.

Creating a symmetric learning-centered problem helps a guiding team see the system and begin to understand differing perspectives. This perspective-taking is especially important if you want to avoid being taken off guard by unexpected developments.

Expect the Unexpected

 Have you ever felt surprised that something happened and then realized that if you had been listening more carefully, you would have seen that the clues were there all along? Developing your ability to understand multiple perspectives requires *listening*, both from your system-level balcony and while you are down on the proverbial dance floor.[4]

To illustrate, consider the reality television show called *Undercover Boss* that aired for ten seasons.[5] Each episode highlighted a high-level corporate executive who posed as an entry-level employee in their own organization. Although the executives often began the episode frustrated by their employees' performance, they usually were surprised to discover that the quality of training for frontline workers was much different than they had assumed. In many cases, they realized that the physical conditions and available resources actually made it nearly impossible for employees to succeed in their roles. By getting down on the dance floor, an executive was able to see how easy it was for information to get lost in a hierarchical organization and feel how implicated they were in the problems that they had only partially understood from their balcony perch.

When you shadow or interview or hold focus groups with people in different roles, you collect data that allow you to understand the emotions and lived experiences so that you can avoid making decisions based on faulty assumptions. Judy's story shows the power of this practice. (See "Judy's Story.")

Manage the Change Process

 When speaking to system leaders, Richard Elmore was fond of reminding them that "if you do not see your work in the instructional core, it does not exist."[6] That means that no matter how busy they may feel, unless system leaders can describe how their actions cause

JUDY'S STORY

In those first couple of years of working as a system team using Data Wise to improve our own practice, we spent a lot of time grappling with who was our "learner." So, by the time I transitioned to a role as the director of curriculum and instruction, I knew that everyone on my team had to be clear about who *their* learners were in order to see change happen in the instructional core. We had a systemwide literacy plan that my team was responsible for implementing. One of my direct reports managed literacy coaches who were responsible for helping school teams build data literacy and monitor the evidence-based instructional practices laid out in the plan.

I'll never forget the time when the manager of the coaches visited a high school that had strong data to observe a data analysis meeting at the school. The meeting was not going as we imagined. The school team hadn't created effective meeting practices in Step 1, and the process that we thought was in place to score and analyze writing samples . . . wasn't. After speaking with the literacy coach, we realized that we made some assumptions that were not founded. Our coaches spent most of their time modeling the process to support implementation at schools that were deemed in need of improvement and did not spend our efforts as sites like this one—one deemed to be "higher flying." Thus, we shifted our strategy to build the instructional capacity of all leaders to lead the literacy plan. We assumed that, just because student scores were higher in some places, leaders were doing the work.

A month later, I got a thank-you message from the school. In short, the team there told us that now that they saw how the process was supposed to work after seeing it modeled, they were moved by the realization that they were too focused on grading and not focused on analyzing for learning and strategy use by students. Nothing beats having your team collect its own direct evidence of seeing the work of a systemwide plan in action.

—JUDITH J. WHITE
Maryland, United States

changes to the relationships between learners, facilitators, and content, they are not actually contributing to the core work of the organization. Michelle Forman and colleagues have offered a conceptual model for acting on that insight from Elmore by mapping the professional learning needs associated with systemwide instructional improvement efforts.[7] When the goal is to integrate the Data Wise improvement process itself across a system, managing the change process in Step 4 requires understanding the shifts that need to happen in the learning cores at each level of the system.

As the guiding team members develop their symmetric learning-centered problem, they must ask themselves questions in order to understand how the learning core must improve if they are to realize the vision of wild success. Let's take the example provided in the Attend to Dimensions of Scale section of this chapter. The team's vision of wild success describes students actively collaborating in tasks that exceed grade-level standards with clear support from peers and teachers. If the default model of instruction in the system is more traditional, where the teacher is the fountain of knowledge and students rarely interact around learning, how does the learning core change when student collaboration is introduced? The relationship between students and teachers must change because teachers are no longer the only experts in the room delivering wisdom. The relationship between students and content must change because instead of only regurgitating what they are told, students must be able to explain the content in ways that make sense to their peers. Finally, teachers must shift from seeing their relationship with content to one of delivery with checks for understanding to one where they facilitate space and scaffolds for students to identify ways to check understanding. The learning core is the tool that allows a System Wise team to describe what teachers already know and what they need to learn in order to be able to realize the vision. This utility continues at each altitude of the system.

The system team can use the same three relationships in the learning core to understand the experience of teachers and the changes that school leaders need to make in order to better support them. In the Greenwood case, teachers are learning how to provide more opportunities for students to collaborate. School leaders need to adjust their relationship with the content to model collaborative learning with teachers and emphasize practices that acknowledge teacher risk-taking to try new things. Trying new things means different teachers will need to engage in different learning. This new way of facilitating is likely also new to school leaders, who may need to shift their relationship with teachers from authority figure to co-learner. Finally, school leaders may need to help teachers work through the fears and mental models that might inhibit giving students the time and space to grapple with ideas together. They may need to help teachers persist with something where success does not happen immediately. The same analysis can be conducted with system leaders and their relationships with the people who supervise school leaders. Figure 4.7 provides a visual representation of this analysis.

The changes necessary to realize our vision of wild success for students are complex and have many moving parts. The learning core provides a framework for *naming* the many shifts required. Michael's story shows the power of *witnessing* what the shift can look like as it happens. (See "Michael's Story.")

Figure 4.7

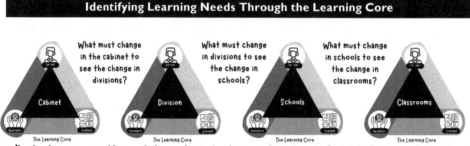

What changes in the relationships between learners, facilitators and content must happen at each altitude in order to cause the desired change in learning?

MICHAEL'S STORY

I support a number of rural school systems in California. We typically do each Data Wise step with grade spans. Kindergarten through second-grade teachers will look at student work and identify trends and priorities, then grades 3 to 5 and 6 to 8. And then we have the groups combine to discuss what patterns are schoolwide. At the end of the day, we get down to one particular challenge around which we can develop a learning-centered problem.

I tell educators that when they eventually get to Step 6, they will address this learning-centered problem by agreeing on one instructional strategy that all teachers in the school will use, and that this strategy might be as simple as deliberately integrating student "partner talk" in all lessons. At this point, they can get a little nervous, worrying, "Well, how is one approach like partner talk going to move my outcomes for my kids and improve student learning?"

But here's the secret: what I've learned over time is that it's not *partner talk* that is the game changer. The game changer is the *collective efficacy* that comes from teachers going through the process together and identifying both a problem that needs to be solved and a strategy for solving it. When teachers implement their strategy, they may discover that they had misconceptions about what was really going on with the relationships between students, teachers, and content. But they will have the confidence and skills to adjust to meet deeper learning needs within the core.

This was a big learning for me that came from being with teachers every step of the way and understanding how change really happens in schools. So I create job-embedded experiences where system-level leaders can have this learning too. If I'm asked to provide training for system leaders at a central location, I tell them they will learn so much more if instead they come alongside me and observe how the process plays out over time in a school. They will build empathy for what it takes to really improve student learning. And they will be able to see how their practice as system leaders is going to have to change if they want their actions to have a clear impact on what happens in classrooms.

—MICHAEL FIGUEROA
California, United States

Practice Radical Inclusivity

 Collectively identifying a problem is an important step if you wish to collectively solve the problem. Yet those in positions of power commonly establish the criteria for high performance and measure others according to their designed standards. Top executives, boards, and government agencies have typically had the responsibility of collecting, analyzing, and reporting data to the community or organization and holding them responsible for results. Even when these leaders collect multiple forms of data, using varied strategies including interviews and surveys, they often interpret the data on their own. But any single individual interpreting data on their own will be unable to see past their own unconscious biases. The only way to mitigate unconscious bias in data analysis is by establishing a collaborative approach to sensemaking. Kerry's story shows how system leaders can tap student voices to broaden their understanding. (See "Kerry's Story.")

KERRY'S STORY

Our Area School Improvement Team looks at data for 120 schools, with each of us responsible for five or six. Area team meetings are essential to helping me do my job . . . but there was a time when I would have said the opposite.

For years, system-level staff felt that meetings were a waste of time: there was no particular purpose, and their voice didn't matter. I was no exception: I would sit there doing my emails because nothing was going to make any difference to my work. What we had was a whole lot of people who cared about what happened in schools who knew they were having no impact. It was so frustrating.

Familiar with Data Wise, I organized for Penny Jayne to deliver a two-day workshop for our executive team where we focused on Step 1: Organizing for Collaborative Work. The experience of sharing our *why* stories was incredibly powerful, some people shed tears, and senior leaders realized how similar their personal *why* stories were. This led to a shared commitment to completely rethink how we used meeting time with a focus on looking at evidence of student learning and hearing all voices.

Now when we meet, we bring lots of different kinds of evidence of student learning and we work to really hone [sic] in on what that data are telling us. This includes everything from data from student well-being surveys to the evidence we collect when doing learning walks at schools, where we each ask students Lyn Sharrett's five critical questions[8]:

1. What are you learning?
2. How are you doing?
3. How do you know?
4. How can you improve?
5. Where do you go for help?

In meetings, we share this evidence and ask one another "What am I not seeing?" When all the ideas are on the table, we discuss how we can support each school.

Our meetings were so profound that regional leaders who work directly with schools, asked for the two-day training too. Over one hundred staff members attended.

As a result, we were able to build symmetry in the way regional personnel worked with one another, and with school leaders.

Now we host similar meetings with school-based mid-level leaders, (such as learning specialists and lead teachers), which impacts what we discuss at a regional level. So, when we provide support, it is much more likely to be what a school really needs, which enables our limited resources to be more targeted. Early impact of our new approach was evident with improved student outcomes in our most recent national data.

—**KERRY WOOD**
Victoria, Australia

System Wise teams ask themselves, "How can we analyze evidence in ways that express our value for diverse voices and working styles?" They are committed to identifying a learner-centered problem that people from across the system truly believe is a priority and worthy of an investment of time and resources. There are many ways System Wise teams can take an anti-bias stance and support collective sensemaking. Figure 4.8 offers four examples.[9]

Collaborative sense-making is anti-biased when you intentionally structure the practice to welcome and value divergent, alternative, and uncommon ideas. The protocols described are radically inclusive when they are structured to elevate the voices of those historically marginalized, including the voices of your students. Do you know who is missing from your table?[10] These protocols create more seats, increasing the collective wisdom needed to fully understand learning gaps.

Your team will want to consider which methods of collective sensemaking are sustainable for your organization. These strategies have the power to build trust. But trying out a strategy and then failing to follow through could signal a wavering commitment to inclusion and cause harm. The very nature of "one and done" initiatives perpetuates cycles of alienation, exclusion, and abandonment. System Wise teams combat these cycles by empowering learners to name their own learning-centered problems and help those in power see how their actions perpetuate learning gaps. How System Wise teams implicate themselves in the improvement work is the focus of chapter 5.

Figure 4.8

Four Ways to Support Collective Sensemaking with an Anti-Bias Stance

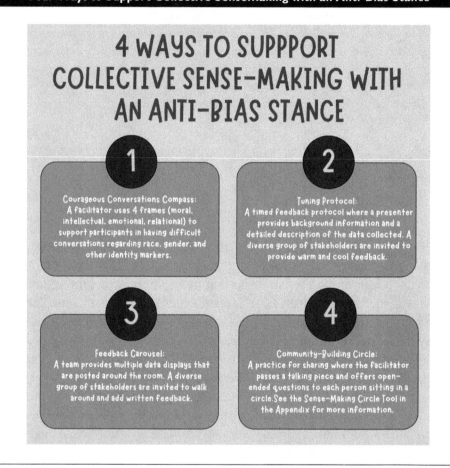

CASE STUDY REVISITED

The guiding team looks at the three pieces of chart paper now on the wall to the left of the wild vision of success.

Reviewing what teachers, school leaders, and system leaders are doing that helps facilitate the vision and what they are doing that gets in the way, a team member laments, "It's a bit embarrassing to see it on paper like this. How could we have been so puzzled before? It makes perfect sense that we are getting the results that we are getting."

"Yes. Through both intentional and unintentional actions, we created the conditions that got us here. I can see how our system divisions, school leaders, and teachers all contribute to both our successes with this learning-centered problem and our barriers."

"OK, so if this is our reality laid out in the symmetric learning-centered problem, where do we show up and what do we do about it, coach?"

Charlie feels the angst of the team members, empathizes deeply, but is not deterred. "This is your question to answer. No one is pointing fingers at you. But the truth is, you are the champions of change. The magic begins here."

REFLECTION QUESTIONS

1. Do we see each learner first through their strengths? Do we believe each learner can do meaningful work?

2. Do we expect enough of our learners? Do we describe the current state of learning with compassion and clarity?

3. How do we see and use our learners' cultural backgrounds to understand their work?

4. What assumptions do we make about learners when we look at their work?

5

EXAMINING OWN PRACTICE

> Does our practice meet the needs of each learner?

SITTING AROUND A U-SHAPED TABLE, the Greenwood guiding team is at an impasse. Emotions swirl. There is a sense of excitement about the insights developed through seeing their work reflected in the system's symmetric learning-centered problem. There is worry that they have identified too many things to do that they do not know how to do. There is frustration about the rate of change being too slow, with not enough time or people to make the shifts the team knows are necessary.

The assistant superintendent brings voice to the moment. "I am stuck. I don't know what to do," Jasmine began. "Over the past three years, this team has allocated multiple professional learning days to using evidence and formative assessment. I have allocated resources and time to these efforts so that teachers can work together with these assessments. I have purchased multiple formative assessment tools that teachers can use. The superintendent and I have shared how this work is important at board meetings and staff meetings. We now have a learning-centered problem that shows how our work connects to change within the learning core. Yet, there are still so many places where this work is not happening. What else can I do?"

ACE HABITS OF MIND IN STEP 5

The stuck feeling described in the case is common for teams as they identify the learning needs of the students and educators they serve and see that their efforts so far have not brought about their desired state for their system. At this step, the ACE Habits of Mind offer teams ways to get unstuck and bring more compassion, clarity, and coherence to improving outcomes for the children and adults who are their learners.

A: Shared Commitment to Action, Assessment, and Adjustment

There is always a legacy of former change efforts that informs how people approach and feel about future actions. Some team members may be skeptical of improvement efforts due to past experiences. This portion of the case illustrates how overwhelmed teams can feel when thinking about the work of improvement. Knowing you need to be doing something differently can generate an urgent impulse to jump into action. *Doing something different* now is prioritized over *understanding what we are doing* now.

Bucking the common trend of analyzing evidence through a deficit lens and attempting to fix what is broken, Jasmine starts by listing the assets already working in the team's favor. She then follows by asking, "What else can I do?" If this question is truly authentic, she is opening the door to self-exploration. The symmetric learning-centered problem that she and the guiding team drafted contains some ideas about why the system is functioning as it is, but at this point they are just hypotheses. As urgent as the call to *action* may feel, the team has some more *assessing* to do before they are ready to start making *adjustments*. At this point their work is to honestly name problems of practice while instilling faith that the collective group can work together to address them.

C: Intentional Collaboration

We see Jasmine use several "I" statements while relaying frustration. This is common: system leaders often feel personal responsibility for the success or failure of an initiative or change effort. Unfortunately, this thinking predictably leads to siloed work and outcomes that are difficult to interpret and reproduce. Effective teams practice empathy and commit to understanding the roles, responsibilities, and perspectives of other team members.

You have probably heard a leader say, "It's lonely at the top." But it doesn't need to be. System Wise leaders recognize the opportunity to build a community of practice through intentional collaboration. In chapters 1 and 3, we discussed the importance of building psychological safety, an interpersonal climate where people feel safe to express ideas honestly and a sense of responsibility to raise important concerns instead of ignoring or hiding them.[1] Psychological safety is absolutely imperative when it is time for educators to examine their own practice together. Just as teachers benefit from peer observation and cultures of feedback, system leaders can best understand their practice if they actually look at that practice as part of their team inquiry. The goal is to get to a place where your team can actually celebrate mistakes by making them teachable moments for everyone's growth and development, but to get to this ideal, sometimes baby steps are required. When Jasmine says, "I am stuck," she is modeling vulnerability, which could be a step toward creating psychological safety for her team.

E: Relentless Focus on Evidence

Jasmine feels exhausted by efforts to bolster educators' use of formative and summative assessments of student learning—especially because, as far as she can see, this work has not paid off. But she has not yet looked at sources of evidence that would provide the rich nuance she needs to understand how her work and that of other system leaders may be contributing to this situation. Defeated, she lists several initiatives that she felt demonstrated the right intentions without the expected impact. Her dismay calls to mind the frustration of a teacher who says about his students, "I taught it, but they didn't learn it." It is time for Jasmine and her team to become curious about how they engaged with others around these initiatives. If they relentlessly collect data about both *what they did* and *how it was experienced*, they will begin to understand what they are doing that is working and where they need to shift their practice.

STRATEGIC TASKS FOR STEP 5

In Step 5, you examine your own practice with the goal of identifying a *problem of practice* that, if addressed, would help you make progress on the learning-centered problem you identified in Step 4. (See figure 5.1.) The idea is to understand how leadership decisions, organizational culture, and the very nature of institutions themselves have worked together to create the conditions that are keeping your system from realizing your vision.

Strategic Task 5.1: Examine a Wide Range of Evidence About Practice

There are many aspects of leadership that require privacy and discretion, often isolating leaders from others in the organization. Some of that work, including performance evaluations and contract negotiations, is intentionally private for legitimate legal and professional reasons. But *when examining practice within the context of collaborative inquiry, the purpose is to learn, not evaluate.* This requires a level of vulnerability as we share evidence of our impact on teachers, students, and

Figure 5.1

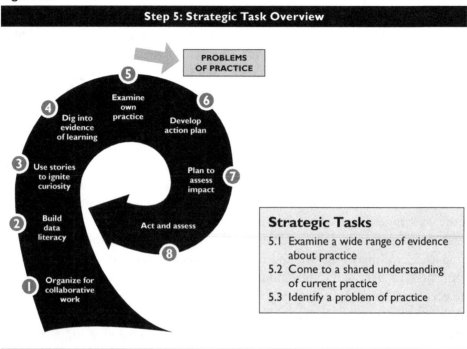

Step 5: Strategic Task Overview

PROBLEMS OF PRACTICE

5 Examine own practice

4 Dig into evidence of learning

6 Develop action plan

3 Use stories to ignite curiosity

Plan to assess impact 7

2 Build data literacy

Act and assess

8

1 Organize for collaborative work

Strategic Tasks

5.1 Examine a wide range of evidence about practice

5.2 Come to a shared understanding of current practice

5.3 Identify a problem of practice

learning. It also requires our openness to receive information from others that can be hard to hear.

System Wise teams typically observe and gather feedback on their practice in five areas: vision and mission, communication, professional development, resource allocation, and accountability structures. The idea here is to *take inventory of current strategies to address the learning-centered problem.* Table 5.1 offers an initial list of domains for gathering evidence of system-level leadership practice, which we hope serves as a starting place and source of inspiration for your teams. There are many other ways to observe adult practice, and we encourage you to choose sources of evidence that most resonate with you.

As we showed in chapter 4, when the Greenwood leadership team used the Data Wise process to improve how their system team supports their learners, who are school leaders, they found that although school leaders were consistently observing teachers and providing initial feedback, they had a learning gap around following up with teachers to support them in integrating that feedback into their practice.

Table 5.1

Domains for Gathering Evidence of System-Level Leadership Practice	
DOMAIN OF EVIDENCE	WHAT EVIDENCE IS GATHERED
Clarifying and leveraging vision, mission, and values	• Video recordings and materials from all-staff presentations • Video recordings and materials from board meeting presentations • Emails, reports, and community letters about mission, vision, and values • Marketing materials, motos, logos • Student assessments
Attending to communication and engaging in storytelling	• Video recordings and materials containing stories shared about instruction • Awards, acknowledgments, and celebrations • Alumni engagement • Community and business partner relationships • Surveys
Support for professional development and coaching	• Video recordings of check-ins with direct reports • Walkthroughs; school or classroom visits • Feedback examples (written and oral) • Anonymized formal evaluation summaries • Work with consultants, contractors, and others with expertise • Recruiting and retention reports
Support for the creation of resources and tools and access to those resources and tools	• Cabinet meeting agendas • Board meeting agendas • Project or task force meetings • Mission-aligned budgets • Calendars
Crafting and use of policy and accountability structures	• School board policy guidelines and norms • State liaison relationships • Evaluation procedures and implementation practices

Given the learning-centered problem, they then asked, "How are we implicated in this learning gap?" and identified evidence sources from the domains in table 5.1 that would shed light on these answers. For example, to address the question, "What guidance do we give school leaders about how to circle back and see how teachers are implementing feedback?" they analyzed video recordings and materials from school leader professional learning sessions on the topic of providing feedback. To explore the question, "To what extent do we model what effective follow-up looks like when we provide feedback to school leaders?" they recorded themselves meeting with school leaders and then took low-inference notes of direct quotes and statements about ways in which they circled back to feedback they had provided in previous meetings.

If you have supervised teachers, you may have developed the skill of taking low-inference notes that capture evidence of *teaching practice* that is specific and descriptive.[2] In Step 5, you need to have a conversation about how best to apply those skills to the observation of *leadership practice*. If your team wants to record how you give feedback to those you directly supervise, you will need to make sure those direct reports understand why in this month's one-to-one meetings, there happens to be an extra body sitting in the corner or a smartphone camera propped up on the desk. Framing might include explaining that the purpose of the observation is to better understand your leadership practice or reassure participants that any notes from the observation will not be used in evaluations. Allocating some time for the observer to interview participants after the observation both allows for additional perception evidence and reinforces that the focus is on the practice of the leader.

If observations are in person, it is well worth the time to thoughtfully consider who will be observing whom. We've seen some teams identify peers in other areas of expertise or departments. Others intentionally seek to disrupt power dynamics and use the opportunity to develop direct reports by having them observe and gather evidence. Whoever is selected, it is important that there is a trusting relationship in both directions and that the observers have enough skill and time to conduct the observations.

If you are on a guiding team scaling Data Wise, you will want to observe the ways the system authorizers establish working conditions. These are the people who lead the organization, decide its priorities, and allocate resources. You will also want to take a step back and notice how the organizational culture itself operates. This can include observing school board guidelines, labor contracts, or evaluation processes.

Strategic Task 5.2: Come to a Shared Understanding of Current Practice

The ultimate goal of collecting evidence is to have a *shared understanding* of what actually happens in leadership practices, instead of relying on our *self-reported sense* of what we think is happening. It is easy to conflate intentions and impact. Creating structures for objective perspectives can help teams minimize bias when examining evidence.

Many teams use the I Notice/I Wonder Protocol introduced in chapter 3 to surface a wide range of perspectives about what the evidence shows. This protocol is incredibly versatile. It can be used to look deeply at quantitative evidence such as content repetitions, time allocations for objectives, or who talks and how much during meetings. It is also illuminating when used with more qualitative evidence sources, such as meeting agendas, schedules, or interview transcripts.

As your team identifies themes across noticings and wonderings, you begin to climb the ladder of inference together by categorizing your ideas as *assets* that you can leverage to address the learning-centered problem or *areas of growth*. If you are on a guiding team that is scaling Data Wise across a system, you will want to do multiple rounds so that you can consider the experience of different groups of learners. One group you want to include is those system authorizers. Some teams use the Affinity Protocol introduced in Step 4 to structure this conversation.[3]

Strategic Task 5.3: Identify a Problem of Practice

Because all the remaining steps in the improvement process will be devoted to addressing the problem of practice you identify in this step, take the time to articulate a problem that is worthy of your energies. A high-quality problem of practice has the characteristics described in figure 5.2.

There are likely to be more areas for growth than you can take on at one time; this is OK. A question that can be helpful to consider is, *If we were to address one of these areas for growth at this moment in time and with the resources available, which one would have a significant impact on our learners and our leadership?* It is also OK to select a problem and have some team members feel that other problems are even more important. What matters is that all members agree that addressing the area for growth is worth the team's investment of time.

With an area of growth selected, you review the assets you found when looking at evidence and then frame your next level of work in

Figure 5.2

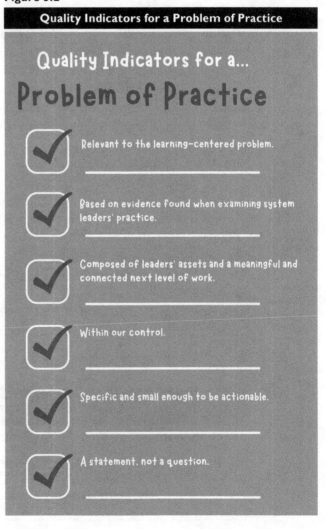

Quality Indicators for a Problem of Practice

Quality Indicators for a...
Problem of Practice

- ✓ Relevant to the learning-centered problem.
- ✓ Based on evidence found when examining system leaders' practice.
- ✓ Composed of leaders' assets and a meaningful and connected next level of work.
- ✓ Within our control.
- ✓ Specific and small enough to be actionable.
- ✓ A statement, not a question.

Figure 5.3

Problem of Practice Sentence Stem

Problem of Practice Sentence Stem

Based upon our review of <insert evidence sources examined>,

as system leaders we <insert strengths relevant to the identified problem>

and our next level of work is <insert one area where system leaders need to improve>.

relation to those assets. You are not starting from scratch; creating a problem of practice that builds on existing excellence will set you up well to select actions in Step 6 that are aligned with your particular context.

Stating your problem of practice succinctly will make it more likely that it is shared and remembered. The sentence stem in figure 5.3 can help ensure that your problem of practice meets the quality indicators described earlier.

Table 5.2 shows an example of a problem of practice the leadership team for Greenwood School System identified as it completed Step 5 of its improvement cycle focused on learners, who are school leaders effective at providing initial feedback to teachers but had a learning gap in following up afterward.

If you are on a guiding team that is scaling Data Wise across your system, each of the strategic tasks for Step 5 also involves looking beyond leader practice to more general forces that may be at play.

That is because there are always enabling and inhibiting conditions that, when identified, provide a richer understanding of the next level of work within the problem of practice. The Greenwood guiding team might ask itself, *What forces already in motion will help us seek school leader input?* It might identify political forces such

Table 5.2

Example of Problem of Practice Developed by the Greenwood Leadership Team	
Problem of practice	Based on our review of professional learning plans, observations of one-to-one feedback sessions with school leaders, and conversations with them afterward, as system leaders we provide professional learning resources and time to improve school leaders' skills in providing feedback to teachers, and our next level of work is to consistently seek input from school leaders about what they need in order to ensure that feedback to teachers leads to changes in practice.

as an environment that values local control. The guiding team might also ask, *What forces already in motion will inhibit our efforts to seek leader input?* The answers could include social structures and habits within the organization that make school leaders fearful of offering opinions. This Force Field Protocol is an activity that helps your team consider the forces that are working in favor of your efforts to scale Data Wise and the forces that work against engaging in continuous improvement. Identifying the conditions in which your problem of practice occurs will support your decision-making in Step 6: Developing an Action Plan.

If you are on a guiding team that is scaling Data Wise across your system, your task is to craft a *symmetric problem of practice* that situates multiple assets and next steps within the ecosystem of your organization. We explain how to do this and give an example in the Attend to Dimensions of Scale section. Table 5.3 summarizes the strategic tasks for Step 5, depending on purpose.

Table 5.3

Strategic Tasks for Step 5, Depending on Purpose		
Step 5: Strategic tasks	**What this task looks like when:**	
	A SYSTEM TEAM IS SUPPORTING LEARNERS IT DIRECTLY SERVES	**A GUIDING TEAM IS SCALING DATA WISE ACROSS A SYSTEM**
5.1: Examine a wide range of evidence about practice	• Decide which evidence to collect • Observe practice with the purpose of learning, not evaluating • Take inventory of current strategies to address the learning-centered problem	• Decide which evidence to collect • Observe practice with the purpose of learning, not evaluating • Observe how system authorizers and organizational culture establish working conditions
5.2: Come to a shared understanding of current practice	• Describe patterns in the relationships between learners, facilitators, and content	• Describe patterns in the relationships between learners, facilitators, and content • Assess the impact of system authorizers and organizational culture on the working conditions experienced by people from multiple positions and perspectives within the organization
5.3: Identify a problem of practice	• List the sources of evidence you used • Identify both the *assets* in leader practice and the *next level of work* that could lead to improved outcomes	• List the sources of evidence you used • Identify both the *assets* in leader practice and the *next level of work* that could lead to improved outcomes • Acknowledge the enabling and inhibiting conditions that affect the problem of practice at each altitude

TAKING A SYSTEM WISE APPROACH TO STEP 5

Attend to Dimensions of Scale

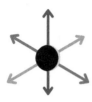

Unlike school teams, system teams work more through *influence* of others than through *direct control* of the change they hope to achieve. Whether you are using Data Wise to examine your practice as a leadership team or whether you are part of a guiding team looking to scale Data Wise across your system, this requires investing more time in attending to the *sustaining* dimension. Similar to the symmetric learning-centered problem, the symmetric problem of practice is a connected story that shows the relationship between practices and outcomes at each altitude of the organization. The arrows in the template in figure 5.4 show how to work back from the teacher problem of practice to describe the next level of work at multiple levels.

System Wise teams start by modeling what it looks like to implicate themselves in a problem of practice. They may form theories or hypotheses about the problems of practice at other levels, but their ultimate goal is to empower educators at those other altitudes to identify their own problems as they learn about the Data Wise process and begin to develop coherent practices. The symmetrical problem provides a general focus for the organization while allowing for differentiation in approaches and priorities for those closest to the work, namely, teachers.

One way to achieve the *depth* dimension of scale is to ensure coherence between the symmetrical learning-centered problems and the symmetrical problem

Figure 5.4

System Wise Symmetric Problem of Practice Template			
Guiding Team Problem of Practice	System Leader Problem of Practice	School Leader Problem of Practice	Teacher Problem of Practice
Based upon evidence, describe what the guiding team does well to support all levels and what their next level of work should be	Based upon evidence, describe what system leaders do well to support school leaders and what the next level of work for system leaders should be	Based upon evidence, describe what school leaders do well to support teachers' problems of practice and what their next level of work should be	Based upon evidence, describe what teachers do well that supports the student learning–centered problem and what their next level of work for should be

of practice. When these line up, the work can have the kind of deep impact that will set the stage well for addressing other dimensions of scale. Figure 5.5 shows what scale with nested learning cores looks like. The learner at the bottom right vertex of each triangle becomes the facilitator in the next triangle over.

Tables 5.4 and 5.5 offer two different examples of symmetric problems of practice, showing that the process works equally well for academics and operations. The first example shows that the Greenwood guiding team's problem of practice about collaboration is enacted and defined in different divisions. The second example is from a guiding team that identified a problem of practice around formative assessment and feedback. As you examine these examples, notice the similarities—including the inclusion of evidence sources, assets, and one next level of work that implicates adults. See how each level of the system is getting clearer about using either collaboration or formative assessment.

Also notice the inconsistencies and messiness in these examples, which show real work of teams at multiple levels, not a guiding team's hypotheses about what they might be. In the first example, not all divisions used the sentence stem. The different school-level problems of practices in the second example were written with differing degrees of clarity since each team was at a different developmental level in their understanding of the improvement process. They are also different in the degree to which they implicate leader practice. And yet because they were authentically

Figure 5.5

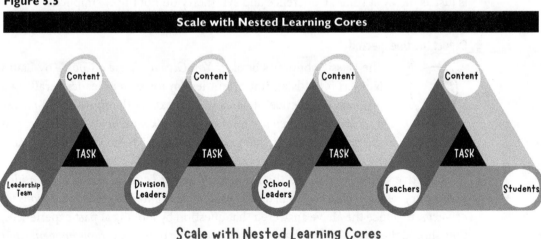

Scale with Nested Learning Cores

Table 5.4

Example of Greenwood School System's Symmetric Problems of Practice		
FOCUS AREA FOR THIS INQUIRY CYCLE: SCALING DATA WISE		
Guiding team problem of practice		
Based on our review of survey data from school and division leaders, focus groups, and our communication audit, as system leaders we are good at communicating that we value collaboration across different parts of the organization. Our next level of work is to align supports and prioritize time in a way that reflects those values and allows for collaboration.		
System division problems of practice		
Operations department	**Curriculum and instruction department**	**Community and family engagement department**
• Based on review of meetings and emails with school leaders, we are good at sharing long-term plans for facilities improvements. • Our next level of work is including school leaders in developing our strategic facilities plan.	• Based on school leader surveys, we are effective at communicating priorities around collaborative learning. • The next level of work is allowing school leaders an opportunity to experience it for themselves.	• We are good at using surveys to gather community input in multiple formats. • Our next level of work is ensuring that families are also part of the teams that make sense of the survey data and identify next steps.

generated by educators seeking to improve their own practice, all are valuable entry points into doing just that. As you do your improvement work, you will likely find it is just as messy at times. Coherence and symmetry do not imply simplicity.

Expect the Unexpected

 The classic children's book *If You Give a Mouse a Cookie* by Laura Numeroff holds an important lesson for system leaders crafting a problem of practice.[4] Just as we can expect that *if we give a mouse a cookie, it will then ask for a glass of milk and then a napkin*, we can expect some of the responses to our change efforts. Figure 5.6 shows questions teams can ask themselves to anticipate responses to change efforts.

Effective systems teams ask themselves: *"If we get better at this area identified within our problem of practice, what are the hopeful and concerning outcome actions we can expect?"* Once they have answered that question by looking at past experiences, they should then ask: *"If those hopeful and concerning outcome actions happen, what hopeful and concerning outcomes are likely to come from those actions?"*

Table 5.5

Example of Academic Focused Symmetric Problems of Practice
FOCUS AREA FOR THIS INQUIRY CYCLE: SCALING DATA WISE

System leadership problem of practice
Based on our review of professional learning plans, budgets, and conversations with school leaders, as system leaders we provide resources and time to implement continuous improvement practices. Our next level of work is communicating our value and practice for consistently seeking feedback from schools about what they need in order to use data more regularly and effectively as a formative assessment to guide our practice.

School leadership problems of practice		
Elementary school	**Middle school**	**High school**
• Based on our observations of collaborative planning time meetings and notes, we are good at getting teacher feedback and responding when teachers provide unsolicited feedback. • We need to work on having structures to regularly gather teacher feedback, particularly from staff that aren't the loudest/typical voices to inform our practice.	• Based on classroom observation notes and cluster team meeting agendas, we are good at informally sharing formative assessment strategies, providing formative assessment professional development as a learning choice, discussing formative assessment in many of our post-observation conferences, modeling formative assessment in administration meetings, and providing resources (software and materials). • Our next level of work is to clarify our expectations around formative assessment and provide feedback on formative assessment practices every time we speak with teachers about instruction.	• Based on our list of high-needs students, state monitoring visit feedback, classroom observations, walkthroughs, and survey feedback, we are able to collect skill-level data, predict students who need support, offer professional development resources, and put data structures in place. • Our next level of work includes supporting teachers with implementing formative assessment and using the results to inform instruction to provide differentiated support.

Teacher team problems of practice (samples)
Primary team: Based on our review of lesson plans and classroom instruction, we (teachers) are good at including mini multiple-choice assessments and student reflections in our lessons and the next level of work for us is to consistently use that information to adjust instruction for our high-need students. **Grade 7 team:** Based on our review of classroom instruction and student interviews, we (teachers) regularly gather and use academic formative assessment to adjust learning and the next level of work is to use more student voice and social-emotional learning formative assessment to provide more culturally responsive learning experiences and classroom environment. **Math department:** Based on our review of student work samples and student surveys, the mathematics team successfully creates formative assessments, reviews them collaboratively to identify patterns and misconceptions, and adjusts lessons to meet the needs of all students. We need to get better at building student ownership of assessment by including students in the formative assessment process.

Figure 5.6

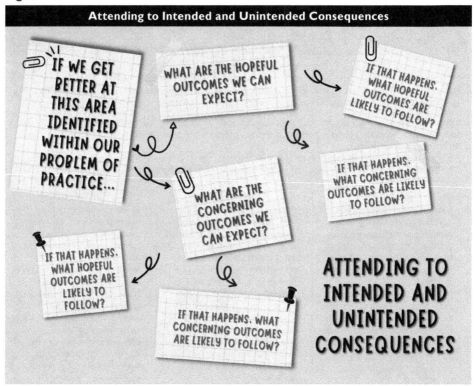

Answering these questions within different time boundaries can be helpful: for example, within the first month of enacting a change, within the school year, or within ten years. Much as geologists use millions of years to measure units of time and biologists studying fruit flies measure in hours, system leaders must consider their efforts over generations, while teachers may focus more on changing learning outcomes over an academic year.

While it is possible to use this process to uncover infinite orders of change, it is rarely helpful to go past one or two rounds of identifying the hopeful and concerning outcomes. Overdoing this strategy can lead to paralysis and inaction or ultimately useless analysis.

Taking time to consider the potential consequences of addressing problems of practice helps to ensure that the need identified has a high likelihood of enabling meaningful change and that there are no surprises. Doing a clear-eyed analysis of the challenges faced when addressing the problem of practice will set you up well for a more nuanced strategy and proactive action plans as you move toward action in Step 6.

A key theme of this book is that collaborative learning is most effective when leaders model vulnerability and risk-taking by making their own learning and mistakes visible. In this chapter, we live this practice by having three of our four authors (David, Carmen, and Adam) each share a story about our own learning (Kathy will share a story in the concluding chapter). We took the risk to help make it easier for you to join us in modeling public learning. David will start us off by sharing a story that illustrates how one team's problem of practice implicated several others in leading differently. (See "David's Story.")

DAVID'S STORY

The twelve-person improvement team that I led landed on a problem of practice after analyzing evidence: while we teach and model the process consistently, we do not engage in specific practices that support school teams in moving steadily through each phase of Data Wise. The root cause for our problem of practice centered on the existence of varying, competing beliefs about how quickly cycles should happen, and who is accountable for ensuring that schools make progress. Relatedly, while school teams engaged in Data Wise, they struggled to document actionable next steps that would support their forward movement. As I reflected on my role, I realized that I had been missing an opportunity to use my biweekly meetings with direct reports to ask focused questions about specific schools and how they were moving through the process with the support of specialists.

I had always used biweekly meetings to connect with each team member to discuss their personal learning goals, consult with them around challenges they were facing, and generally be a thought partner. Once we landed on a problem of practice for our team, though, it became clear that I needed to adjust my meeting structure to support me in working in a way that was *not* my workstyle preference. Leading this type of improvement was going to require that I have consistent conversations about specific schools and prioritize my school visits to see evidence of how the improvement specialists were following through. The reality was that their problem of practice was my problem of leadership.

(continues)

DAVID'S STORY (*continued*)

With support from my assistant, I redesigned my one-on-one meeting agendas with the improvement specialists so each agenda began with a discussion of the evidence from actions taken at schools that were stuck in the process. From there, we planned how the improvement specialist would engage moving forward to keep the school-based teams moving. And given that my supervisor, the deputy superintendent, was highly engaged in the work of improvement, her coaching to me focused on how I was maintaining a focus on the work of the improvement specialists for those schools. Through shared agendas and notes, all of our practice became public. It was hard to be so transparent at first because exposing *my* practice exposed *other people's practice*, but we really did learn a lot about improvement and adult learning at scale through this approach.

—**DAVID REASE, JR.**
Maryland, United States

Manage the Change Process

 When examining the effectiveness of system-level improvement, the default response of many system leadership teams is to emphasize the technical and intellectual aspects of the process. This includes a hyper-focus on action-step accountability and quick measures of compliance like report submission, walkthrough checklists, or performative accountability.[5] Teams often go deeper into the weeds by making expectations even more detailed and less flexible. This leads to dysfunctional, compliance-centered, fear-based cultures and actions that do not easily adapt to local conditions, have minimal impact, cause harm, or even lead to furtive rebellion and independent action that happens below the radar of system leaders.

System Wise leaders consider the adaptive nature of challenges and emphasize the relational and emotional aspects of change, examining the ways in which their practice contributes to an enriching organizational culture with strong relationships among all members. One way to do this that is responsive to those relationships is to gather evidence about the emotions surrounding the focus area and past change efforts.

Dr. Mary Lippitt developed a useful framework for considering the emotional impact of change management.[6] This model includes five areas that must work in concert for a change effort to have its intended effect:

- The change effort has a clear and shared vision.

- The right people have the right skills to enact what is expected of them in their role.

- The incentives for compliance with the change efforts are aligned and support implementation without unintended consequences.

- The team has adequate resources (time, people, and stuff) to implement the change.

An action plan encompasses all the critical moves required for the change effort. What is most helpful for system leaders is that this model identifies the emotional or practical outcome if any of these elements are missing. For example, a change effort where everyone has the skills and resources, is properly incentivized, has an action plan, but does not have a clear vision tends to confuse people. When folks are asked to enact change for which they do not have the skills, they will respond with anxiety. When incentives are missing, there is a lethargic lack of urgency in the effort. A lack of resources leads to frustration, and a lack of plan leads to constant restarts and skepticism. This framework is summarized in figure 5.7.

By gathering emotional data as part of the development of a problem of practice, leaders can diagnose what sorts of actions may be most helpful to those responsible for enacting the change. System leaders can examine feedback responses from surveys given during professional learning about the change priority. When participants engage in the Plus/Delta Protocol to share what supported their learning and what they would have liked to change, they often provide information about their emotions. Leaders can also conduct focus groups or one-on-one interviews with those enacting or experiencing change efforts. It can also be helpful to review team meeting agenda notes, topics, and Plus/Delta

Figure 5.7

Framework for Managing Complex Change

MANAGING COMPLEX CHANGE

CHANGE REQUIRES · IF THIS ELEMENT IS MISSING... · EMOTIONAL EXPERIENCE

☑ VISION ·······► CONFUSION
☑ SKILLS ·······► ANXIETY
☑ INCENTIVES ·······► LETHARGY
☑ RESOURCES ·······► FRUSTRATION
☑ ACTION PLAN ·······► FALSE STARTS

Source: Inspired by the version published in Richard Villa and Jacqueline Thousand, *Restructuring for Caring and Effective Education: Piecing the Puzzle Together* (Baltimore, MD: Paul H. Brookes, 2000).

reflections. Leaders can categorize these responses to see patterns and priorities in where shifts in vision, skills, incentives, resources, or action plans could help improve implementation. Carmen shares how this attention to emotional impact is one way in which leaders can identify blind spots in their practice. (See "Carmen's Story.") Table 5.6 is a graphic organizer that can help system teams with this analysis.

Table 5.6

Analyzing Emotional Experiences of Change		
EMOTIONAL EXPERIENCE	**EVIDENCE**	**IMPLICATIONS FOR YOUR SYMMETRIC PROBLEM OF PRACTICE**
Confusion (lack of vision)		
Anxiety (lack of skills)		
Lethargy at gradual change (lack of incentives)		
Frustration (lack of resources)		
Skepticism/feeling of "we've already done this"; false starts (lack of action planning)		
Confidence in sustainable change		

CARMEN'S STORY

Starting as a central office leader in my previous district, I found it didn't take long for me to recognize that there was a complex history of relating and relationships among leaders. As in other organizations, distinct departments, roles, and budgeting practices were structures that inherently created silos of work and, consequently, barriers to developing meaningful relationships. Our leaders worked closely with the people they supervised or to whom they were physically proximal. The day-to-day interaction within a building or department afforded many opportunities to engage deeply. However, our system leaders were brought together with intention only once per month. Yes, leaders were serving the same districtwide mission and vision, and yes, they were collaborating within a community. However, there was a lack of communication and understanding. Leaders had little empathy for their colleagues' workload, successes, or challenges because we didn't have a routine or protocol for sharing and building authentic relationships.

I was concerned that leaders would resist being vulnerable when it was time to examine our practice. I thought that the leaders felt pressure to always put their best foot forward and maintain their status as effective rather than implicate themselves in a problem. I noticed evidence of anxiety and hesitation to lean into the process. At the time, I didn't realize that I was dealing with the same fear. I was the new person and hadn't yet developed meaningful relationships. Could I be vulnerable with this group I was leading and acknowledge that this was new territory?

To prepare for this step, I decided to take a risk and introduce a peer coaching protocol in order to develop a rhythm of being together. The coaching protocol created a smaller space where a leader could focus on one self-selected area, then use their coach as a mirror and guide to deeply understand the root causes of the problem and see opportunities or paths forward. Developing these communication skills with support helped to build the capacity of the group. The protocol also provided a strategic way of talking and being together, reducing fear of shame.[7] It was empowering for leaders to see that they were not alone in the work or victims of circumstances outside of their control. Instead, their collective experience and wisdom were exactly what was needed to begin solutioning. The leaders now have data indicating that someone else *sees* them, understands, and cares enough to offer support through thought partnership.

—**CARMEN WILLIAMS**
Massachusetts, United States

Practice Radical Inclusivity

 It is imperative that leaders have the opportunity to own their problem of practice and deeply consider the changes in their own practice. This is an empowering step that reestablishes the team's identity as a change agent, and leaders should model it for everyone in the organization. This step is about self-actualization; however, it is also an opportunity to give various stakeholders the opportunity to make an investment in relational trust.

As authors, we hope the readers of this book upend the ways in which problems are identified within systems. Our systems are structured to privilege the voices of those at the top of the hierarchy. Many systems have built cultures where the expectation is that the leadership names problems and provides a plan for what to do. In the best cases, those experiencing the problems of the organization are asked for their input and may even get updates on decisions or results. In contrast, System Wise leaders develop their problem of practice through co-analysis with those they seek to influence. (See figure 5.8.)

The larger community must be involved in all three strategic actions in Step 5. At this step, we can ask the question, *How can we automate feedback loops and action steps that express our value for diverse voices and working styles?* Members of the community must both engage in the observation of practice and have their experiences and perspectives captured as additional sources of evidence. Community engagement in the process of developing shared understanding will help you refine your problem of practice. By gathering their experiences and perspectives, we can reveal the improvement practices they value and champion.

Figure 5.8

Leaders Need Multiple Perspectives to Fully Understand Their Problem of Practice

System Wise teams use existing stakeholder meetings in service of their goals to analyze evidence of current practices. It is likely that leaders regularly meet with unions or associations, student councils or cabinets, and caretaker groups to discuss current, urgent problems. The meetings typically focus on perceived problems of practice that one of these groups presents. System leaders are expected to do something about it with their positional power. However, System Wise leaders shift the energy toward using these meetings to foster ownership of an important problem of practice and seek further evidence or feedback to substantiate their hypotheses about why the problem exists. This humble stance increases the team's ability to gain a deeper understanding from multiple perspectives. Additionally, System Wise teams use this platform to allow others to hold them accountable for addressing the problem. Relational trust is built in this vulnerable space. Adam shares his story about how he learned this the hard way. (See "Adam's Story.")

ADAM'S STORY

As a system leadership team, we were trying to figure out why so many of our actions did not translate into the expected changes in schools. We identified through interviews and building walkthroughs that while we were good at coming up with possible improvements for schools, we did not successfully enlist school leaders into making changes.

In regularly scheduled meetings, we shared this problem of practice with our principal's union and our principal cabinet (a group of school leaders who provided feedback in an advisory capacity to the superintendent's team). These leaders helped us see that our problem was not that we did not enlist school leaders, but that we enacted strategies that were not informed by what school leaders experienced in their schools and that school leaders did not believe would be effective. We also learned that many leaders were not even aware of what changes we were trying to make. These leaders gently shared that I was making assumptions based on my experience as a former principal and not based on an understanding of the current state of these schools and their leaders' perspectives. For a leader who aspires to an inclusive grassroots approach, this was hard to hear.

(continues)

ADAM'S STORY (continued)

With this problem of practice revised through feedback from those closest to the problem, we shifted our approach. We developed a district policy of principal task forces where highly effective school leaders could lead a district change effort for which they had passion without having to leave their current role. These leaders were positioned to tackle system priorities such as how our schools support youth in foster care and identifying pathways to increase the number of leaders of color within the system with much more knowledge of local conditions.

—**ADAM PARROTT-SHEFFER**
Illinois, United States

CASE STUDY REVISITED

After the assistant superintendent shared her feelings and the guiding team members reflected on their own emotions, Charlie, the coach, asked, "If we don't know what to do, who can we ask?" A principal shared that when teachers are stuck, she recommends they ask the students. "What if you asked the school leaders what they need from our guiding team in order to really organize for collaborative work?"

The assistant superintendent smiles and stands to her feet, "I see it now! We ask our leaders what they need through the budget process every year and find the resources to do something *for* them instead of *with* them. We can't expect them to collaborate unless we model genuine collaboration, and they experience it. We are trying to improve collaboration practices in each classroom, and we haven't partnered with the people best positioned to help us understand what we need to do differently."

REFLECTION QUESTIONS

1. Does our practice meet the needs of each learner?

2. Do we take responsibility for meeting the needs of each learner?

3. Do we expect enough of ourselves? Do we describe our current practice with compassion and clarity?

4. What is our vision for our equitable practice?

6

DEVELOPING
AN ACTION PLAN

How much are we willing to change?
How much is our organization willing to change?

HAVING A CLEARER SENSE of the role of system leaders in the problem of practice brings energy to the guiding team that is supporting Greenwood School System in scaling Data Wise. A school leader on the team shares that the process is allowing him to see his school and the system as a whole through new eyes.

But the energy dissipates as the team begins to identify actions to take. Many members feel like they are back where they have been so many times during improvement efforts over the years. There is a fear that they will once again build action plans that create more work for everyone, but nothing will change.

"Whenever we have a meeting, the deliverable is always some sort of action plan. We fill in the boxes and then come to the next meeting with none of the items having happened—and that is the best-case scenario! Usually, we never look at them again. We are addicted to *making* plans for ourselves and our teachers, not to *implementing* them."

"It isn't from a lack of desire that we don't get anywhere with our plans. I leave our meetings genuinely excited about all the things we come up with. In our last strategic planning session, I had seven items I had some responsibility for and I planned to do all of them. However, I had two major grant reports due before the end of the quarter, and a key team member left to take a job closer to their home. Our actions were all great ideas, perhaps lofty, but definitely student focused. I feel horrible dropping the ball, but I couldn't hold it any longer."

Several heads in the room silently nod and it gets really quiet until someone asks, "How will this time be different?"

ACE HABITS OF MIND IN STEP 6

System Wise leaders embrace the challenge of building equitable schools: places where learners of any age feel celebrated for who they are, have access to rigorous learning experiences, and have outcomes that are not predictable by their demographic data. Meeting this challenge requires that educators develop sound, implementable, and measurable action plans and also take time for the introspection and reflection needed to ensure high-quality professional learning. Once again, keeping the ACE Habits of Mind at our fingertips supports this reflection.

A: Shared Commitment to Action, Assessment, and Adjustment

Action often requires us to denounce fear and embrace hope through strategic adjustment. The Greenwood team members are vulnerably sharing their concerns about writing yet another action plan. The content of the action plan is not the problem; problems come when they need to respond and act on items that are not on the plan. One team member shares how excited she was to get started on the previous plan; however, other unexpected priorities interrupted her workflow, and she was unsuccessful in completing her assigned tasks. Working in a dynamic organization means that team members are balancing their time between responding proactively and reactively, shifting their focus and prirorities as needed. In the past, team members felt unable to make adjustments in real time, creating the false choice of either succeeding by following the plan as written or choosing to fail.

Our case team sees the value in establishing an action plan, but the fear of failure in implementing the plan causes them to hesitate. System Wise teams enacting plans recognize the need to be flexible in implementation. Flexible thinking is far from conceding or giving up. It is strategic preparation that accounts for the unknown and creates the conditions for teams to pivot, making necessary adjustments. Similarly, during the COVID-19 pandemic, many organizations recognized the need to extend grace and understanding due to the complex nature of maintaining distance and safety in communal learning spaces. A halt to all education services would have had significant consequences. Instead, many systems used a steady flow of data and information to learn how best to navigate the situation and persist. Flexible thinking, grace, and understanding are not the same as lowering expectations or letting go. They represent instead a heightened consciousness of your goal that allows you to develop adjustment strategies and put care at the center of your work.

C: Intentional Collaboration

How often do we make assumptions about collaboration? Action plans are an opportunity to be explicit. Many action plan templates strive to provide clarity by encouraging clear tasks that are aligned to shared goals and assigning work to specific individuals and small teams. Unfortunately, if you aren't intentional in your practice, action planning can be alienating. As we see in this case, the grants director expresses her shame at not being able to fulfill her commitment. While most would appreciate her taking responsibility for dropping the ball, she's not the only one who failed to fulfill a commitment. Where was the team support?

 Traditional action plans often employ a divide-and-conquer approach, divvying up work to complete a big task. Unfortunately, that approach can create silos of work, responsibility, and interests. When your team develops a shared *why* and commits to engaging in an inquiry cycle on a focus area, you are committing to a journey of shared values, interests, and action. Unleashing the full weight of the diverse talents of a collective group offers richness and greater capacity to complete tasks. There is no evidence in the case that the grants director relied on other members of her team to show empathy and understanding of her increasing demands, or that her team members checked in to help. Intentional collaboration requires systematic lines of communication that enable each individual to flourish in an attentive and supportive community of practice.

E: Relentless Focus on Evidence

Know thyself! Socrates, the Greek philosopher, left us with this profound phrase and charged us with exploring knowledge of self as a path toward wisdom. It is important to use evidence to inform decisions, but equally important to acknowledge that evidence does not exist in a vacuum: we interpret it through our values. One team member in the case says, "We are addicted to making plans for ourselves and our teachers." The other members could receive this statement as an invitation to collect evidence on how they work together. Is their addiction to "filling in the boxes" but seldom following through driven by a respect for compliance-based activities? Or a belief in the sufficiency of well-meaning intentions? Self- and team awareness can help them understand why they are stuck.

We can use past experiences and stories to support our ability to develop an action plan we can implement with integrity. When we give members of the team the opportunity to share their stories, we learn more about their backgrounds and perceptions. Members of the case team silently agreed by nodding their heads to the statement regarding the failure to implement previous action plans. As this team builds and enacts its action plan, it would benefit from creating space to reflect on not just the intentions, but the actual leadership moves it plans to make and the impact it means to have. A team member asks, "How will this time be different?" Focusing on evidence of how they have approached implementation in the past will help them understand how to mitigate barriers moving forward.

STRATEGIC TASKS FOR STEP 6

The goal of Step 6 is to create an action plan that all stakeholders are invested in implementing. Strategic tasks include choosing a strategy for addressing the problem of practice, agreeing on what the strategy will look like in practice, identifying the professional learning needs related to the strategy, and creating an action plan that specifies who will do what by when. (See figure 6.1.)

Figure 6.1

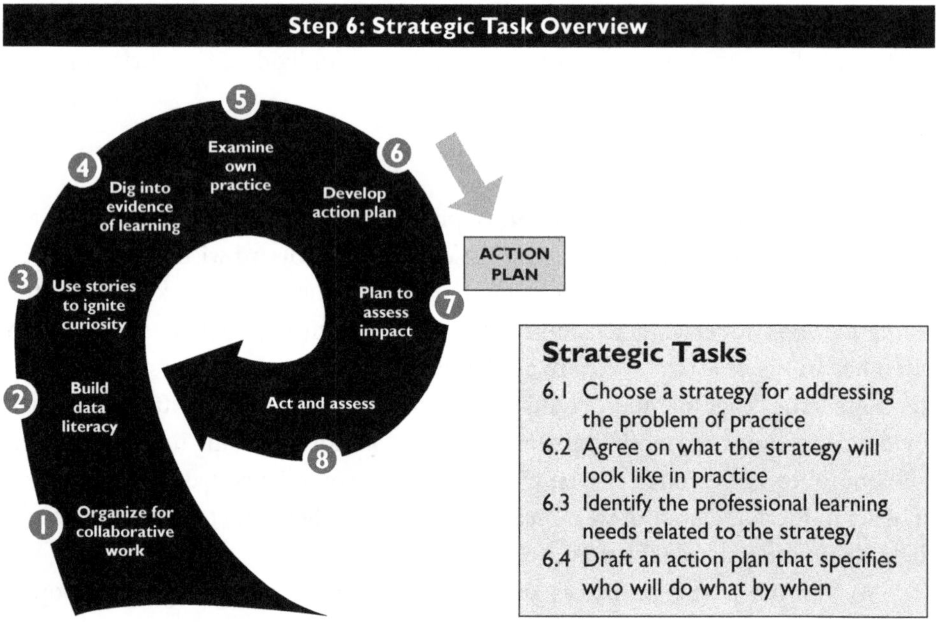

Step 6: Strategic Task Overview

5 Examine own practice
4 Dig into evidence of learning
6 Develop action plan
3 Use stories to ignite curiosity
ACTION PLAN
Plan to assess impact 7
2 Build data literacy
Act and assess
8
1 Organize for collaborative work

Strategic Tasks

6.1 Choose a strategy for addressing the problem of practice

6.2 Agree on what the strategy will look like in practice

6.3 Identify the professional learning needs related to the strategy

6.4 Draft an action plan that specifies who will do what by when

Strategic Task 6.1: Choose a Strategy for Addressing the Problem of Practice

There is a default mindset in improvement work that identifying a strategy to address a problem of practice requires adding something completely new to the plate of those assumed to be responsible for the problem—usually school leaders and teachers. In our experience, this leads to ever-expanding and unrealistic expectations. System Wise leaders recognize that the most effective strategies are built within the context of what is already happening within the organization and reflect savvy application of the organization's assets. For our purposes, a *strategy* is a generalized approach to how one will take action, and *action steps* refer to the specific and measurable actions that are coherent with the strategy.

A strategy hits the sweet spot when it is specific enough that it offers good guidance for those closest to the work to make aligned decisions when confronted with future choice points, but not so prescriptive that those closest to the work are unable to adapt it to meet contextual needs. Table 6.1 shares some examples of things that people may *say* are strategies but are not. It also offers examples of strategies that demonstrate a useful level of specificity.

Table 6.1

Examples of Strategies	
THINGS PEOPLE MAY SAY ARE STRATEGIES	**EXAMPLES OF SYSTEM WISE STRATEGIES**
"Our strategy is implementing the ABC Literacy Curriculum." *Why this is not a strategy: this is a resource masquerading as a strategy.*	"Our strategy is using a common, vertically aligned literacy curriculum with sufficient time for planning that we support through professional learning, coaching, and feedback." *Why this is a strategy: it gives a description of what people will do with the resource.*
"Our strategy is that 100% of students attend preschool." *Why this is not a strategy: this is a goal masquerading as a strategy.*	"Our strategy is to leverage parent coordinators and multiple means of communication to share prekindergarten options with families, simplify the application and enrollment process, and offer materials in multiple languages." *Why this is a strategy: it uses verbs that describe how that goal will be achieved.*
"Our strategy is local control for decisions." *Why this is not a strategy: this is a value masquerading as a strategy.*	"Our strategy is to clarify decisions made at each altitude of the system, align resource allocation to decision-making authority, and respect and support decisions made at the school level." *Why this is a strategy: it provides specificity about the actions that will be taken in service of the value of "local control."*

When choosing a strategy to address your problem of practice, start by focusing on what is going well at the level of the organization closest to the work. For example, if you are choosing an instructional strategy, the first place to look is at the school-level curriculum and instruction across the system. Are there aspects of the curriculum that are not being used? Are there elements that are being used incorrectly or infrequently? If you are not able to identify a strategy by looking at schools, consider system-level resources next. Are there tools, professional learning opportunities, curricular supports, or other resources that could address the problem of practice effectively? If so, look no further. It is fine to name something that is already available but underused as the strategy. If your team is still coming up short, consider the counternarratives. Look for places across your system where people are getting results that are different from most. Are there teachers or departments who do not share the problem of practice? If so, what are they doing differently and how might that inform the problem of practice? All three of these approaches focus the organization on building on strengths instead of taking on something completely new. This is often a more effective approach because folks are more inspired and have more energy to build on things they are already doing. Just as it is easier for a driver to change direction by using a roundabout than by coming to a complete stop, it takes a lot less emotional, political, and financial capital to adjust momentum in progress in a school system than to stop and pivot.

There will be times when you examine local practice, system resources, and counternarratives and still come up short. In those rare instances, the final step is to select a strategy from beyond the expertise of the organization. To identify a strategy, look to research centers, professional organizations, and similarly situated systems that achieve different results. This tiered approach to asset-based strategy exploration is summarized in figure 6.2. This approach supports teams using an asset-based frame when reviewing current practices while taking a learning stance.

Figure 6.2

Tiers of Strategy Exploration

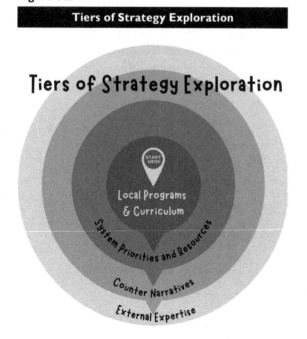

Whichever tier eventually leads to a strategy, the important deliverable for this step is to articulate a strategy the whole team can get behind.

Strategic Task 6.2: Agree on What the Strategy Will Look Like in Practice

The learning core has been central to how we talk about the work of improvement through Step 5; Step 6 is no different. It is one thing for your team to agree on a strategy. It is a much more complex task for your whole team to agree on what that strategy looks like in practice. To achieve this level of understanding, you work together to describe what it will look, sound, and feel like when the strategy is enacted (similar to the kind of description you may have created for your vision of wild success). Taking the time to create this description of actual practice helps ensure that everyone means the same things when they use the same words.

If you are using Data Wise to support learners you directly serve, you begin by adjusting the vertices of the learning core to fit your situation. Figure 6.3 offers two examples of what the adaptation could look like. You then describe how your intended strategy will impact the relationships between your learners, yourselves, and the content that your learners are working on. If your learners are system-level divisions, that content may be core work like hiring a diverse faculty or making sure the buses run on time. If your learners are school leaders, that content may be leadership tasks like providing instructional leadership or engaging families.

Figure 6.3

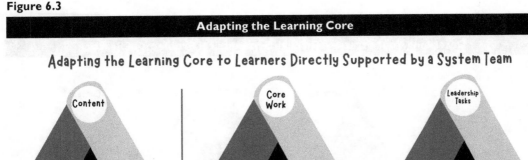

Adapting the Learning Core

Adapting the Learning Core to Learners Directly Supported by a System Team

If you are seeking to scale Data Wise across your system, you will be working to influence learners at multiple altitudes. Therefore, agreeing on what the strategy looks like in practice involves considering a series of "nested learning cores" as shown in figure 6.4. You first describe how the strategy will impact all three relationships in the core that includes the learners you directly serve. Then you describe how those changes will impact all three relationships in the learning core where your learners are the facilitators. This process continues until you get to the classroom core.

The artifact you and your team create as you have this conversation could be a whole wall of multicolored sticky notes organized on four pieces of chart paper. It will likely look messy to anyone who sees your work and was not there for the discussion. We share the image of the abstract symmetric learning core because there is no way we could succinctly capture the end result of Greenwood's process within a book without either oversimplifying the product or sharing pages and pages of what might look like gibberish. However it looks in the end, so long as your team has a shared understanding of how the strategy impacts the learning core relationships at each altitude of the system, you are ready to move to the next task.

Strategic Task 6.3: Identify the Professional Learning Needs Related to the Strategy

The purpose of this strategic task is to identify the knowledge, skills, and mindsets that you need to support educators in developing so that they can implement the strategy well. For example, if the next level of work for your learners is providing effective peer feedback, you may need to *build knowledge* by planning professional

Figure 6.4

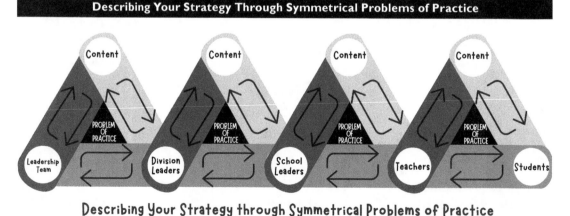

Describing Your Strategy through Symmetrical Problems of Practice

learning about the different purposes and types of feedback. This learning could include providing opportunities for educators to *build skill* by practicing taking specific and descriptive notes that can serve as evidence during feedback. It may also involve reflection activities that allow people to *build a growth mindset* about themselves and their colleagues. As you consider professional learning needs, you can evaluate the work you did to organize for collaborative work in Step 1 to see if you need to adjust any practices for teaming effectively.

Strategic Task 6.4: Create an Action Plan That Specifies Who Will Do What by When

This task is critical because things that aren't written down tend not to happen. In this task, you specify the actions that will allow your team to enact your strategy. We recommend focusing on the actions that your team can commit to in the next four to eight weeks (and we'll explain more about this in the Expect the Unexpected section of this chapter). You can put actions more than eight weeks out in a future actions section of the plan. This allows you to focus on what is most immediate. As you learn from your first set of actions and the future gets closer, you can refine your understanding of what you need to do next.

There are many different types of action plan templates; if you already have one that works for your team, we encourage you to use it—especially if it includes includes a summary of the overarching strategy, a place to capture current and future action steps, an owner for each action step, a due date for each stem, and impact measures.

Table 6.2 provides a sample action plan template that supports system teams with attending to all aspects of an effective action plan. A rolling action plan is a live document where your team can list intended actions and track learning and progress as they unfold.[1] Two places where we find teams especially need to build their skills are in creating action steps that are specific enough and in defining success criteria for each step.

The general rule for an action step is that a professional colleague in a similar role could be handed the action step and do something substantially similar to what the writer of the action step had in mind. Does this sound silly to mention? The fact is that too often the step when enacted looks a lot different from what the writer intended. And worst of all is when the person getting it wrong is our future self, who can't remember what was originally meant. To prevent this, System Wise leaders evaluate their action steps against the quality indicators for action steps in figure 6.5. To illustrate what it looks like to apply these quality indicators, table 6.3 offers some examples of things that people may *say* are action steps but are not. It also provides examples of action steps that provide a helpful level of specificity.

Table 6.2

Rolling Action Plan Template

ROLLING ACTION PLAN COMPONENTS

1 Strategy summarized in 1–2 sentences

2 Current Actions

Focus action steps that will happen in the next 4 to 8 weeks. Be specific enough that someone else could take the description and complete it independently.

3 Future Actions

Capture any possible action steps that may need to happen beyond the 4 to 8 week window. Be as specific as needed to remember what the step means when you return to it.

4 Historic Action Steps completed in previous rounds

Strategy: **1**					
CURRENT ACTIONS Focus Action Steps:	Person Responsible	Completion Date	Criteria for Success	What Happened	What We Learned
2					
Historic Action Steps	Person Responsible	Date Completed	Criteria for Success	What Happened	What We Learned (Continue, Stop, Adjust)
4					

Figure 6.5

Quality Indicators for Action Steps

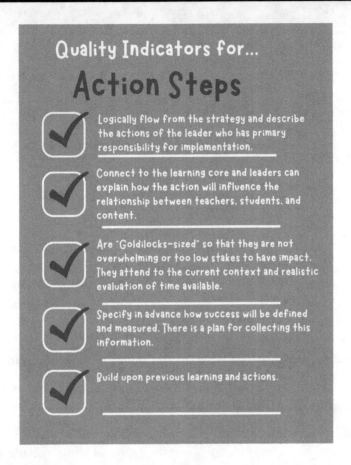

Quality Indicators for...

Action Steps

✓ Logically flow from the strategy and describe the actions of the leader who has primary responsibility for implementation.

✓ Connect to the learning core and leaders can explain how the action will influence the relationship between teachers, students, and content.

✓ Are "Goldilocks-sized" so that they are not overwhelming or too low stakes to have impact. They attend to the current context and realistic evaluation of time available.

✓ Specify in advance how success will be defined and measured. There is a plan for collecting this information.

✓ Build upon previous learning and actions.

After identifying the person responsible and the due date for each action step, you then specify its success criteria: what it will look like to adequately complete that step. For example, if your action step is "Observe three schools weekly and provide affirming feedback and one question via email or face-to-face," then your success criteria could be that observations are conducted in each school for at least sixty minutes and that three school leaders receive affirming and curious feedback that they report to be valuable. In Step 8, when you act and assess, you will use these criteria to evaluate the extent to which you implemented your plan. In Step 6, this level of specificity is helpful in ensuring that the team feels the action steps are

Table 6.3

Examples of Action Steps	
THINGS PEOPLE MAY SAY ARE ACTION STEPS	**EXAMPLES OF SYSTEM WISE ACTION STEPS**
"Observation/coaching"	"Observe 3 schools weekly for at least 60 minutes and provide affirming feedback and one question via email or face-to-face." "Practice using system coaching protocol with each cabinet member in the next month. Revise tool."
"Provide stipends"	"Allocate $500 stipends for 100 teacher leaders from enrichment grant to support extended day meeting time."
"Hiring interview requirements policy"	"Adjust hiring protocol to include a 30-minute task that requires participants to present data and make one recommendation based on their findings." "Develop performance criteria and share with evaluators." "Set minimum scores for candidates to be considered for leadership roles."

realistic and feasible within the time available in the coming weeks. For an example of Greenwood's action plan, please see the Data Wise website.

In addition to clarifying the deliverables of the action plan, System Wise teams are attentive to their process. They ensure the action plan creation process includes conversation about:

- what the team hopes to learn from engaging in the action plan

- a pragmatic assessment of the time available compared to how much time the action steps will likely take

- whether there is a balance of action steps that will: a) implement the strategy, b) gather evidence about the degree of implementation, c) gather evidence of learning from implementation and impact, and d) communication about progress

- intuitive ways the team will regularly check in to start/stop/adjust action steps

- ways to format and communicate the plan for different purposes or audiences such as leaders, educators, and external stakeholders.

Table 6.4 summarizes what the strategic tasks for Step 6 look like depending on purpose.

Table 6.4

Strategic Tasks for Step 6, Depending on Purpose		
Step 6: Strategic tasks	What this task looks like when:	
	A SYSTEM TEAM IS SUPPORTING LEARNERS IT DIRECTLY SERVES	A GUIDING TEAM IS SCALING DATA WISE ACROSS A SYSTEM
6.1: Choose a strategy for addressing the problem of practice	• Choose a strategy for addressing the problem of practice, ideally drawing on knowledge from within the system.	• Choose a strategy for addressing the problem of practice, ideally drawing on knowledge from within the system.
6.2: Agree on what the strategy will look like in practice	• Describe the concrete behaviors leaders will exhibit. • Confirm that the action steps address all relationships in the learning core.	• Describe the concrete behaviors leaders will exhibit. • Confirm that the action steps address all relationships in the learning core. • Discuss how the strategy will influence the learning core for learners at all altitudes within the system.
6.3: Identify the professional learning needs related to the strategy	• Identify the learning needs around knowledge, skills, and beliefs. • Revisit Step 1 and identify strategic tasks that need to be strengthened to implement the strategy well.	• Identify the learning needs around knowledge, skills, and beliefs. • Revisit Step 1 and identify strategic tasks that need to be strengthened to implement the strategy well.
6.4: Create an action plan that specifies who will do what by when	• Include specific action steps that relate to providing professional learning about the strategy and enacting the strategy. • Include person responsible, due date, and success criteria	• Include specific action steps that relate to providing professional learning about the strategy and enacting the strategy. • Include person responsible, due date, and success criteria. • Include action steps related to preparation for communication.

TAKING A SYSTEM WISE APPROACH TO STEP 6

Attend to Dimensions of Scale

Action planning offers you a powerful opportunity to work toward the dimension of scale that involves a *shift* in ownership toward the people who work most closely with students. To foster this shift, it is wise to practice humility about the limits of your own power and cultivate positive regard for those charged with actually doing the day-do-day work of improving their instructional practice.

When leading change, too often leaders rely on tried but truly ineffective actions, including:

- Simply announcing what they expect to change (or the name of the initiative)

- Making organizational chart changes with new reporting structures, new names, or new departments

- Hiring and firing (typically at the senior or mid-management level)

There is no evidence that these actions are helpful; in fact, they are likely harmful, given the uncertainty they infuse within the organization and mistrust they engender. But because they *feel* like they are doing something, leaders assume they *are* doing something.

Figure 6.6

In contrast, System Wise leaders are pragmatic. They think about their actions in terms of what they can do to influence the learning core from a role that is multiple positions removed from the classroom. The following five actions support scaling Data Wise (or any initiative, for that matter) (see also figure 6.6). We have organized them from those that most rely on influence and persuasion to those that most assert organizational power.

- **Clarify and leverage vision, mission, and values.** These actions focus on identifying what matters and explaining why leaders do what they do, why change is needed, and what wild success looks like.

- **Attend to communication and engage in storytelling.** These actions focus on telling stories about how others are enacting the change.

Stories often include "rut to river" messages that describe times when people got stuck when enacting a change and how they overcame the challenge.

- **Support professional learning and coaching.** These actions focus on providing opportunities for people within the organization to acquire knowledge, practice skills, engage in sensemaking, and transfer concepts to their own work.

- **Support the creation of resources and tools and ensure access.** These actions focus on providing time, people, and materials that reduce friction when implementing a change.

- **Craft and use policy and accountability.** These actions focus on creating rules, consequences, and written procedures informed by the principles of behavioral science to "nudge" people toward compliance.[2] Table 6.5 offers key ideas from behavioral science that can inform action planning.

By focusing the action plan on these moves, system leaders are more likely to see their scaling efforts become more effective. These moves also make a good playbook when determining actions in seeking to improve the practice of those one directly supports.

Table 6.5

Key Ideas from Behavioral Science That Can Inform Action Planning

Behavioral science is the study of decision design and how the design can influence individual behavior. The practices have been made accessible through the work of Richard Thaler and Cass Sunstein in their book *Nudge.* "Nudges" are organized by the degree to which they are transparent or nontransparent and the degree to which they change the decision environment or make additions to the decision environment. Here are several examples that are applicable for System Wise leaders:

	CHANGE THE DECISION ENVIRONMENT	ADD TO THE DECISION ENVIRONMENT
Transparent	• Simplify messaging • Remove friction from preferred decision • Provide social proof of other's choices	• Use commitment devices • Tap into social norms • State rewards and punishments
Nontransparent	• Limit the number of options • Create friction for undesired decision • Default to opting people in • Frame to emphasize loss or gain	• Use norms of reciprocity • Activate social identities • Tap into the fear of missing out

Source: Richard H. Thaler and Cass R. Sunstein, *Nudge: Improving Decisions About Health, Wealth, and Happiness* (New Haven: Yale University Press, 2008).

Expect the Unexpected

 Investing time in developing action plans in organizational contexts where things are constantly changing can seem futile. Nevertheless, System Wise leaders take comfort in Dwight Eisenhower's counsel that "*plans* are worthless, but *planning* is everything."[3]

System Wise leaders maximize the utility of action planning in uncertain environments in two ways. First, they narrow the time horizon for which they make plans and leverage an emergent action-planning strategy. Second, they rigorously scrutinize their plans with a healthy dose of skepticism in order to anticipate likely barriers.

The default improvement culture of many school systems is focused on annual improvement plans and three- to five-year strategic plans. If your team finds value in these documents, by all means continue to use them. However, the time frame of these documents is usually too long for folks who are doing the day-to-day work of improving things. These are the sorts of documents that, in our experience, tend to sit on shelves, except when higher-ups or evaluators stop by. Instead of these long-term action plans, System Wise teams create plans that go into great detail for what actions to take in the next four to eight weeks. Within that time frame, teams identify and prioritize the actions most important to move the strategy forward and can predict with greater accuracy the context they are working in. They can account for how much time is available for the effort, the phase of the organizational year they are in, and the resources available. By focusing on shorter cycles, teams can be more responsive to changes and the *adjusting* aspect of the ACE Habits of Mind.

The other way in which System Wise leaders enhance their action plans is that they predict failure before starting and move to anticipate and address it. We find teams can best identify and proactively address challenges by engaging in four thinking exercises with peers, which are captured in the Push with Peers Protocol in the appendix.[4] (See figure 6.7.)

André's story illustrates the tensions that come into play as leaders think about the consequences of acting or not acting. (See "André's Story.")

Figure 6.7

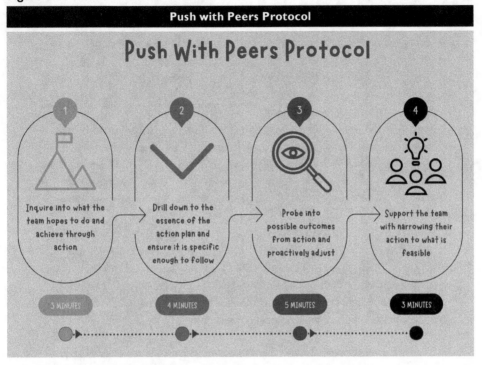

Push with Peers Protocol

Push With Peers Protocol

1. Inquire into what the team hopes to do and achieve through action — 3 MINUTES

2. Drill down to the essence of the action plan and ensure it is specific enough to follow — 4 MINUTES

3. Probe into possible outcomes from action and proactively adjust — 5 MINUTES

4. Support the team with narrowing their action to what is feasible — 3 MINUTES

ANDRÉ'S STORY

I joined our system, one that already had many years of experience with Data Wise, as the director of opportunity, access, and equity. One of my initial tasks was to review evidence from an equity audit, which made it clear that we weren't using data as effectively as we could to inform decision-making. The key driving questions for my work in the system have been, "How do we strengthen the sense of belonging for all students and how can we create access for students who are falling—or have fallen—through the cracks?" We needed to create a plan of action around this.

(continues)

ANDRÉ'S STORY *(continued)*

Survey data showed that 96 percent of students felt that it was important to be engaged in conversations about race, 5 percent reported experiencing discrimination based on race or gender, and 12 percent felt that their voices didn't matter in shaping school policies. We knew it would be critical to have student leaders shape the next steps we'd take to improve their experiences.

To address this, we elevated preexisting work through a curriculum from the Anti-Defamation League and paired it with other initiatives. We customized the program to include three tiers: educator training, peer training, and peer leadership. Each tier focused on topics related to race/ethnicity, gender, religion/culture, disability, and orientation. Deepening the existing work made some people uncomfortable, and there was resistance from some staff.

People were engaged in their own identity work at the same time that we were pushing for access for marginalized students . . . This helped us see into a deeper culture of the system. There was a tension here for me. We wanted to impact students' experiences immediately, but I felt that we couldn't wait for adults to address their beliefs, better understand themselves, and be compelled to change. The change timeline adults needed was longer than our students could wait.

—**ANDRÉ MORGAN**
Massachusetts, United States

Manage the Change Process

Organizations heavily rely on those in positional power to make critical decisions. Leaders within a hierarchical system are charged both formally and informally with making decisions that alter the trajectory of the organization. The metaphor from William Shakespeare's *Henry IV*, "uneasy is the head that wears a crown," is often used to describe the great responsibility that falls on an individual leader.[5] When we aren't in that position of power, we often jest and say, "That's above my pay grade," or "That's why you get paid the big bucks." Members of the organization who are not in a position to make critical decisions have often graciously accepted that they are not responsible and feel a sense of relief that they won't be blamed if something goes wrong. What does the path forward look like if we embrace more inclusive decision-making practices?

In Step 6, the focus shifts from using evidence to look back to planning actions that look forward. Managing change requires that you and your team attend to power and make thinking visible, asking yourselves: *Have we created conditions where individual team members believe they have decision-making power? Have we established relational trust and psychological safety for members to take risks?*

Consider two actions as you answer these questions and shift the culture of decision-making in your action-planning process. The first is to consider the continuum of making decisions *for* others and *with* others that is shown in figure 6.8. Decisions can fall anywhere along the wide range between one person dictating decisions and group consensus. The goal for your team is to commit to intentional collaboration as

Figure 6.8

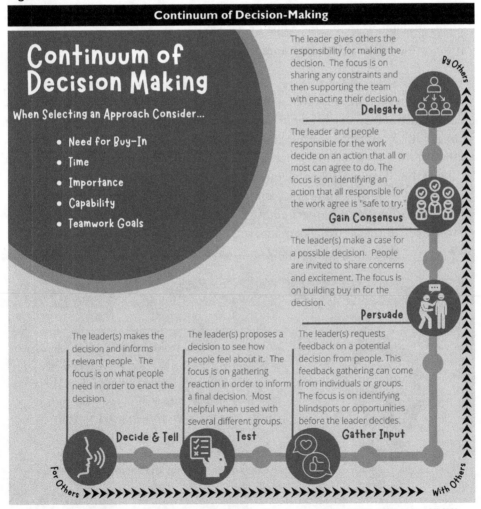

Source: Adapted from Jakada Imani, Monna Wong, and Bex Ahuja, *Management in a Changing World* (Hoboken, NJ: Wiley, 2023); Interaction Associates, Inc., *Levels of Involvement in Decision Making* (Boston: Interaction Associates, Inc., 2012).

a habit of mind and discuss how a decision will be made rather than relying on past practice. When might it be most appropriate to vote, propose a decision for feedback, or make adjustments until everyone agrees? Engaging in this conversation will support your team's ability to reimagine your decision-making practices. Your conversation to determine how to make a decision may include these questions:

- Who is implicated in this decision?
- Who is empowered by this decision?
- Who has the capacity to make this decision and understand the ramifications?
- What information or professional development would support individuals in making a quality decision?
- How will decisions be communicated?

The second action at this step is making your thinking visible. System Wise leaders understand the importance of transparency in decision-making and work to relieve fears that there might be a hidden agenda or ulterior motive. They demonstrate vulnerability by making their thinking visible and mapping how their thinking shifts as they learn. They share the "what" and "why" of the decision and name emotions as they arise. Likewise, when members of your team map your thinking back to your shared *why*, they build trust among themselves and others in the system as they demonstrate faith in others' ability to listen and understand. And when it is up to you to make a challenging decision, you create space for empathy. As Rob's story shows, managing change is all about trust. (See "Rob's Story.")

ROB'S STORY

My organization has extensive experience with supporting systems in implementing the Data Wise improvement process at scale. We've found that successful systems attend to purpose, people, and process. They provide a level of specificity about deliverables that allows others in the system to take action. They are clear about the scope of the work and the time it takes people to learn to change their practice, and they use that learning time really well.

We teamed with one state department of education that wanted to use Data Wise to deeply support its schools in need of improvement. The department was really clear about the problems it was trying to solve and what it hoped to see. Ultimately, it wanted to take the compliance out of improvement and make it more human-centered.

The department felt conflicted since it was tasked with turning around schools urgently, but it also needed to create conditions by which schools could improve their own practice. This work is messy. One way the department shared decision-making was to create opportunities for schools to opt in, whether that was around which process to use or when to start. This approach worked best when combined with an investment in 1:1 relationship-building. When I think about the people that opted into Data Wise, in almost every case it was direct outreach by the people at the state level that made the difference.

But even when people opt in, it *stays* messy. I think the mess comes because of organizational dynamics that happen between the different levels of the system. Do they trust each other? Do they believe that they have the same shared interests? This trust takes time to build and sustain.

We understand this tension because even in our own organization, we experience it. So, we've put in place a strategic planning process where the leadership team does some initial thinking and proposing, then our full team does idea generation, then the leadership team synthesizes. We don't do change *to* people; we have people be involved in the change.

—**ROB WESSMAN**
Massachusetts, United States

Practice Radical Inclusivity

 In this chapter, we have established the importance of determining a key strategy for implementation and building the capacity of the team as well as other members of the organization to understand what implementation will look and feel like. Building the capacity of others begins with an acknowledgment of assets, but we can't stop there. In Step 6, we allow our essential question for radical inclusivity to support our efforts of building coherence: *How is our vision of equity reflected across all levels of the organization?*

Many organizations have recognized the need to hire diverse staff and provide capacity-building professional development to offer ongoing support and increase retention. However, when leaders of organizations seek diverse candidates to fill identified gaps or balance teams in some way, they are approaching their process from a deficit frame. They are focused on how the individual can help them achieve their goals, and therefore the relationship appears transactional in nature. Unfortunately, this dynamic creates a narrative in which both the leaders and the employees pursue wins and if the win is not clear or deferred, the professional relationship tends to deteriorate. System Wise leaders believe organizations can rewrite this narrative and shift their orientation of team-building from transactional to transformational. How teams function then reflects the system's vision of equity.

Figure 6.9

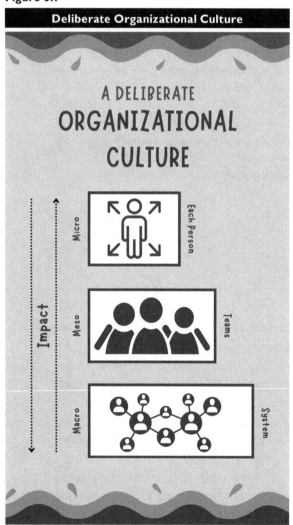

Robert Kegan and Lisa Laskow Lahey have developed a conceptual structure for creating an organizational culture where every person is on the path to deliberate personal and professional development.[6] Equity is at the center of the framework because it departs from common notions that adults are static in their ability to change and adapt, that systems are inevitable, and that individual growth and organizational growth are separate. A "deliberately developmental organization" is one that reinforces adult developmental growth by establishing foundational routines for working together, intentionally engaging in activities that foster trust, and encouraging if not incentivizing risk-taking. As individuals commit to self-development, the team develops; thereby the organization continues to grow and develop. Rather than asking members of the team to simply align their values and working styles with the established majority, the idea is to build system coherence by embracing a culture where continuous improvement depends on everyone. (See figure 6.9.)

Practicing radical inclusivity through action planning is developing a keen awareness of the mental models that have historically produced our processes for working together. Mental models around inputs and outputs, investments and returns on investments, and wins and losses have informed how your team enacted action plans in the past. But with each action plan, you have an opportunity to think critically about the limits of these mental models and consider how the act of committing to a shared experience—a journey—is a transformative practice. Your team learning is no longer reduced to checking a completion box or reporting percentage points in terms of positive or negative growth. It also includes a story of deliberate development and a culture shift toward radical inclusion. (See "Kelly's Story.")

KELLY'S STORY

In Tasmania we have a streamlined approach to school improvement. Each school is required to align their improvement journey to the department's strategic plan. Schools have choice in their improvement models; some use Data Wise, and there are other models also used across the system. What's important is that we link and elevate the work we do to the instructional core, emphasizing data collection about what students are saying and demonstrating with the content and the instruction they receive.

One method we employ is to capture exactly what students say, leveraging their agency as a key improvement strategy. We review the trends to determine what our next leadership and instructional actions should be based on what we are learning from students. We often use these data as a temperature check to see what it looks like when teachers implement agreed action plans.

At one school, there was a relatively inexperienced staff who were like sponges. We moved through the first cycle quickly and saw significant impact by the third cycle. Another school had a more established team with seasoned teachers. It took longer for that staff to see the value, and we had to break through barriers to create professional trust. Once trust in the process was established, we saw a massive impact on student learning in our second cycle. Deeply understanding context and the nuance of true collaboration in each setting was essential for future success.

(continues)

KELLY'S STORY (*continued*)

Experienced teachers bring a wealth of knowledge to each team. Part of the success is leaning in on their experience and using this wisdom to grow a belief in an untested, agreed practice. This requires a rigorous process to capture evidence of impact on student learning and outcomes (sooner rather than later). Impactful teachers will often question the "why" of change if they are already experiencing positive outcomes for *their* students regardless of effect size or evidence of impact on *all* students.

Experienced teachers have witnessed and, on some occasions, been subjected to needless change resulting in minimal or no impact. Growing belief must become a compelling evidence-based undertaking.

Strategically planning an improvement process that deeply captures context and carefully articulates the *why* of the improvement process is crucial. While it may take more time to have all stakeholders integral to the design process, shared ownership and investment is guaranteed.

—**KELLY DYER**
Tasmania, Australia

CASE STUDY REVISITED

Jasmine begins the leadership meeting by reviewing the pluses from last meeting's Plus/Delta Protocol. She is determined to use the same meeting practices that have been keeping things on track in the guiding team meetings that Charlie has been coaching. Today, she has asked Charlie to observe how the work of the leadership team is going.

"At our last meeting, there were several things that we said really supported our learning," she says, listing the pluses from the last meeting. "There were also some things that we wanted to change. Top on that list was that it is getting hard to see how all the new actions we committed to fit with everything else that is on our plates. How could we address that "delta" in today's meeting?"

"It would help me if we could put some of this in a shared calendar," suggests one team member.

"Yes, great idea! We will add 'creating a shared calendar' as a meeting objective."

"And if we make revisiting the calendar a routine, we can assess and adjust along the way," volunteers another member.

Jasmine smiles to herself. The team's action planning used to be about filling out a template once a year and then letting it just sit and collect dust. Now every meeting the team is sharing its progress, reflecting together on what it is learning, and clarifying next steps.

When the meeting is over, Charlie is feeling proud of how far Jasmine has come in her leadership. The team is living its norms and understanding its role in action planning. Wondering if Jasmine can feel the progress, Charlie asks, "How is this team doing? What evidence from today's meeting is speaking to you?"

REFLECTION QUESTIONS

1. How much are we willing to change? How much is our organization willing to change?

2. Have we created conditions where individual team members believe they have decision-making power?

3. Have we established relational trust and psychological safety for members to take risks?

7

PLANNING
TO ASSESS IMPACT

Are we measuring what matters? Who decides?

THE GREENWOOD LEADERSHIP team members are meeting after a month to review the progress they have made on their action plan, which involves using school leader input to improve how they provide feedback efforts to improve literacy performance in their schools. As the team reflects about their most recent actions and the success criteria they have met, they congratulate each other on the effort.

They note what they have learned from their focus groups with school leaders and from their new ways of working together as a team, and they see progress. Several people share that they now come to these meetings excited. Then a team member asks, "We have gotten good at capturing evidence of implementation, but how will we know if we are having any impact on things that matter?"

Jasmine glances up at the top of their action plan and the list of goals for the year they copied from the improvement plan they had made last year. She remembers how they had spent so much time making their first action steps specific that they hadn't had much time left to really think about how they would know if their action plan had been successful. They had scribbled a few measures including "10 percent increase on state literacy assessment" and "improved use of literacy screener results," but hadn't really discussed them.

One team member bravely shares, "I am not sure I care too much about whether we meet these goals at the end of the year. I am not convinced these measures are that helpful. Trying to meet them is not informing my day-to-day practice."

"And how rigorous or useful is that short-term measure of 'seeing new assessment practices in teacher lesson plans'?" adds another team member.

"These measures are all too limited, too infrequent, and take too much time to collect," says a third person. "There has to be a better way to gather information that can help us do our work better."

ACE HABITS OF MIND IN STEP 7

In Step 7, System Wise teams set themselves up to realize their shared commitment to action, assessment, and adjustment; it clarifies how the team will assess the impact of their work so that they know how and when to adjust. Our definition of "impact" includes measuring how people's experiences, behaviors, and learning change along the way; it is not just about measuring the end goal.

A: Shared Commitment to Action, Assessment, and Adjustment

This portion of the case opens with a moment of celebration. We can visualize the bright eyes, smiles, and perhaps even a high five or two as the team members come together to acknowledge that they are already making progress on their action steps. The evidence in the form of meeting their success criteria is significant, yet the team recognizes that a piece of this puzzle is missing. The team reviewed its action plan, which reflects a clear intention to do meaningful work, but what connection the team's actions have on changes in student learning is unclear.

System Wise teams commit to reflection as an individual and collective practice. The Greenwood team members have much to celebrate in terms of implementing their plan and engaging in a reflective process. Their curiosity has led them to want to learn more about the impact of their plan. Formalizing their plan for assessing impact would set them up to gather all the puzzle pieces they need to understand the relationships between their intended actions, actual implementation practices, and the results they hope to see.

C: Intentional Collaboration

We see a greater level of camaraderie as team members congratulate one another on their ability to enact the plan. Seeing and acknowledging the assets and contributions of each team member builds psychological safety within the group. They are able to push one another's thinking and ask provocative questions to move the group forward. Just as the team is mid-celebration, a member offers a candid reality check by saying, "We have gotten good at capturing evidence of implementation, but are we having any impact on things that matter?" Fortunately, the team is now at a place where it can embrace complexity, leaning into dialogue about practice instead of becoming defensive or retreating into the safety of avoidance.

While the Greenwood team members have built meaningful relationships and a strong sense of community, they are recognizing that they can't complete this puzzle on their own. The questions they want to answer require a partnership with those who work most closely with students. The team will have to think about the quality of relationships and the ways in which they have communicated with school leaders and teachers. Their action plan is attempting to replace the one-way communication they used to have with people in schools. Collaboration at this level must be built on relational trust because the team is counting on truth and honesty as it collects evidence of implementation practice.

E: Relentless Focus on Evidence

The Greenwood team members have created space for sensemaking and reflection in their meeting, leading them to a few key questions. They are reviewing the evidence sources they had hastily considered and are willing to admit that they may need different evidence. Their outcome measures may not be the most useful ones, and they still need to learn how to set strong targets. They recognize that they have the power to drive evidence selection, and they are going to use it. It takes courage to admit that they were actively collecting data, but not the evidence they needed to measure impact.

STRATEGIC TASKS FOR STEP 7

The goal of Step 7 is to create a plan to assess your impact on addressing your learning-centered problem and problem of practice. (See figure 7.1.) Steps 6 and 7 often happen simultaneously. In fact, the authors of *Data Wise* had a lively conversation about whether to combine the two steps into one. We settled on separating them, though, because we knew well the temptation to just get started once you have a strategy and some action steps in place. By giving Step 7 its own place in the improvement process, we hoped to signal that planning to assess impact is an important activity in its own right. Strategic tasks for Step 7 include identifying what evidence about impact would be helpful, deciding what tools to use to gather evidence about impact, and setting impact goals.

Figure 7.1

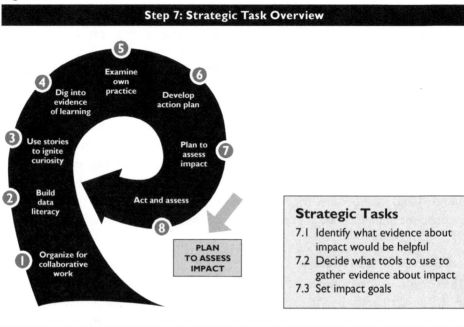

Step 7: Strategic Task Overview

⑤ Examine own practice

④ Dig into evidence of learning

⑥ Develop action plan

③ Use stories to ignite curiosity

⑦ Plan to assess impact

② Build data literacy

Act and assess

⑧

① Organize for collaborative work

PLAN TO ASSESS IMPACT

Strategic Tasks

7.1 Identify what evidence about impact would be helpful

7.2 Decide what tools to use to gather evidence about impact

7.3 Set impact goals

Strategic Task 7.1: Decide What Evidence About Impact Would Be Helpful

System teams, particularly those who are working through nationally or state-mandated school and district improvement planning processes, often default to selecting evidence about student performance on annual nationally normed assessments. This is problematic for many reasons, but we will cite two here. First, it narrows the purpose of school to increasing student performance on tested subjects, which typically overemphasizes language and mathematics instruction. Second, for most system teams, these assessments offer only a lagging indicator of improvement; it could take at least a couple of years for system-level actions to measurably impact performance on state assessments.

System Wise teams have a broader understanding of the type of information that will help them assess and adjust their action plan. Figure 7.2 shows the importance of considering impact in terms of both learner experience (How does it feel?) and learner performance (What are people doing differently?). Evidence about experience is typically collected by asking people about their perceptions; evidence about performance is gathered by either directly observing what people do or the work products they create. Figure 7.2 also shows that you can think of impact in terms

Figure 7.2

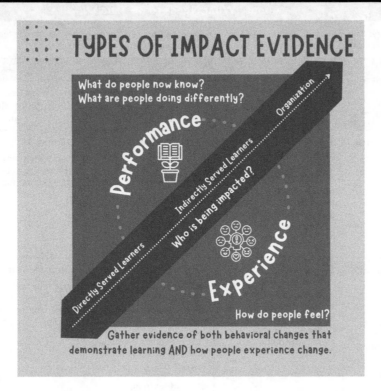

of *whom* you are trying to impact. Not surprisingly, you will need to think in terms of multiple levels. You are certainly trying to have an impact on the adults whose learning you directly serve, but your ultimate purpose—which is quite likely captured in your shared *why*—is to have an impact on students. In addition, you also have your eye on the organization itself, which can (and must) also learn in order for the improvements to be sustainable.[1]

When your team is thinking about the evidence for impact that would be helpful, ask yourselves, "What would need to be true for us to be convinced that the learning-centered problem is resolved?" You may hear a colleague say something like, "I'd need to see X, but I have no idea how to measure that." This is a good spot for engaging in strategic task 7.1. At this point, you are just trying to identify what is persuasive to you, not what evidence you can easily gather. Table 7.1 shows how the Greenwood leadership team answered the "What needs to be true?" question.

Table 7.1

Examples of Greenwood Leadership Team Statements About "What Needs to Be True"			
Strategy: As a leadership team, we will use school leader input to improve how we provide feedback to school leaders about their efforts to improve literacy performance in their schools.			
WHAT IS BEING IMPACTED?	**WHO IS BEING IMPACTED?**		
	Learners directly served by our action plan	**Learners indirectly served by our action plan**	**Our organization itself**
Experience (how do people feel?)	**School leaders' experience** is that the leadership team provides the kinds of feedback that are most helpful to their efforts to increase teacher use of evidence to improve literacy.	**Teachers experience** school leaders' changed feedback practices as being helpful. **Students experience** teachers' changed instructional practices as better supporting their learning.	**Culture** Everyone experiences Greenwood as being a place of continuous learning and trust.
Performance (what do people now know or what are people doing differently?)	**School leaders' practice** involves following up with teachers to provide support that allows them to more effectively use evidence to improve literacy instruction.	**Teacher practice** Teachers use common planning time to plan improvements to literacy instruction. Teachers enact improvements to literacy instruction. **Student learning** Students' literacy skills improve.	**Sustaining shifts** System authorizers increase budget for school leader and teacher professional learning.

Strategic Task 7.2: Decide What Tools to Use to Measure Impact

The goal of this strategic task is to adopt measurement tools that can give you and your team a rough sense of impact. While strategic task 7.1 is about identifying persuasive evidence unbounded by reality, strategic task 7.2 is where your team pragmatically confronts its current limitations.

The greatest pitfall in this task is selecting tools that provide information that is highly accurate but time consuming to collect and analyze. Remember, the purpose of assessing impact is not to publish a randomized controlled-trial research study. Instead, it is to show your team what might be working and how you might need to adjust. Tools that pass a professional gut check will usually do the trick. A blurry impressionistic painting is enough; you do not need a high-resolution photograph.

Work products, surveys, specific observation indicators, and interviews all make excellent impact measures. Figure 7.3 offers criteria for determining whether a measurement tool is a good fit for use in Step 7.

With a tool selected, the next thing your team needs to decide is sample size. In many instances, you don't need to include everyone. Trying to survey all teachers or observe in every classroom is overwhelming at a school level and is close to impossible at a system level. Instead, your team determines what is the smallest set of evidence team members can collect to feel confident as professionals about the inferences drawn. The team may decide to choose a random sample of participants or to select a target group of division leaders, schools, or grade levels. What matters most is that your team makes the decision collaboratively and intentionally. Finally, your team decides how frequently to use the selected measurement tool. Table 7.2 summarizes the four main decisions your team makes about each tool selected.

Figure 7.3

Quality Indicators for a Measurement Tool

Quality Indicators for a...
MEASUREMENT TOOL

- ✓ Is quick and easy to administer and analyze.
- ✓ Is oftentimes things you are already collecting.
- ✓ Provides useful and timely information about what's working and what can be improved.
- ✓ Can be collected in an ongoing way to assess change over time.
- ✓ Is viewed as legitimate by the team.

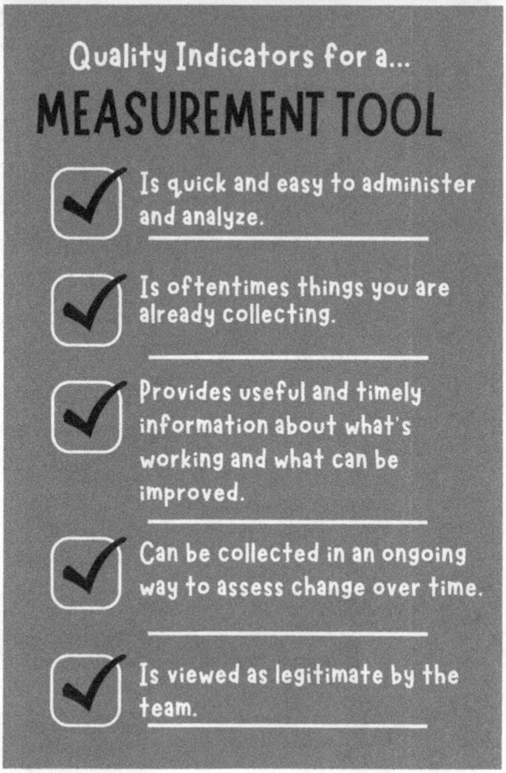

Table 7.2

Decisions to Make About Each Measurement Tool			
HOW TO MEASURE?	HOW MANY TO MEASURE (N)?	WHOM TO MEASURE?	HOW FREQUENTLY TO MEASURE?

• Interview/focus group/case study
• Observation
• Work products
• Performance tasks
• Formative/summative assessments
• Survey
	• 1–5
	• 5–10
	• 10–50
	• 50–100
	• 100+
		• Random sampling
		• Targeted sampling:
		  - Specific schools/departments/grades
		  - Early adopters
		  - Priority populations/historically disempowered
		• Volunteers
			• Biweekly
			• Monthly
			• Quarterly
			• Yearly

Strategic Task 7.3: Set Impact Goals

Most people, most of the time, are doing the best they can. But even so, when implementing an action plan, some action steps on the plan will not get done because other priorities or emergencies arise. There are aspirations for improvements in learning that they will not realize. When those realities combine, a team naturally looks back on the work accomplished and in retrospect defines whatever happened as "good." This is why strategic task 7.3 is so important. This task requires that teams define the impact it is trying to have *before* the work begins.

When setting impact goals, you and your team need to engage in the following thought exercise: *Imagine that you have to present your impact to a group of your peers. What results would convince them that you have addressed the learning-centered problem?* Figure 7.4 summarizes the quality indicators for impact goals. The main idea is that when future you brings your evidence to your next meeting, deciding whether what happened was good should not require additional judgment.

As you complete all three strategic tasks of Step 7, be sure to go back to your action plan and include your decisions about how to measure impact. The editable action plan

Figure 7.4

template available on the Data Wise website has a tab for this purpose. Table 7.3 is a copy of this template; table 7.4 shows the Greenwood leadership team's impact goals.

It is OK if the goals you create do not feel achievable in one, or even a couple, iterations of your action plan.[2] While the ultimate goal of your action plan is to improve the learning-centered problem identified in Step 4 and address the problem of practice identified in Step 5, the short-term purpose of setting impact goals is *learning*. Setting goals in advance sets up your team in Step 8 to be curious about any variation between your goals and the desired impact.

Table 7.5 shows that the strategic tasks for Step 7 are the same whether your team is working to improve how you support the adults whose learning you are responsible for or if you are using the process to scale Data Wise across your system.

Table 7.3

Action Plan Impact Goals Template			
VISION OF WILD SUCCESS			
SYMMETRIC LEARNING CENTERED PROBLEMS			
System leaders	**School leaders**	**Teachers**	**Students**
IMPACT GOALS			
	WHO IS BEING IMPACTED?		
WHAT IS BEING IMPACTED?	**Learners directly served by our action plan**	**Learners indirectly served by our action plan**	**Our organization itself**
Experience (How do people feel?)			
Behavior (What do people now know or what are people doing differently?)			

Table 7.4

Example of Impact Goals for Greenwood Leadership Team			
Strategy: As a leadership team, we will use school leader input to codesign how we provide feedback to school leaders about their efforts to improve literacy performance in their schools.			
	WHO IS BEING IMPACTED?		
WHAT IS BEING IMPACTED?	**Learners directly served by our action plan**	**Learners indirectly served by our action plan**	**Our organization itself**
Experience (how do people feel?)	80% of school leaders agree or strongly agree on quarterly surveys that support from the leadership team has improved their feedback practices.	**Teachers' experience** 70% of teachers in quarterly focus groups share positive feedback about their relationship with their school leader. **Students' experience** 70% of students in monthly pulse check survey share that their teacher can explain things in ways they understand. There is not more than a 5% gap between different racial groups.	**Culture** Annual culture survey for families, students, and teachers shows district is organized for success in the continuous learning and trust domains.
Performance (what do people now know or what are people doing differently?)	Recordings of 3 out of 3 school leaders' feedback sessions with teachers show that school leaders follow up on how teachers are implementing previous feedback.	**Teacher practice** 90% of teachers in priority schools achieve a *meets* rating with 30% at an *exceeds* rating in "communicating with students" domain. **Student learning** Students' literacy skills improve so that 90% achieve proficiency on benchmark assessments.	**Sustaining shifts** Both the school leaders' union and the teachers union approve 8-hour increase in professional learning time in contract. Human resources department includes a "performance competency on feedback" expertise as school leader hiring requirement with task, rubric, and norming professional learning.

Table 7.5

Strategic Tasks for Step 7, Depending on Purpose		
Step 7: Strategic tasks	**What this task looks like when:**	
	A SYSTEM TEAM IS SUPPORTING LEARNERS IT DIRECTLY SERVES	**A GUIDING TEAM IS SCALING DATA WISE ACROSS A SYSTEM**
7.1: Identify what impact evidence would be helpful	• Consider impact on experience and performance • Consider impact on direct and indirect learners • Consider impact on the organization	• Consider impact on experience and performance • Consider impact on direct and indirect learners • Consider impact on the organization
7.2: Decide what tools to use to gather evidence about impact	• Decide how to measure • Decide how many to measure • Decide whom to measure • Decide how frequently to measure	• Decide how to measure • Decide how many to measure • Decide whom to measure • Decide how frequently to measure
7.3: Set impact goals	• Include specific performance target	• Include specific performance target

TAKING A SYSTEM WISE APPROACH TO STEP 7

Attend to Dimensions of Scale

 Earlier in this chapter we offered an example of the impact goals for Greenwood's leadership team, which was focused on improving its support of school leaders. In this section we'll offer an example of what impact goals look like when the goal is scaling Data Wise across a system. While there are many possible ways to measure each category, these measures each provided enough information to get a sense of the impact of the strategy without being too complicated or time consuming to use regularly.

When the Greenwood guiding team collects data to measure progress toward the goals captured in the six cells in table 7.6, it will paint a picture of how the scaling effort is going. These indicators provide evidence for the depth of impact by measuring whether participants apply their knowledge. Shift of ownership can be seen in the analysis of the agendas because the team can observe independent creation and sharing of roles and, therefore, responsibility. Sustainability is most

Table 7.6

Example of Impact Goals for Greenwood Guiding Team			
Strategy: Increase collaboration across the system by providing professional learning and resources on the strategic tasks of Data Wise Step 1			
WHAT IS BEING IMPACTED?	**WHO IS BEING IMPACTED?**		
	Learners directly served by our action plan	**Learners indirectly served by our action plan**	**Our organization itself**
Experience (How does it feel?)	**School leaders** 80% of school leaders are "net promoters" of our approach to improvement.*	**Teachers** 80% of teachers are "net promoters" of our approach to improvement.* **Students** 80% of students agree or strongly agree with the survey prompt: "I have frequent opportunities to learn with and from my peers"	**Organizational culture** 80% of employees agree or strongly agree with the survey prompt: "I feel I can effectively do my job."†
Performance (What are people doing differently?)	**Leading indicator** In a random sample of 10 agendas, 9 show use of the rolling agenda format, meeting roles, meeting norms, and plus/delta feedback. **Mastery indicator** 90% of instructional leadership teams complete a summary of their work for each step of the process where each artifact meets the criteria and 75% of teams complete a full Data Wise cycle within the year.	**Teacher learning** 75% of grade-level teams complete a summary of their work for each step of the process where each artifact meets the criteria and 50% of teams complete a full Data Wise cycle within the year. **Student learning** Literacy benchmark scores of students taught by teacher teams implementing the practice exceed the scores of students taught by teacher teams not implementing the practice.	**Sustaining shifts** Continuous improvement using data continues as one of the three priorities on the annual improvement plan with an annual budget of at least $100,000 attached.

*To determine our net promoter score, we will survey school leaders, asking them to rate their likelihood of recommending our approach to improvement on a score of 0 to 10, with 0 being extremely unlikely and 10 being extremely likely. The prompt we will use is : "I would recommend Data Wise to a colleague seeking to improve collaboration and data informed practice." To calculate the net promoter score, we will follow the standard practice of finding the percentage of people who respond with a 9 or 10 and subtracting from that the percentage of people who respond with a 6 or lower. See https://www.qualtrics.com/experience-management/customer/net-promoter-score/ for more information.

†Internal research finds high levels of agreement with this statement to be predictive of whether people remained in their role in future years, and it becomes a quick proxy for retention.

obviously captured in the sustainability measure, but it is also understood through the participant reactions because educators who value the learning are more likely to continue it. The team will be able to assess the degree of spread and evolution by comparing responses across divisions or schools to see where there is evidence of commitment and adaptations to meet particular contexts.

Teams that include action steps in their action plan that are about regularly collecting and analyzing impact evidence are much more likely to build their capacity for scale over time.

Expect the Unexpected

 When scaling an instructional initiative such as Data Wise, we know that there will be confusion. We know that action plans will be executed with great variability or not at all. We know that some measures and impact goals may not be useful or the infrastructure to gather and analyze these measures may never be developed. Similar to how teams identify their success criteria for action steps and impact goals before enacting their action plans, System Wise leaders prepare for disparate outcomes before they occur. Figure 7.5 shares some questions to plan for related to different aspects of impact.

We are certainly not advocating that you have a plan for all these questions. But even selecting one, such as "What evidence will you gather to better understand why people do not apply learning from the change effort?" can set you up to get ahead of potential problems, as Felice's story shows. (See "Felice's Story.")

FELICE'S STORY

 As educators, we are better at identifying how students progress in their learning over time than we are at assessing the improvement of adult practice—whether teachers in classrooms, school leaders, or system-level leaders. I have found that a big reason why we fail to capture evidence of adult practice improvements connects to having too few tools that can help us capture and analyze the adult practice connected to the professional learning we receive. As an improvement specialist in my school system, we had to support system teams engaging in Data Wise to support their learners in creating tools to track data.

(continues)

FELICE'S STORY *(continued)*

I've seen teams have strategies to increase proficiency through coaching to support math teacher's efficacy in understanding mathematical practices. The challenge was that in math, we measured progress based on *student performance*. Nothing existed to capture either teachers' *perception of the impact* of the coaching on their practice or *how the teachers used the mathematical practices* when instructing their students.

Saying that we provided professional development wasn't giving us the right data to measure our impact on our adult learning strategies. In order to capture adult impact data better, we sent out online surveys to ask teachers to share what they noticed about students' experiences in the classroom and how their own instruction had shifted as a result of their new learning. Instructional coaches could then use these data to plan future learning for teachers and follow up more directly in specific classrooms.

After engaging in this data collection for a number of months, we all saw the benefit of taking time to reflect on what we were learning and make new adjustments. The biggest pushback I received in the beginning was about the amount of time it took to determine how to collect data about adult practices, but these were the data that we needed to ultimately help students learn math better.

—**FELICE DeSOUZA**
Maryland, United States

Figure 7.5

Questions That Expect the Unexpected

Questions to Ask
That Expect the Unexpected
When Planning to Assess Impact

Experience

What will you do when a group is not enthusiastic about the change effort?

What will you do about those who are openly hostile?

How will you support those who feel change is not happening fast enough?

Figure 7.5

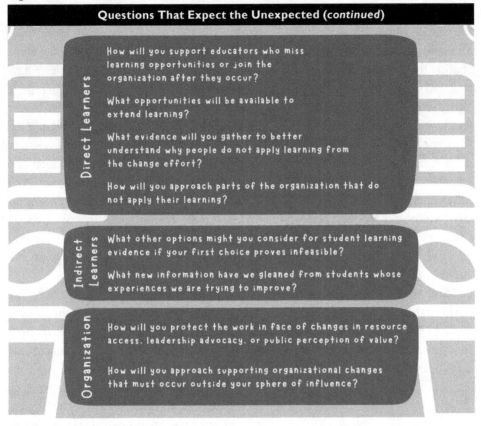

Questions That Expect the Unexpected (*continued*)

Direct Learners

How will you support educators who miss learning opportunities or join the organization after they occur?

What opportunities will be available to extend learning?

What evidence will you gather to better understand why people do not apply learning from the change effort?

How will you approach parts of the organization that do not apply their learning?

Indirect Learners

What other options might you consider for student learning evidence if your first choice proves infeasible?

What new information have we gleaned from students whose experiences we are trying to improve?

Organization

How will you protect the work in face of changes in resource access, leadership advocacy, or public perception of value?

How will you approach supporting organizational changes that must occur outside your sphere of influence?

Manage the Change Process

It's common to greet a friend or colleague we haven't seen in a while with a genuine "How's it going?" The informal check-in is well intended and creates space for brief, off-the-cuff updates. One would rarely expect a significant amount of detail, but rather an honest overview of a friend's current status. As your team leads continuous improvement efforts, think strategically about how you use communication to champion the implementation of your change efforts. Consider the communication style and frequency that will keep your team and members of the community engaged and committed.

System Wise teams communicate their learning as they assess the impact of their strategies. Committing to learning opens possibilities for authentic growth and transformation. Your identity as a team and organization will begin to shift and reorient as you develop new skills and mindsets. If you desire to build broad ownership of the change, you will need to create opportunities for them to see, if not experience, all that your team sees so they can learn and take this journey with you. Consider a routine for communicating impact so that members of the community don't have to spend energy focusing on the mode of communication or the rationale behind it. You create psychological safety when you prepare others for communication, even if it has undesirable content. Creating routines for communicating your learning has the power to build trust as you manage the change process.

Consider three things when planning communication (see figure 7.6). First, determine the appropriate frequency of your communication. We check in with our physicians annually, and shareholders can typically expect a financial report quarterly, while teachers often review student benchmark assessments three times a year. Choose a reporting interval that will keep the members of your community curious, engaged, and active. This will be based on the time frame for your action plan and your plan to assess impact.

Second, decide whether to give updates on the *how* of implementation (Are we meeting the success criteria for each of our action steps?) and meeting the *what* of impact (Are we reaching the impact goals we set?). You could decide to share both the *how* and the *what* if you believe a particular action step and impact measure are tightly aligned.

Finally, capture *your* learning at each interval. You may want to share this in the form of an individual team member's testimony, or as a conclusion that you came to as a team during a sensemaking session. Communication cycles should be clearly identified within the plan to assess impact, and we encourage you to share your intentions around communication with stakeholders before you begin implementation. As Robin's story shows, although at first you may think of communication as something that you do for others, you may discover that it also really supports your own learning. (See "Robin's Story.")

Figure 7.6

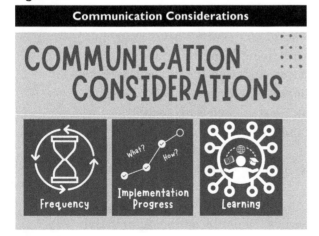

ROBIN'S STORY

Because I was one of the first school leaders to use Data Wise in my school and our first certified coach, district leaders invited me to be a member of our system guiding team. My work in multiple areas allowed me to be a bridge between Data Wise practices, the district's priorities, and our building leaders' experiences as we faced obstacles of implementation. I could help explain how these practices work in a school setting and think through how district decisions would play out at a school level.

I shared my school's progress both in large group presentations and in one-on-one conversations. We are a system with a lot of autonomy for school leaders, and people do not do things unless they find them to be worthwhile. We have to work through influence.

The presentations were a learning curve for me. The first year I presented our progress, I stuck close to the data and the district priorities and tools. There weren't a lot of questions and not too many additional schools signed up. The next year I coupled the data with my story. I talked about what we actually did and what it looked like. I explained who the kids and adults were and what happened. That shifted curiosity in folks. All the remaining schools except one signed on to train teams to launch Data Wise the following year.

The one-on-one conversations were easier. I could explain to colleagues the impact we saw at my school and how they could adapt these practices for anything they wished to improve in their buildings. I was able to identify leaders through our assessment of implementation who would be great coaches and encourage them to take that step in order to expand our system expertise. They needed to hear from a veteran leader that I saw that they were good at improvement work and they were the right person for the role.

Ultimately understanding our system efforts and impact made me a more effective leader in my building. I drew connections to what we were doing across the district and began thinking of my school as a smaller system with different elements needing different support.

—**ROBIN FINN**
Massachusetts, United States

Practice Radical Inclusivity

Radical inclusivity is the very intentional practice of recognizing the assets among a diverse team and creating a strong sense of belonging so that each member can bring their whole self and do their best work. It is a recognition that we are stronger together. We use radical inclusivity to name systems and structures that have traditionally alienated, disenfranchised, or intentionally caused harm to specific groups and then actively pursue ways to repair harm and restore humanity. Every Data Wise step, protocol, and tool offers opportunities to live intentionally collaborative practices and transform your organizational culture as you pursue continuous improvement. But Step 7, specifically setting impact goals, may be the most significant in actualizing true inclusivity. It allows us to answer the question, *How is our vision of equity reflected across all levels of the organization?* Radical inclusive practices challenge traditional power structures.

We recommend that you revisit the Step 1 strategic tasks, especially your shared *why*, as you develop your impact goals. Returning to your shared *why* and the core values that guide your decisions can support your team in balancing the urgency of your continuous improvement goals with the complexity of the strategic path to get there. As you develop your impact goals, considering who will be measured and the degree to which you hope they will be impacted, review your shared *why* and consider how you can authentically engage those at each altitude. This will be a challenge if you have not invested in trust-building rituals and routines. Trust-building routines typically involve clear expectations, balanced participation, and an invitation to bring your whole self to the process. Throughout this book, we have emphasized the importance of sharing your values, communicating clearly and frequently, and sharing decision-making power. With consistency and competency, your team will develop rituals of trust-building. Cultural rituals like weddings, birthdays, and funerals often create safe spaces for the individual, even when facing challenging emotions. Rituals of trust will embolden members of

Figure 7.7

Trust-Building Routines

Trust Building Routines

- Clear Expectations
- Balanced Participation
- Sharing Whole Self

your team and those across the organization to deeply consider their role in the continuous improvement effort.

Development of success criteria for action steps and impact goals is traditionally reserved for those in power. Authorizers, governing bodies, and chief executives have the privilege and responsibility of establishing goals, standards, benchmarks, and other forms of success criteria. However, the System Wise approach empowers those implementing the change to do this important work. Specifically, this means involving teachers and students in creating impact goals and deciding how to measure them. This countercultural approach may feel new and uncomfortable for teams. But let's face it: if our ultimate goal is to improve student learning, teachers and the students themselves are the ones in the best position to determine what success looks and feels like. Kentaro's story gives a glimpse of the power of including students in the improvement process. (See "Kentaro's Story.")

KENTARO'S STORY

I had the opportunity to work in a system that, like many, was focused on mathematics achievement disparities among racial groups. Fortunately, the system had partnered with an organization that supported the development of student voice, and students were facilitating a discussion with educators in a virtual meeting space, analyzing the math landscape and data regarding ninth-grade math placement.

At one point, students presented data indicating that 71 percent of Asian students and 15 percent of Black students were placed in geometry, the higher-tracked math class, when entering ninth grade. One student, who I recall was White, asked, "Why are Black people less likely to take geometry?" I later reviewed a recording of the meeting and counted the seventeen seconds of silence after the student posed her question.

The answer to this question rested in practice and policy that was laden with bias. Teachers in the eighth grade made recommendations for placement, and those recommendations were generally followed. When we reviewed the placement guidelines, we noticed that they favored students "with a strong work ethic, good organizational skills, and willing to get help before or after school." The first two criteria were subjective, with

(continues)

CASE STUDY REVISITED

"I left our last meeting frustrated that we didn't have a handle on measuring what matters," Jasmine shares at the Greenwood leadership team meeting. "So during my coaching session with Charlie, we looked at our leadership team's action plan and reflected on ways to think differently about how we assess impact. I'd like to share my learning with you all and see what you think."

Jasmine shows the leadership team members how they can identify measures to provide ongoing information about how things are going. They discuss ways in which they can capture evidence of impact on school leaders, teachers, students, and the organization itself.

Team members become especially animated when they realize that the school climate surveys that students and teachers already complete could help them learn how adults and students feel about the changes the team was putting in place.

"It is nice to know we don't have to make more work for ourselves," offers one team member. "We can get new insights from our existing measurement tools. For the more time-consuming school visits, giving ourselves permission to sample instead of trying to observe everyone is so freeing."

"But since we aren't seeing everyone, are our results accurate enough to make decisions? We couldn't exactly publish these results in study," adds another.

"That isn't our purpose," explains Jasmine. "It's OK to have a blurry impressionist painting of what is going on. What matters is that we use our own professional gut check to decide whether we know enough to feel confident to start climbing the ladder of inference and drawing some conclusions about the impact we are having. The good news is that if we figure out that we're not heading in the right direction, we can always adjust course."

The team members continue their discussion until they feel they have a strong plan to assess impact. Right before the meeting ends, they realize that they need to go back and add action steps to their action plan about gathering and reviewing the evidence.

"I hadn't considered that our action plan has to include both actions that *implement the plan* and actions that *help us understand how it is going*," shares a team member. "There sure is a lot to stay on top of when you are both learning the improvement process for the first time *and* trying to actually improve something."

REFLECTION QUESTIONS

1. Are we measuring what matters? Who decides?

2. How varied are our sources of evidence of impact?

3. To what extent are learners involved in assessing their own learning and our learning?

8

ACTING AND ASSESSING

> Who benefits from our actions?
> Who does not benefit, and what are we going to do about it?

■ **JASMINE SITS DOWN** to meet with the guiding team that has been working all year to lay the groundwork for scaling Data Wise across Greenwood School System. She takes a deep breath and says, "I know some of you have already heard this from her, but our superintendent shared at last night's school board meeting that she would be retiring at the end of the year."

Team members' expressions show whether or not this announcement comes as a surprise. A sense of loss and disappointment settles over the room.

Knowing they are still in the early phases of integrating Data Wise practices and habits, Jasmine realizes that this is a critical moment for their change efforts. She celebrates how the guiding team has built among themselves a real sense of shared ownership of the scaling effort. But she also acknowledges that many people outside this room do not yet see the work as their own. She invites team members to share what is on their minds and think together about how to keep the work strong.

"What does this mean for our work as a team?" asked one of the newest members of the team. "We have come so far this year . . . but we are only just getting started. What if the new leader has other priorities?"

ACE HABITS OF MIND IN STEP 8

A: Shared Commitment to Action, Assessment, and Adjustment

"What does this mean for our work as a team?" asks a team member with some trepidation. After several months of deep engagement as a team, they express clear concern for the team's ability to maintain momentum. Developing ownership and staying the course took a concerted effort all year. The experience had great value for those involved and the organization as a whole as the leaders began to work in new ways. But a change in guard commonly derails all improvement efforts.

Looking closer, there is an acknowledgment that while the guiding team was very committed to becoming System Wise, other members of the organization had not yet had the opportunity to fully embrace this goal. The shared commitment to action, assessment, and adjustment cannot be achieved in a vacuum. This team may not yet have considered, "How have we provided others with the opportunity to act, assess, and adjust with us?" Intentionally expanding the team's circle could have given others in the organization experiences that would increase their personal commitment to the work of continuous improvement. And when the new superintendent arrives, the team will need to do more than inform or seek permission. This guiding team needs to identify ways for the new superintendent to join them in embracing the ACE Habits of Mind.

C: Intentional Collaboration

The members of the Greenwood guiding team recognize that they are at a critical moment as they consider how to scale their change efforts effectively despite a change in leadership. They have a strong sense of being overwhelmed here and need to surface and acknowledge these feelings. Too often, leaders ask individuals to quietly shoulder the emotional weight of the team and just get down to business. But System Wise leaders create space in their agendas for affective conversations. Jasmine has made this topic a portion of the meeting agenda. Inviting members of the team to bring their whole selves to the work supports their ability to be resilient and sustain practices.

Surfacing the emotions of team members during reflective conversations also provides the team with more data points. When intentional collaboration is the goal, teams are constantly considering evidence to improve how they collaborate. If you recall, when we first met Jasmine, she was attempting to tell the team what needed to be done rather than listen first to their concerns. Now we see her creating space to listen. Instead of taking on all the transition work herself, she provides an opportunity for the team to collaborate on ideas.

E: Relentless Focus on Evidence

This team is tormented by the idea that one person in a position of power has the ability to undermine all their efforts to integrate continuous improvement in their system. For generations, we have seen education systems make it possible for a handful of leaders to exert power over those closest to the work of creating equitable student outcomes. While it is important to surface the fear and concern, we caution against being paralyzed by it. This team has reason to be proud of its work. As the members reflect, they will see the complexity of their journey. Now is the time to share with others how they have learned from their successes and failures. A relentless focus on evidence will help them tell a compelling story to stay the course.

Our case team members would benefit from documenting their implementation through a description of their leadership moves, collaboration practices, and progress on meeting the success criteria for their action steps. They could then show evidence of the impact they have had on the performance and experience of the learners they directly and indirectly serve—as well as their impact on the organization itself. "We have come so far this year . . . but we are only just getting started. What if the new leader has other priorities?" asks a team member. A relentless focus on evidence would allow the team to shine a light on how it has navigated all year toward the North Star of equitable student achievement and well-being. What better way to engage the new superintendent in a conversation about priorities than to be clear about their own?

STRATEGIC TASKS FOR STEP 8

Step 8 is what transforms this work from a line to a circle. (See figure 8.1.) The goal of Step 8 is to transition from "this is something we did" to "this is something we do." The focus is on capturing what the team learned during the implementation of the action plan in order to apply that learning to planning additional cycles related to this focus area or to selecting a new focus area. The strategic tasks include implementing the action plan, analyzing evidence, celebrating success, and determining the next level of work.

Strategic Task 8.1: Implement the Action Plan

This task is the easiest to describe and hardest to do. Here you complete the action steps listed on your plan and determine whether you have met the success criteria you set for each of those steps. Each person must do their best on the tasks to which you have collectively committed—and to ask for help if they need it.

That said, System Wise teams do not follow action plans without thinking and reflection. They recognize that learning emerges even before the team meetings, when there is an explicit objective to assess progress, so they adjust accordingly. They might add, remove, or adjust action steps midcourse so long as the changes address their

Figure 8.1

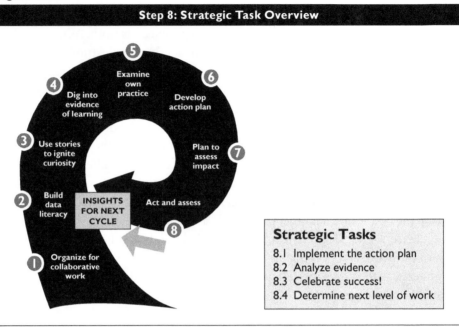

Step 8: Strategic Task Overview

⑤ Examine own practice

④ Dig into evidence of learning

⑥ Develop action plan

③ Use stories to ignite curiosity

⑦ Plan to assess impact

② Build data literacy

INSIGHTS FOR NEXT CYCLE

Act and assess

⑧

① Organize for collaborative work

Strategic Tasks

8.1 Implement the action plan
8.2 Analyze evidence
8.3 Celebrate success!
8.4 Determine next level of work

learning-centered problem and problem of practice or get closer to realizing their vision of wild success. When they make adjustments, System Wise teams capture the evidence and learning that caused them to deviate from their intended action. They bring this evidence and learning to team meetings so that they can examine their practice collaboratively.

System teams seeking to scale Data Wise have an additional consideration when implementing their action plan. Because they are seeking to change practice at multiple altitudes within the system, they need to both *implement* their own action steps and *monitor* the implementation of action steps at other altitudes. (See figure 8.2.) This can require a delicate balance because what one team considers support might not feel like support to those receiving it. In our experience, systems tend to default to the extremes of benign neglect or micromanagement, when what is needed is more nuanced support determined through dialogue.

An effective way to find this middle ground is to codesign how teams will receive support from the guiding team or other system leaders. Discuss with each team the frequency of check-ins and whether they will be with the whole team or through a point of contact. Decide on face-to-face, virtual, or asynchronous communication

Figure 8.2

Using the Action Plan in Step 8					
Strategy:					
Current Actions:					
Focus Action Steps:	**Person Responsible**	**Completion Date**	**Criteria for Success**	**What Happened**	**What We Learned**
Historic Action Steps	**Person Responsible**	**Date Completed**	**Criteria for Success**	**What Happened**	**What We Learned (Continue, Stop, Adjust)**

of updates. Create a routine that allows time to surface celebrations, challenges, support requests, and two-way feedback, and to iterate as you learn more about what is helpful. Whatever the design, keep the goal of empowering the team at the center of your decisions.

With these routines in place, guiding teams have a much lighter lift when they get together to analyze evidence from their action plan, the next strategic task in this step.

Strategic Task 8.2: Analyze Evidence

As you drafted your action plan in Step 6, you identified the *success criteria* for each action step. As you planned to assess impact in Step 7, you set *goals* that clearly described the changes in performance and experience that would persuade you that you had addressed your learning-centered problem. In strategic task 8.2, you work with colleagues to make sense of what all this evidence is telling you.

In the Twi language of Ghana, the word *sankofa* is often used to represent the need for human beings to reflect on the past in order to build a brighter future.[1] System Wise leaders heed the importance of this teaching and appreciate that those who do not know their past are doomed to repeat it. The challenge for teams is to identify *how* to learn from the past. The following tasks can lead to especially fruitful discussions.[2]

To systematically capture learning that can be used to improve practice over time, System Wise teams do the following:

1. Confirm the *goal* they were trying to achieve

2. Accurately describe the *reality* of what happened

3. Identify *options* for adjusting their work

4. Select a narrow set of adjustments as a *way forward*

5. Request the *support* they will need

See the GROWS Protocol to Evaluate Action in the appendix for a structured way to capture team learning. If your team is using Data Wise to improve your support for learners you directly serve, you can use this protocol on your own or with the help of a coach or peer network. If you are scaling Data Wise across a system, we recommend you use this tool to have teams support each other and transfer learning across your system.

Another kind of evidence that can be helpful to explore in Step 8 is information that you get from using frameworks. When you were laying the foundation for instructional improvement, you may have decided to use an improvement framework (like Data Wise) and an instructional framework (like Multi-Tiered System of Supports). The end of a cycle is a good time to review and revise the frameworks. This can involve discussing what is essential versus what is nice to have and what adaptations to each framework (including Data Wise!) are required to meet the needs in your particular setting.

Strategic Task 8.3: Celebrate Success

This task is different from all previous tasks in this book because it is likely easier to complete when scaling Data Wise across a system compared to when you are using Data Wise to support learners you directly serve. This is because people, particularly educators, often struggle to celebrate their own work. We are quick to elevate the wins of our peers and our teams and continue on as though celebrating our own wins is not as important for the sustainability of our efforts.

If the preceding pages of guidance, frameworks, and resources have not made it abundantly clear, we are going to say it again: this is hard work. Our promise to you is not that you will solve all your problems; it is that you will see improvement and learning. This journey requires that you recognize and appreciate forward movement. Determine how you will celebrate your learning, your progress toward achieving your vision of wild success, and your growth as a collaborative team. Decide what can happen each time you meet, each time you review your action plan and annually. This investment will buffer your team during times of uncertainty and disappointment. And it feels kind of nice in the moment too.

If you are a guiding team scaling Data Wise across your system, you will also be responsible for celebrating people across the organization and creating space for them to celebrate and acknowledge themselves. An important

Figure 8.3

consideration is how public you make your celebrations. Some folks are leery of public recognition—especially if it separates them from their peers. Others are motivated by public praise. Design practices that will both land as intended for the recipient and feel authentic to you.[3]

Oftentimes it can be helpful to focus on celebrating the learning of *teams*. We have worked with systems that have an internal conference where teams share the story of their work and the lessons learned, like an adult science fair or professional organization poster session. Others gather stories documenting what teams have learned and place them in a searchable online repository of the organization's professional knowledge. In addition to celebrating the work and demonstrating how efforts will be valued in the future, this approach also provides opportunities for knowledge sharing and aligning around common practice.

Strategic Task 8.4: Determine Next Level of Work

The purpose of assessing your work is to capture learning that your team can then feed forward into your improvement process. As you finish Step 8 you need to decide where to go next. (See figure 8.4.)

The following items are your options:

- **If you feel like your problem of practice is still active** but you have not fully addressed it, you may decide to go back just as far as Step 6 in your inquiry process, where you choose a new strategy for the same, but likely more nuanced, problem of practice.

- **If you feel like your learning-centered problem is still active** but your problem of practice needs to change, you go back to Step 5 and collect more evidence that allows you to shift to a problem of practice that feels more appropriate, and then finish out the cycle from there.

- **If you are satisfied that you have addressed your learning-centered problem**, congratulations! Depending on your needs, you can head back to Step 2, 3, or 4 and start a new cycle with a new focus area, priority question, or learning-centered problem.

This decision is easiest to make when you have clear evidence that you have resolved the learning-centered problem. It is time to look for new urgent needs to address. It is also pretty easy to decide to continue with the same problem of practice when the need remains urgent and the actions taken to date have not had a

Figure 8.4

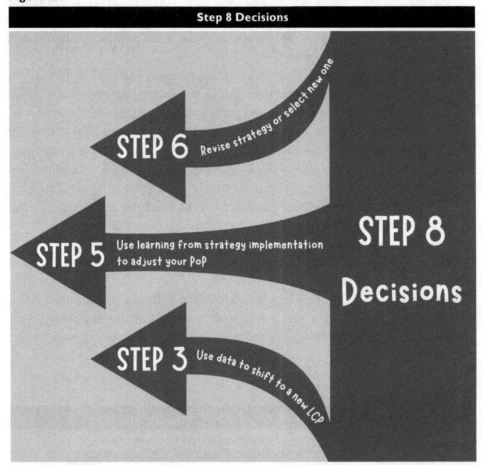

significant impact. The challenge is when your team begins to see enough progress that other needs now appear more urgent, even if the team has not fully addressed the learning-centered problem. In those cases, your team must decide whether the progress is good enough or whether to persevere still longer. In general, we recommend you consider how many cycles you have completed on this particular problem of practice. If it is the first cycle, we would usually suggest going deeper with consistency. If you are on round five, perhaps see where new inquiry might lead. However, you should take this guidance as a light suggestion. What matters most is that your team wrestles with these questions and comes to its own consensus. The good news is that while some choices might be better than others, there are no wrong decisions. Trust yourselves as a team.

As you consider which direction you are taking, be sure to capture the next level of work for both the *team* and for *each member of the team.* As you implement Data Wise, the deepest improvement happens when you attend to both collective growth and each individual's development.

If you are scaling Data Wise across your system, you also need to capture the next level of work for improving the systems and structures of the organization. How will the system learning improve the ways in which it supports individuals who are leading and teaching in new ways? Additionally, identify the next level of work for school-based teams and the support you provide them. How are you building the capacity of teams at different altitudes to improve and learn from each other? The following section will help you think more deeply about this.

When describing the System Wise approach to managing the change process in Step 7, we talked about the importance of planning for regular communication about how the action plan is progressing. As part of the acting and assessing you do in Step 8, you will be communicating both your successes and your next level of work with stakeholders.

Table 8.1 summarizes the strategic tasks for Step 8 depending on whether your team is working to improve how you support the adults whose learning you are responsible for or if you are using the process to scale Data Wise across your system.

Table 8.1

Strategic Tasks for Step 8, Depending on Purpose		
Step 8: Strategic tasks	**What this task looks like when:**	
	A SYSTEM TEAM IS SUPPORTING LEARNERS IT DIRECTLY SERVES	**A GUIDING TEAM IS SCALING DATA WISE ACROSS A SYSTEM**
8.1: Implement the action plan	• Implement the action plan	• Implement own action steps • Monitor and support action plan implementation at each altitude
8.2: Analyze evidence	• Analyze evidence about implementation • Analyze evidence about impact	• Analyze evidence about implementation at all altitudes • Analyze evidence about impact at all altitudes
8.3: Celebrate success!	• Celebrate own success • Celebrate the success of those closest to the work • Enact communication plan	• Celebrate own success • Celebrate the success of those closest to the work • Enact communication plan
8.4: Determine next level of work	• Adjust action plan based on learning or begin a new cycle	• Adjust action plan based on learning or begin a new cycle

TAKING A SYSTEM WISE APPROACH TO STEP 8

Attend to Dimensions of Scale

Step 8 is a good time for teams that are scaling Data Wise to reflect on how their scaling efforts are going. Ask yourselves:

- What evidence do you have that teams have *deepened* their knowledge of the work?

- Are the structures strong enough to *sustain* the work more independently?

- Do you see opportunities to *spread* the work to new parts of the organization? Which ones are most primed for adoption?

- Where do you have evidence of a *shift* in ownership of the initiative toward those closest to the work?

- Have you *evolved* the work in meaningful ways that allow it to be more effective within your context?

As your team examines your scaling efforts, you'll be less overwhelmed if you decide to be opportunistic in prioritizing certain dimensions. Go where you are wanted. Do the actions that will be the lightest lifts. It is OK to select one dimension of scale to consider during an improvement cycle. It is also OK to focus on several. What matters is that it is an intentional decision.

As you make scaling commitments, the same advice we provide for action planning holds. Prioritize scaling efforts that you can adopt in the next four to eight weeks. The waters outside that time frame are murky, uncertain, and constantly churning. This horizon is the most manageable and where you can most likely predict outcomes with the greatest success.

Expect the Unexpected

One of the most predictable challenges that System Wise teams face when scaling Data Wise is the possible transitions of team members—especially senior leadership. Like any comprehensive reform effort, integrating Data Wise across a system requires five to ten years of committed practice. Given the average tenure of school and system leaders, this means that leadership and key stakeholders will change during the course of implementation.

Talented people will be promoted or move on to new challenges. When people leave, System Wise leaders are ready with contingency plans. Leaders build redundancy into roles and systematize knowledge-sharing and cross-training structures. They leverage transitions to provide stretch assignments to junior leaders in order to ready them for more senior roles in the future. The goal is not a seamless transition (there is no such thing) but a solid plan for sustaining momentum and learning. Tricia's story provides some reflections on preparing for these three predictable transition scenarios. (See "Tricia's Story.")

While functional tasks can be reallocated, we reject the conventional business-sector wisdom that people are replaceable. The loss of a community member is a loss—even when it is for good reasons. As you prepare for the technical work of shifting team members during a transition, you also have to prepare for the relationship shifts. You can anticipate that people (including you) will feel loss, grief, anxiety, and uncertainty. System Wise leaders create space to acknowledge and feel these emotions both privately and collectively. You can also anticipate that there will be feelings of joy and pride for colleagues. System Wise leaders ensure that the contributions and humanity of those transitioning are celebrated and honored. Those who leave will define their time with you by how you treat them when they depart, and those continuing the work will look to how others are treated as they decide how they will allocate their most precious time.

If you lead this work long enough, eventually your authorizers will change. Whether it is a superintendent you report to or a board, organizations identify new priorities and new leaders have differing values. People also just get tired, and "the new" is a strategy for infusing energy into an organization. This will happen no matter how effective your continuous improvement efforts are. We are going to

Figure 8.5

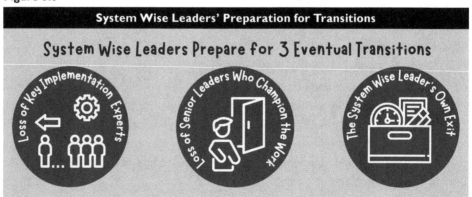

TRICIA'S STORY

Our district's efforts to improve learning through the use of Data Wise have now spanned three superintendents. Each transition meant we needed to articulate why this work mattered, why we needed it, and what we were doing. I had to adapt our implementation approach based on the different strengths of each leader. At times, learning our Data Wise work was what drove our meetings as a senior leadership team. At other times, I prioritized working directly with schools one-on-one.

Over time, as our collaborative work became the norm, district-level ownership was less important. We went from district leadership focusing on providing resources and training to focusing on ensuring that schools and teachers could protect time for improvement work and build relationships.

Our guiding team also experienced transitions each year. There were people who left who were powerful champions for this work. We're a place that supports people with growth in their careers and part of that is celebrating when effective leaders take on new challenges in new districts. When people left, I ensured our hiring process centered the skills that team members would need in order to scale our improvement work. This included leading the hiring committee and ensuring we asked all candidates about their experience using data and assessments. We drilled into both what they used and how they used it. When onboarding new senior leaders, as the assistant superintendent and their supervisor, I had to learn that they needed similar support as new teachers. I adjusted my priorities to provide more time for observation, providing feedback, conducting instructional rounds together, and mentoring. All new leaders meet with me every other week for informal conversations about the work.

These days I think a lot about what it will look like to sustain this work beyond my leadership. I know I need to build our bench of coaches. My focus is on current teachers and teacher leaders in these efforts, as I know they will be our future principals and assistant superintendents when I am gone. This work can weather the storms of leadership change when the focus is on supporting and empowering teachers. We hold focus groups to hear from both folks who support change efforts and those who are critical of them. My job is to harness my passion for the work so that it will sustain me, but to do so without coming across as angry to team members who do not share my same passion.

—**TRICIA CLIFFORD**
Massachusetts, United States

assume that, like us, you believe that the practices captured in this book describe how equitable organizations improve strategically. You believe that this is the work that should happen in your organization regardless of priorities. If so, you, like all System Wise leaders, should have a strategy for how you will proceed when trying to do this work with differing levels of authorization. Decide what your approach will be when you have leadership that champions continuous improvement, leadership that is neutral, or leadership that is openly hostile to this practice.

Effective long-term leaders become strategically multilingual. They learn how to communicate about improvement work in a way that aligns with the values and priorities of the day. Like the work of teaching and learning that happens in schools, Data Wise is complex. It is a multifaceted approach that gives you an opportunity to prioritize various aspects based on your community and context. Different facets are of different value to different stakeholders. System Wise leaders connect the relevant facet to the values of their stakeholders. Those seeking greater coherence across their system and those seeking local decision-making and autonomy have embraced the Data Wise habits, processes, and practices. This is why the work of aligning improvement efforts to the priorities of key authorizers that we first shared in chapter 1 is a "forever task." Regardless of framing or leadership priorities, effective champions can move improvement work forward that advances equity through the ACE Habits of Mind. For this reason, we began each chapter with an analysis of the values embedded within these habits at each step of the process. Consider the ACE Habits your touchpoint when you champion this work during more challenging times.

System Wise leaders know that someday they will no longer lead the work. So they have thought through how the organization can handle their departure, whether planned or sudden and unexpected. In either case, developing a written plan in collaboration with other leaders is a best practice. Part of that plan is coming to peace with the fact that the work will continue differently without you.

Manage the Change Process

 Most change efforts begin with an urgent problem. A team has a common experience or shared data point that is of concern because it is not aligned with the organization's mission and vision. Worse yet, the team might acknowledge that current systems or structures are actually causing harm. System Wise teams engage in our data inquiry cycle with great expectation that committing to the ACE Habits of Mind and strategic tasks will move them to solutions capable of addressing their urgent problem. If you have been able to work with integrity, you can find yourselves exhaling with relief as you get to Step 8. This moment is special and an opportune time to reflect and celebrate the intentional focus on shared goals and initial outcomes. Yet, System Wise teams understand that there is no finish line.

The journey of continuous improvement can be long and difficult. Therefore it is necessary to pause and take a collective cleansing breath to reenergize the team. System Wise teams create intentional spaces for team and organization-wide celebratory exhaling. This time of reflection and celebration reinforces the relentless focus on evidence by

Figure 8.6

capturing individual and collective learning. (See figure 8.6.) Teams are motivated to persevere when they see that their work has value. We recommend that your reflection and celebration include the following prompts:

- What do we see now that we didn't see before?
- In what ways did we take risks and experiment with leadership moves?
- What advice do we have for our future selves?
- How have our relationships with people, process, and content shifted?

These reflection prompts reveal learning in a manner that perpetuates movement rather than awards completion or status. Surfacing your learning is a data collection activity, and the evidence collected can build momentum and trust.

While creating a sense of urgency is a first step when embarking on a change initiative, continuous improvement cycles are not about fighting fires. It is true that in many aspects of the work of system leaders, there will be a need to respond to urgent matters. But working through a deliberate improvement cycle ensures that you have some protected time to think strategically and proactively create strategies to meet visionary goals even as you also handle anticipated concerns. Now is the time to deepen your values for inquiry, curiosity, and perseverance through iteration and systems-level learning. Deirdra's story shows the power of taking time to reflect deeply on learning. (See "Deirdra's Story.")

DEIDRA'S STORY

We have nearly thirty schools in our system, and at the time I became the deputy superintendent, we didn't have a systemwide school improvement process. Each school engaged in planning differently, depending on how the state accountability system classified its improvement status, which meant that, across all our schools, teacher teams did not have a consistent approach to using student assessment and learning data during their meetings.

To address this clear problem, we implemented a three-year phase-in process to ensure all school leaders learned the Data Wise improvement process. We started with those the state deemed in need of improvement, followed by middle schools, then all schools. We mandated that a principal plus one other staff member engage in ongoing professional learning about the process, and our guiding team (who was also engaging in Data Wise to improve our own work) used the Data Wise rubric to assess how each school was progressing. We collected baseline data against the rubric during their initial year, and tracked changes over time in how school leaders responded to questions such as "How well have you been supported?" and "How comfortable do you feel leading the process?"

We also regularly reviewed the notes that teams wrote in their meeting agendas. That is where the most powerful data have come from. There is a school where, early on, meeting notes showed that the school leader was asking a lot of clarifying questions, which seemed to indicate confusion. We now see that the leader was asking more insightful questions, arriving at more meaningful action steps connected to instruction, and has higher levels of ownership.

I've found that celebrating success and managing the change process can go hand-in-hand. Following guidance from *Strategy in Action*, we have teams give real evidence for what they should start, stop, continue doing, and tell us *why*.[4] When they get specific about why they need to continue doing certain things, I find that they learn more about their assets and strengths. With a heightened consciousness of why they are being successful, they are empowered to keep pushing forward to try new things.

—**DEIDRA JOYNER**
Delaware, United States

Practice Radical Inclusivity

 As discussed in previous chapters, committing to radical inclusivity is an intention to address systemic inequities that perpetuate along the lines of race, gender, socioeconomic status, and other sociopolitical categories. Our commitments to action have provided recommendations to support organizations in shifting toward a more inclusive culture. In Step 8, we want to ensure that our intentions have in fact delivered their desired impact. Yes, we are concerned about the shared goals explicitly linked to the learning core and the ultimate impact on student outcomes. However, we also want to reflect on the actions and implementation practices that support the development of an inclusive culture.

Many organizations in the business, health and wellness, and education sectors have created an organization chart to illustrate the traditional hierarchical system of leadership and workflow. Top executives, including the chief executive officer, chief financial officer, and now even a chief equity officer, are positioned at the top of the chart and are referred to as the "C-suite." We recommend that your team consider a new C-suite organizational chart as a reflection tool. Here, C-suite means *collective.* (See figure 8.7 on p. 180.)

Most organizational charts fail to include students and families, yet the work of creating a radically inclusive, data-rich culture means prioritizing and centering these voices. As you reflect on your progress, consider the opportunities you may have taken to mirror this collective-suite org chart by including voices that have been previously excluded. What value has this added to your process? How might you share responsibility for progressing toward your goal? How will your data collection methods inform your next data cycle? It is important to acknowledge, celebrate, and advance the work of developing a radically inclusive culture. (See "Carolyn's Story.")

Figure 8.7

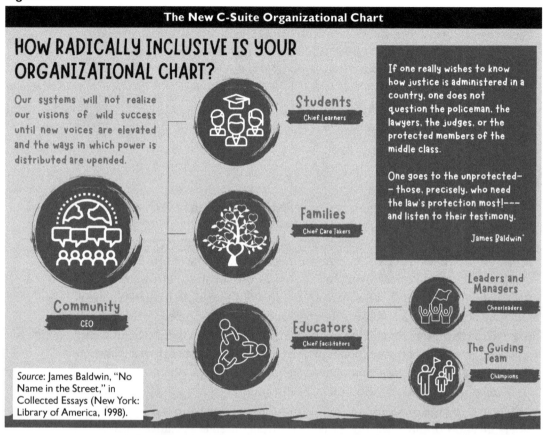

The New C-Suite Organizational Chart

HOW RADICALLY INCLUSIVE IS YOUR ORGANIZATIONAL CHART?

Our systems will not realize our visions of wild success until new voices are elevated and the ways in which power is distributed are upended.

Students — Chief Learners

Families — Chief Care Takers

Community — CEO

Educators — Chief Facilitators

Leaders and Managers — Cheerleaders

The Guiding Team — Champions

If one really wishes to know how justice is administered in a country, one does not question the policeman, the lawyers, the judges, or the protected members of the middle class.

One goes to the unprotected—— those, precisely, who need the law's protection most!——— and listen to their testimony.

James Baldwin*

Source: James Baldwin, "No Name in the Street," in Collected Essays (New York: Library of America, 1998).

CAROLYN'S STORY

 A big part of my work is establishing strong, long-term relationships, co-constructing a vision for new ways youth can experience school, and developing plans for how our district partners can achieve that vision. We worked with a state team that sought to use continuous improvement practices to strengthen its school turnaround process. As we implemented the plan for the work, I noticed that there were different understandings among state, district, and school leaders about how each group defined improvement.

This led to different stakeholders seeing or not seeing the purpose of various parts of the plan.

Bringing people back to the shared *why* rooted in their vision was critical to moving forward. This allowed us to examine actions and make adjustments. When teams that were used to an "already knowing what we need to work on" culture struggled with the slower pace of looking at broad sources of evidence, we created space for the group to realize how the additional time increased trust and empowered them to solve their own problems instead of reacting to system demands.

We also used the shared *why* to help remove work that was not as purposeful. State improvement structures were making schools complete multiple plans that were somewhat duplicative and that oftentimes did not center strategies for improving learning. While the current template is still a work in process, we were able to help remove some of these redundancies by getting all stakeholders to agree on a shared definition of what needs to be true in order to support student learning. The improvement template we designed was built to address pain points that school leaders elevated in empathy interviews. It was then refined through codesign and feedback sessions with the school teams responsible for completing the school improvement plans and in partnership with state leaders. By listening to those doing the work, this effort was focused on changes that would make the jobs of educators simpler and more effective.

Describing the current state with evidence is only powerful if you do the work to set a vision. The shared *why* inspires people to act in order to get closer to the vision. We can do our best to create and implement plans, and the plan can still end up getting in the way of achieving our vision. Getting school leader and teacher voices at the table throughout implementation helped us see what needed to be true for our plans to work as intended.

—**CAROLYN CHEN**
Massachusetts, United States

CASE STUDY REVISITED

Jasmine prioritizes communicating to all stakeholders the importance of the work of creating an inclusive, data-rich culture focused on student learning.

It helps that the school board had engaged in some of the early data analysis work with the guiding team and that Jasmine had regularly shared with them updates on their inquiry process and the learning it generated. The board invites the guiding team to suggest interview questions and tasks for superintendent candidates and has guiding team members sit on the interview committee. They even have finalists complete school learning walks with guiding team members and discuss their insights using the I Notice/I Wonder Protocol.

At the same time, the assistant superintendent shares her optimism with the guiding team: "The power of this work comes from its ability to apply to any initiatives that come our way or that we identify a need for through evidence. We have built a way of working that will support any new leader who enters instead of creating barriers." She continued, "And the Data Wise knowledge and skills are distributed across teacher teams within the system. Our most important next step is to share our journey so far with the incoming superintendent and to engage them in our next inquiry phase."

✳ ✳ ✳

Charlie and Jasmine have a brief check-in. "We have been on quite the journey. How do you feel?" asks Charlie.

"I have to be honest, though we are technically on Step 8 of the process, I feel like I am ready to get started!" says Jasmine. "I have learned so much about the process and about my team. Not to mention, I learned so much about myself and how I learn. I should probably be exhausted, but I feel more prepared than ever for whatever is coming."

Charlie couldn't help but smile. "I can relate. People would say things like, 'Just trust the process,' but I didn't have a personal reference for that quote until I began coaching. The process can be trusted."

REFLECTION QUESTIONS
1. Who benefits from our actions? Who does not benefit, and what are we going to do about it?
2. How well did we connect to our shared *why* as we executed our action plan?
3. What did we learn about improvement and equity?

CONCLUSION

A SCALING STORY

If you have read this far, you have likely anticipated you wouldn't find an actual conclusion here. You realized this book is intended to get you to the beginning of this work.

Our challenge as authors has been to share with you the tools and approaches that have been successful as teams attempted the noble, important, and challenging work of scaling an instructional improvement practice like Data Wise that is focused on building equitable schools. If any part of the book makes it seem this work is easy, remember it is not.

In this final chapter, we aim to drive this point home by turning the mirror on the Data Wise Project itself. So we will share some stories of where we stretched, where we stumbled, and how we used our values to steer us toward our shared *why*, which is *educators collaborating so each learner thrives*.

When we lived these stories, the term "System Wise" did not exist. But as we look back on our experience, we realize that we were learning our way toward four components of what we now call the System Wise approach.

ATTEND TO DIMENSIONS OF SCALE

First thing to admit: when we published *Data Wise* in 2005, scale was the furthest thing from our minds. We were deeply concerned that the focus on high-stakes assessments would exacerbate the inequities in schooling and economic outcomes that were widening each year. We wanted to share the fruits of the two-year collaboration among nineteen researchers and practitioners that Harvard Graduate School of Education (HGSE) faculty member Richard Murnane had convened. We hoped that our call to give teachers the leading role in instructional improvement would resonate beyond our campus, but we didn't have any plans to expand our teaching beyond the one degree-program course we offered at the HGSE for twenty to thirty participants each year.

And yet, as of the publication of *System Wise* nearly two decades later, we have five books, a massive open online course (MOOC) that has enrolled over 150,000 people, a professional learning portfolio that has served over 6,000 educators, and a coach development program that has certified over 150 Data Wise coaches on four continents. These members of our community influence the learning of millions of students around the world. How did this ecosystem come into being?[1]

Part of the answer is that we had colleagues who encouraged us to *attend to scale*. Our first step in this direction was to offer our course each summer to a hundred practitioners willing to come to Harvard's campus. When we studied how alumni from this program had integrated Data Wise into their daily work, we were inspired by how many had used the process to improve teaching and learning. But we also learned that although the process may have looked easy in the book, educators really struggled with organizing for collaborative work and examining practice. To offer some strategies for dealing with these particularly messy steps of the process, we wrote *Meeting Wise: Making the Most of Collaborative Time for Educators* and *Key Elements of Observing Practice: A Data Wise DVD and Facilitator's Guide*. As we integrated these resources into our professional learning program, we realized that teaching people how to use data wisely was even more complex than we had originally thought. It seemed that the only way we could do right by our learners was to continue our intensive and interpersonal teaching approach.

Around this time, some HGSE colleagues invited us to participate in the Scaling for Impact institute that they were hosting on campus. When we learned about Coburn and Dede's scaling framework at their institute, it was like someone turned on the lights.

Until then, we had understood scaling to be about getting *bigger,* and we were hesitant to embrace growth for growth's sake. Discovering that scaling could involve depth, sustainability, spread, shift, and evolution helped us see that scaling didn't mean we needed to water down our model in an effort to serve more people. So we began working toward scale in all its dimensions, and this is what happened.

 DEPTH. A group of school-level educators who embodied the ACE Habits of Mind and had participated in our institutes came back to us "on fire," about describing the way the Data Wise process had transformed teaching and learning in their schools. Some system-level leaders were similarly on fire about the potential of a teacher-centered approach to guide improvement more broadly. When we brought these passionate educators together to serve on the teaching team for our weeklong institute, we found that iron sharpened iron. In the crucible of living our dawn-to-dusk commitment to our participants and one another, team members learned together about how to effectively coach others in the messy work of improvement. From this insight, the idea of developing a coach certification program was born. No, we wouldn't look for a way to give "Data Wise lite" to lots of people. We would instead invest in creating a cadre of coaches who would feel authorized to replicate our highly relational teaching approach with depth and integrity.

SUSTAINABILITY. Developing a coach training program meant that we could offer schools and systems a strategy for making the work live on in their own settings. Systems that invested in having one or more of their own educators engage in the yearlong certification process wouldn't need to keep sending people to our campus. And as our Data Wise coach network expanded, we were comforted to know that we had built enough expertise at Harvard and beyond that the work we were doing did not depend on any one individual.

SPREAD. When US school systems like those in Boston and Prince George's County committed to developing their own in-house coaches, they worked directly with many more schools than we had any hope of serving from our campus. When we released our *Introduction to Data Wise* MOOC, coaches had a free resource that they could offer to all of their schools and systems. And once educators in Australia, Brazil, Chile, China, and Colombia became certified, teachers and leaders from these countries could learn the Data Wise improvement process from someone who could contextualize their experience. Two examples: our first coach from Australia wrote a book with colleagues from her school that taught assessment literacy using examples from Victoria; our first coach from Brazil translated *Data Wise* into Portuguese and created materials from his own school's improvement work that showed that *sim, Data Wise pode acontecer aqui.*[2]

SHIFT. Those of us based at Harvard started to see our role shifting. We were spending most of our time facilitating educators in assuming ownership of the work. Our most useful teaching materials included student work, teaching videos, and candid testimonials from people in the field. When any number of us gathered—to deliver professional learning, create a resource, or engage in an equity workshop—we felt a kinship with others whose commitment to action, collaboration, and evidence resonated with our own. So we engaged with members of our "Data Wise family" as co-evaluators, codesigners, and co-scalers. And when members of our coach network founded their own organizations focused on teaching continuous improvement, we viewed them as partners, not competitors.

 EVOLUTION. We found new ways to tap the Data Wise Coach Network and our advisory board to help integrate educators' adaptations into our materials and courses so that we could share innovations back in the field. This very book and all the stories in it are examples of how Data Wise has now become what our community of learners has told us they need it to be.

✳ ✳ ✳

Looking back, it is easy to make it sound like each step along our scaling journey was obvious. But the truth is that we were unsure at every decision point about *how* to scale. And at the same time, we were also transforming *what* we were offering. Political and cultural shifts and growing racial opportunity gaps in education were pointing to a need to integrate a more explicit equity lens into the Data Wise framework. This brought its own challenges, as Candice's story illustrates. (See "Candice's Story.")

CANDICE'S STORY

As the director of Data Wise research, I am responsible for making sure that, as a project, we are always cultivating the habit of mind of maintaining a relentless focus on evidence. I do this by both studying how Data Wise is being used in the field and collecting evidence about our own practice so that we can make adjustments.

The last several years presented a deep challenge and opportunity for our Data Wise leadership team to live our values and act based on the evidence we were hearing from participants in the

United States and around the world. There was increased consciousness about the impact of historical inequities that caused us to confront questions we were getting from our coaches and colleagues in the field. We began to ask, could we use a collaborative improvement process to face issues of implicit racial bias in schools? Could we talk directly and honestly with one another about systemic injustices that led to our schools not serving all students well? How could we be more explicit in naming our value that we believed every single learner should have access to an equitable and supportive learning environment?

Honestly, early on it felt frustrating that people didn't see the connections between Data Wise and equity, because it was so clear to *me*. As a woman of color and the daughter of immigrants, I tend to question systems that only work for some groups and not others. It was hard to hear that we were not doing enough, but our learners were telling us that the equity content felt "added on" at the beginning. These data were hard to ignore. By listening over time to the perspectives of our teaching team, coach candidates, and school teams—at times through tears and deep emotion—we were able to center new questions, elevate different stories, and create tools that allowed us to explore how identities, culture, and beliefs show up in our practices and decision-making. We tapped the deep experience of people inside our coach network and embraced learning from texts like *Street Data* and *Unconscious Bias in Schools*.[3] Now, we feel much closer to a point where "the equity lens" is truly embedded at each step of Data Wise.

When I first became involved with Data Wise, we were building a team that was skilled at using evidence for continuous improvement. But when we realized we needed to shift to talking directly about race, power, and the sociopolitical environments that impact schools, we had to look at new kinds of evidence and find new ways of talking about it.

—**CANDICE BOCALA**
Massachusetts United States

EXPECT THE UNEXPECTED

The next thing we have to admit is that, for at least the first fifteen years, our team at the Data Wise Project never uttered the words "expect the unexpected." But the unexpected just kept happening anyway.

In particular, a global pandemic swept the earth, threatening health and disrupting teaching and learning in every classroom, in every school. Before we could even wrap our heads around the loss of life and well-being caused by COVID-19, a man named George Floyd was brutally murdered in the street by a police officer in Minneapolis, leading to a long-overdue racial reckoning in the United States and countries around the world.

To cope with these unexpected events, we discovered that we needed to become tightly attuned to emotions and the need for healing. This meant learning how to recognize and express our own emotions and then use them to connect us to our broader Data Wise community. We also needed to open our hearts to new lessons that these events could teach us. The inequities that we were hoping to confront with Data Wise ran deeper than we had even realized. Jae's story highlights the importance of being aware of the weight that people can carry based on their identities and how that impacts how they work. (See the sidebar "Jae's Story.") For some, working to assimilate to the norms of the dominant culture limits the depth of the teaching they do and learning experiences they can create for others.

JAE'S STORY

I thought I understood the habit of mind of a shared commitment to action, assessment, and adjustment, but cochairing Data Wise Coach Certification during the pandemic helped me understand it even better and become more confident as a coach and instructor.

We had a virtual coach network event scheduled for the end of March 2020, when the world first shut down. As facilitators, we knew we had to throw out our whole lesson plan for the session and just be responsive to the moment, because our hearts were aching. When my cofacilitator began the event by inviting us all to take three deep breaths, it felt so right: we were a community, and we needed each other. I brought this lesson with me and adjusted my plan in another class I was teaching to borrow this strategy. I learned that putting aside my plans to care for my colleagues and students first was an adjustment that did not put us behind. Instead, the pause allowed us to become stronger as a community, which prepared us to step forward despite the uncertainties.

Another lesson I gained using the "A" ways of being from the ACE Habits of Mind was the power that comes from imperfection as a leader. We had coach candidates who were dropping out because of the difficulty adjusting to the new normal. I remember speaking with a coach candidate who told me about the challenges she was having in identifying which team she would coach as part of her certification process. But then we shifted to talking about her role as a mom and trying to manage work while also caring for her son. Normally, I would have kept us on track with our agenda. Also, I would have known how to support a struggling candidate and would have offered some advice and strategies to help her.

However, things were different during the pandemic. I was as clueless and helpless as she was, with similar challenges as a working mom. I decided to put aside my *professional self*, who wanted to do my job well, and be my *full self*, to connect with her. I told her that I was also struggling, feeling lost and behind. I wanted her to know that I understood what she was going through. I had never had to show the nonprofessional side of me until that point, and this led to me building a different type of relationship. Seeing that this other part of me was also viable, it made me, as a non-native-English-speaking immigrant, have more comfort to bring myself to the work.

I didn't expect that not trying to be perfect would release so much anxiety for me. I also learned that not being perfect in my role also brings connection with others. Now, I'm able to admit to making mistakes when I don't know certain words. Before I used to always use scripts to talk to be perfect.

It's so interesting; one of my colleagues saw me presenting a couple of weeks ago and shared that I seemed much more comfortable in my teaching role now than I had been before. I like that being me makes me a better teacher.

—**JAEIN JOSEFINA LEE**
Massachusetts, United States

MANAGE THE CHANGE PROCESS

Looking back, one thing we did as we scaled Data Wise was think deeply about how we would manage the change process. We knew we needed to be *responsive to relationships* since people are the core of what we do. We also thought about how to engage a broad set of stakeholders inside and outside Harvard to *champion the change* that would allow each learner to thrive. We developed an elaborate data dashboard in an effort to *map the movement*, only to discover that our fancy interactive graphics weren't enough to help us chart our course. Instead, we needed to invest comparable time in collecting stories about what it looks, sounds, and feels like when educators from a wide variety of contexts act for equity. And through it all, we tried to *attend to power*, which as Cate's story shows was mostly about resisting positioning ourselves as the Harvard experts and instead doing our best to be good partners. (See "Cate's Story.")

When I think about engaging with systems as the portfolio director for Data Wise, I go back to my *why*, which is helping people be as effective as possible in their work. I try to always remember that we're collaborating with systems on one particular aspect of their much bigger ecosystem. What may seem simple and straightforward to me as an outsider may be more complex to the partner as they consider their broader context. I go into conversations just trying to be a good thought partner. I want to listen and learn and help them improve. I feel privileged to get to know educators in different parts of the world and connect people as they work through challenges.

When we partner with other organizations to help us deliver Data Wise content, I like to identify our shared goal. Some of it is calibrating to make sure we are moving in the same direction, but always there is this sense that we are all in this bigger work together. We have the lane that we are in, but if I can share something that is going to be helpful in another dimension of a partner's work, I'm going to do that.

We have teams who make significant investments in our programs; thus, they want to see impact and bring learning to scale. Scale can feel intimidating because people think scale is *big*. But that's not quite it. You might take one part of the work and deepen that and do it really well. Whatever you do today is not what you have to do forever. I often share something Candice said that really helps teams manage their performance anxiety as they try to implement this learning and change process: "The goal is not to implement Data Wise with 'fidelity' because you are always adjusting and modifying it to make the process work for your organization."

I've found this framing helpful because it allows teams to release themselves from the pressure of having to get it right, a mindset that can prevent them from making the adaptations needed for a successful experience. When I get overwhelmed in my own life, I take a step back. So when systems feel overwhelmed, I try to help them make sense of things from a big-picture point of view.

—**CATHERINE GARDNER**
Massachusetts, United States

PRACTICE RADICAL INCLUSIVITY

Let's go straight to Kathy's story here, in the hope that storytelling can best convey our learning about what radical inclusivity can feel like. (See "Kathy's Story.")

KATHY'S STORY

Our early efforts to integrate an equity lens fell short in part because I made an error that I had spent years teaching others to avoid: mistaking an adaptive challenge for a technical one. We realized that we needed a bigger, more diverse team that could learn its way into a new way of teaching about improvement. Thankfully, Candice was willing to co-lead this effort and Jae committed to joining us for the long haul. We engaged a teaching team of racially and socioeconomically diverse graduate students and practitioners who were passionate about building schools where each student thrives.

But guess what? The deeper we went, the harder the work became. At first, our new members were hopeful, but many were deeply disappointed as the institute unfolded. Some were dismayed that in a weeklong institute focused on equity, there was no acknowledgment of the news headlines about deep injustices. Others believed that the best way to work for equity was to stop wringing our hands about what to *say* about equity. Instead, we needed to focus on equipping participants and coach candidates with the collaborative inquiry skills that would allow them to *do something* about equity back home.

It hurt to hear our own community's frustration, and it was hard to see that we didn't even agree among ourselves. There were days when my stomach would sink as I realized I had missed yet another opportunity to confront racism, homophobia, and classism. There were nights when I lay awake wondering, "Who am I to try to make a difference in such a broken world?"

One thing I did was commit to doing my own personal work. I went to every training I could find that would help me better understand my own identities and the historical and contemporary context I lived in. I needed to come to terms with how my privilege (as a white, highly educated, cisgendered, able-bodied, neurotypical, and economically secure woman) had made it so hard for me to grasp what real equity work entailed.

(continues)

KATHY'S STORY *(continued)*

We turned an important corner after Darnisa Amante-Jackson, one of our certified coaches, led a workshop for our coach network.[4] We were shifting power to our coach community, knowing that we had to trust collective wisdom. At that workshop, Darnisa helped us see we needed an "equity swoosh" that called out the equity issues at each step, and we spent the next five years hearing from our network about what that could look like. We were learning that real equity work required intentional collaboration, at a much deeper level than we had previously expected of one another.

Even so, as director of the Data Wise Project, I spent a lot of emotional energy worrying that I was doing things wrong. So I tightened up when a new student came to my office and said, "I have a lot of questions about how you are thinking about equity." I was scared to hear what he would say next and then relieved when he framed his questions in a way that helped me feel that he was coming from a place of curiosity. He was there to engage me as a learner, not criticize me as a human being. For years I had been teaching a process grounded in inquiry and encouraging others to ask each other tough questions. When I was the one being asked the questions, I developed more empathy for what that experience felt like. I think that is when I started to believe we were on the right track. We were creating an inclusive space for dialogue, and that space held hope for healing.

—**KATHRYN PARKER BOUDETT**
Massachusetts, United States

WORDS TO THE WISE

Our hope is that you will find value in the ideas shared in these pages. Although we have focused this book on scaling Data Wise, we have also used these practices to scale other instructional improvement approaches. Our partners have used System Wise concepts to scale writing programs, intervention models, and school culture efforts, to name a few. Some have even used the concepts in noninstructional areas including hiring processes and school bus routes. If your goal is to help lots of people get smarter together, these tools are for you.

Our final gift to you is the wisdom of song leader, composer, scholar, and social activist Bernice Johnson Reagon that is our touchstone when we get stuck or disillusioned in the murky waters of systemic change:

If, in moving through your life, you find yourself lost, go back to the last place where you knew who you were, and what you were doing, and start from there.

In moments when things are not going the way we hope, we return to the ACE Habits of Mind. Through these habits, we can diagnose our current state and wrestle with the gap between reality and our values. System work is values work. By engaging *your* values, your team learns how to do the things described in this book.

This is hard work.

You can do it.

Accept that you'll get stuck . . . and that returning to your values and the ACE Habits of Mind will help you find a way forward.

If, in moving through your life, you find yourself lost...

go back to the last place where you knew who you were, and what you were doing, and start from there.

—Bernice Johnson Reagon

SYSTEM WISE TOOLS

In each chapter, we introduced at least one tool to support the teams seeking to be System Wise. Our goal in this appendix is to offer resources that you can return to as you work to continuously improve instruction at scale. We provide the tools in the order referenced within the book and with additional framing and details so that they can be used independently. It can be hard to pick up a book and try to recall where the resource you want is located—we hope this appendix makes it easier for you to find what you need.

Tools for System Wise Leaders:

EXAMPLE SYSTEM WISE INQUIRY THROUGHLINES

In this example, the learners served by the leadership team are school leaders.

Table A.I

Example of Data Wise Cycle Throughline Developed by the Greenwood Leadership Team	
Focus area	School leader support of teacher teams' use of evidence to improve literacy instruction
Priority question	Why do we see so much variation in student performance across schools with so many of the same schools at the bottom levels of performance year after year?
Learning-centered problem	Based on our review of school improvement plans, observations of school leaders, and student and teacher surveys, our school leaders are effective at consistently observing teachers and providing initial feedback and the learning gap is in following up with teachers to support them in integrating feedback into their practice feedback after observations.
Problem of practice	Based on our review of professional learning plans, observations of one-to-one feedback sessions with school leaders, and conversations with them afterward, as system leaders we provide professional learning resources and time to improve school leaders' skills in providing feedback to teachers, and our next level of work is consistently seeking input from school leaders about what they need in order to ensure that feedback to teachers leads to changes in practice.
Sample action plan steps	• Conduct empathy interviews and focus groups with school leaders to get input on how to better support them with providing feedback to teachers • Integrate insights from school leaders into a revised school leader observation feedback protocol • Engage in professional learning around providing feedback to school leaders • Collect evidence described in our plan to assess impact
Example of impact goals from plan to assess impact	• **80% of school leaders agree or strongly agree on quarterly surveys** that support from the leadership team has improved their feedback practices. • **Recordings of 3 out of 3 school leaders' feedback sessions with teachers** show that school leaders follow up on how teachers are implementing previous feedback. • **Teachers' experience**: 70% of teachers in quarterly focus groups share positive feedback about their relationship with their school leader. • **Students' experience:** 70% of students in monthly pulse check survey share that their teacher can explain things in ways they understand. There is not more than a 5% gap between same and different racial groups. • **Teacher practice:** 90% of teachers in priority schools achieve a *meets* rating with 30% at an *exceeds* rating in "communicating with students" domain. • **Student learning:** Students' literacy skills improve so that 90% achieve proficiency on benchmark assessments. • **Culture:** Annual culture survey for families, students, and teachers shows system is organized for success in the "continuous learning and trust" domains. • **Sustaining shifts**: Both the school leaders union and the teachers union approve 8-hour increase in professional learning time in contract; human resources department includes a performance competency on feedback expertise as school leader hiring requirement with task, rubric, and norming professional learning.

Table A.2

Example of Data Wise Cycle Throughline Developed by the Greenwood Guiding Team				
Focus area	Scaling Data Wise across our system			
Priority question	What is helping and hindering realizing our vision of wild success?			
Symmetric learning-centered problem *These examples are of problems at multiple altitudes within the curriculum and instruction division*	**System leaders** Based on school leader surveys, our system leaders are effective at communicating priorities around collaborative learning and the learning gap is allowing school leaders an opportunity to experience it for themselves.	**School leaders** Based on school visits, our school leaders are effective at monitoring the pacing of curriculum and the learning gap is adjusting support based on differing needs of teachers.	**Teachers** Based on classroom observations, our teachers are effective at communicating what high-quality work looks like and the learning gap is providing collaborative peer learning experiences to practice giving feedback.	**Students** Students work collaboratively with peers and help each other master grade-level content.
Symmetric problems of practice *These examples are related to learning-centered problems for system leaders*	**Operations division** Based on review of meetings and emails with school leaders, we are good at sharing long-term plans for facilities improvements. Our next level of work is including school leaders in developing our strategic facilities plan.	**Curriculum and instruction division** Based on school leader surveys, we are effective at communicating priorities around collaborative learning. The next level of work is allowing school leaders an opportunity to experience collaborative learning for themselves.	**Community and family engagement division** We are good at using surveys to gather community input in multiple formats. Our next level of work is ensuring that families are also part of the teams that make sense of the survey data and identify next steps.	
Example of action steps from action plan	• Implement meeting agenda template and roles in all system-level meetings. • Provide professional learning on collaborative practices using the Data Wise improvement process and habits of mind. • Organize school leader around similar problems of practice at meetings.			
Example of impact goals from plan to assess impact	• **School leaders:** Net promoter prompt: "I would recommend Data Wise to a colleague seeking to improve collaboration and data-informed practice." • **Leading indicator:** In a random sample of 10 agendas, 9 show use of the rolling-agenda format, meeting roles, meeting norms, and plus/delta feedback. • **Mastery indicator:** 90% of instructional leadership teams complete a summary of their work for each step of the process where each artifact meets the criteria and 75% of teams complete a full Data Wise cycle within the year. • **Teachers:** Net promoter prompt: 80% of teachers are "net promoters" of our approach to improvement.* • **Students:** 80% of students agree or strongly agree with the survey prompt: "I have frequent opportunities to learn with and from my peers" • **Teacher learning:** 75% of grade-level teams complete a summary of their work for each step of the process where each artifact meets the criteria and 50% of teams complete a full Data Wise cycle within the year. • **Student learning:** Literacy benchmark scores of students taught by teacher teams implementing the practice exceed those of students taught by teacher teams not implementing. • **Organizational culture** • **80% of employees agree or strongly agree with the survey prompt:** "I feel I can effectively do my job." • **Sustaining shifts:** Continuous improvement using data continues as one of the three priorities on the annual improvement plan with an annual budget of at least $100,000 attached.			

✳ SHARED *WHY* PROTOCOL

Timing

This protocol takes sixty minutes to complete assuming a group size of five.[1] Add ten minutes for each additional group member and consider completing over two meetings.

Purpose

This protocol is for teams that are newly forming, adding new team members, or beginning their first inquiry cycle. The purpose is to support teams in *organizing for collaborative work* by learning about one another, identifying connections, and developing a shared *why*. It also helps participants cultivate the habit of mind of *intentional collaboration*.

Benefits

*   Helps team members see one another's humanity as they listen to stories

*   Provides opportunities to practice Data Wise norms, especially "speak your truth and be open to different perspectives" and "take an inquiry stance"

Goals

*   Learn why each member of the team does the work they do

*   Develop a shared *why* for the team

*   Agree on a vision for what an equitable school or system would look like

Facilitation Guidance

To prepare for the first part of the protocol, ask participants to spend at least fifteen minutes thinking about their responses to the following questions, and to come to the meeting ready to share their reflections in three uninterrupted minutes.

WHO AM I? This question invites you to reflect on your own social identities. Dimensions of identity include (but are not limited to): race/ethnicity, age, gender identity, religion, national origin, ability status, political beliefs, education level, socioeconomic status, sexual orientation, first language. For each person, certain dimensions will be more or less salient than others. Sometimes the dimensions of identity that feel most salient to you may not be the dimensions your colleagues may ascribe to you.

WHAT DO I BELIEVE ABOUT EQUITY? Here you have an opportunity to clarify how you define equity. When you hear this term, do you immediately think of racial equity? Gender equity? Socioeconomic equity? Do you see a distinction between equality, which involves treating all children the same, and equity, which entails making sure all children can reach high standards, which could involve giving students different kinds of support? What are your values and beliefs about how students learn, what role their background plays in their learning, what is possible, what is important in teaching?

HOW DOES THIS CONNECT TO WHY I DO MY WORK? This question allows you to connect to your purpose. You are working in the field of education for a reason. What is it that animates your efforts, allowing you to justify for yourself the times when you get up early or stay up late or make other choices that lean into your priorities? What actions do you take to advance your beliefs about equity? For example, how does your approach to teaching, assessment, or communication with families reflect your beliefs in action?

For the third part of the protocol, which involves describing the team's vision for an equitable school, it can be helpful to point participants to Meira Levinson et al.'s article on conceptions of equity or to share examples of how other organizations have described their vision of an equitable school.[2]

Relevant Information

It can be helpful to have sticky notes and chart paper for this activity, but it is not essential.

Steps

1. **THIRTY MINUTES:** Share personal *why* stories[3]

    a. (Six minutes)

       i. (Three minutes) While listeners silently take notes, first storyteller shares their response to these questions:

          1. Who am I? What do I believe about equity? How does this connect to why I do my work?

       ii. (Two minutes) Each listener has no more than thirty seconds to offer a connection and wondering to the story. The storyteller responds to each person by saying thank you.

       iii. (One minute) Storyteller speaks to whichever connections and wonderings they choose.

    b. (Twenty-four minutes) Repeat for the remaining four people.

2. **FIFTEEN MINUTES:** Develop a shared *why* for the team

    a. (One minute) Facilitator reminds the team that a shared *why* statement is a short (four to eight words) phrase that captures why the team does the work it does. For example, the shared *why* for the Data Wise Project is "so each learner thrives."

b. (Five minutes) Each person shares a word that they heard when people shared their stories that could be particularly important to include in the shared *why*, writes it on a sticky note, and puts the note randomly on the poster paper.

c. (Eight minutes) Participants work together to rearrange the words to see if they make sense, feeling free to add or delete words.

d. (One minute) When the statement feels right, the scribe writes it above the sticky notes on the poster paper. This is the team's shared *why*.

3. **FIFTEEN MINUTES:** Agree on a shared vision for an equitable school

a. (Three minutes) Facilitator gives silent time for team members to consider their vision for an equitable school.

b. (Five minutes) Team members go around the circle and share their vision.

c. (Seven minutes) Team members work together to create a shared vision of an equitable school. For example, for the Data Wise Project, the vision is, "In equitable schools each student is respected and celebrated for who they are, each student has access to rigorous learning opportunities, and student outcomes are not predictable by demographic data."

 **DATA WE VALUE PROTOCOL**

Timing

The protocol described here takes sixty-five minutes to complete, assuming a group size of five. Add ten minutes for each additional group member and consider completing over two meetings.

Purpose

This protocol is for teams that are newly forming, adding new team members, or beginning their first inquiry cycle. The purpose is to share individual perspectives and values regarding data in education and to find common patterns and trends. It also helps participants cultivate the habit of mind of *intentional collaboration.*

Benefits

* Gets team members to think about their beliefs on what sources of evidence matter and broaden their understanding of how different data sources provide different kinds of information

* Shows how beliefs about data dictate actions leaders take

* Provides a deeper shared pool of data that can inform team thinking and learning

* Provides opportunities to practice listening more deeply

Goals

* Participants share an artifact of a data source they use and describe how it informs their work.

* Participants identify commonalities and points of difference among the members of the team.

Facilitation Guidance

Some groups need encouragement to think broadly about what constitutes data. (See figure A.1.) They can share standardized or quantitative data sources if they truly value them and use them to make decisions. However, their data sources can also be more qualitative or emotion-based. Observation records, notes from students or teachers, and financial records are all possible data sources that people value.

Consider capturing notes on the types of evidence team members share or the value words people use when describing why the artifact is important to their work. Post photographs of the artifacts in a shared document. These data sources are ideal for identifying a system focus area or priority question rooted in evidence that is important to the organization.

Figure A.1

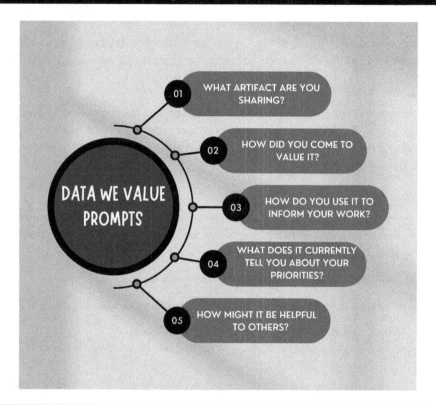

Prompts for Data We Value

DATA WE VALUE PROMPTS

01 WHAT ARTIFACT ARE YOU SHARING?

02 HOW DID YOU COME TO VALUE IT?

03 HOW DO YOU USE IT TO INFORM YOUR WORK?

04 WHAT DOES IT CURRENTLY TELL YOU ABOUT YOUR PRIORITIES?

05 HOW MIGHT IT BE HELPFUL TO OTHERS?

Relevant Information

Participants need to bring an example of the evidence source as an artifact. The artifact should be an example of evidence they use in order to do their job. Encourage everyone to bring something that they would create or use *even if their organization did not provide it*. The protocol works best when people print the artifact or take a screenshot so the artifact is easy to share.

Steps

1. **FIVE MINUTES:** Facilitator explains that each member of the group will share their artifact and their answers to five prompts about it.

2. **FIFTY MINUTES:** For five participants; add ten minutes for each additional participant:

   a. (Seven minutes) First team member responds to the following prompts:

      i. What artifact are you sharing?

      ii. How did you come to value it?

      iii. How do you use it to inform your work?

      iv. What does it currently tell you about your priorities?

      v. How might it be helpful to others?

   b. (Three minutes) Team members ask clarifying questions (the presenter can remain silent until all questions are asked and then respond to all questions at once).

   c. (Forty minutes) Repeat for the remaining four people.

3. **FIVE MINUTES:** Facilitator invites team members to reflect silently on the presentations, encouraging people to write notes about themes heard, values and beliefs about data, and places where they agreed or disagreed with others.

4. **TEN MINUTES:** Discuss the patterns you heard in the presentations.

   a. Where are we in agreement about data?

   b. Where do we see differing opinions?

READINESS GUIDELINES FOR SYSTEMWIDE INSTRUCTIONAL IMPROVEMENT EFFORTS

Table A.3

Readiness Guidelines for Systemwide Instructional Improvement Efforts		
STRATEGIC TASK	**GUIDELINES**[a]	**SOURCES OF EVIDENCE**
1.1: Establish the structures of inquiry	**System leadership support** The system leader, cabinet, and governing board have given explicit support for adoption of the initiative. The system leader or an appointee regularly communicates progress on the initiative.	• Board approval • Communications from leadership • Cabinet agendas, minutes • Strategic plan
	Vision of improvement The system-level instructional improvement team has articulated a clear vision of comprehensive improvement for teaching and learning and how the initiative fits into that vision for all stakeholders. The initiative is framed as balanced ownership rather than as a mandate or non-negotiable. The initiative is positioned to be a long-term approach.	• Organization website • Notes from agendas • Leadership communications
	Strategic plan Leadership has articulated a strategic plan (or theory of action) for achieving the vision of improvement at scale, and how the instructional initiative will help carry out that strategic plan	• Strategic plan • Organization's theory of action • Notes from agendas
	Collaborative time Leadership designates and protects time (at least monthly) for teacher, school, and system teams to engage in collaborative team work.	• Calendars • Professional learning schedules • Staff surveys
1.2: Prepare to team effectively	**Guiding team** A guiding team composed of key school improvement stakeholders with decision-making authority and diverse perspectives has been formed at the system level. This team reviews evidence of school team progress, provides support to schools, coordinates logistics and schedules, and makes adjustments to plans based on evidence.	• Team roster • Guiding team agendas • Guiding team communications
	Structures and Routines Guiding team has established structures and routines for working together, including norms of collaboration, division of responsibilities, communication strategies, task management, decision-making processes, conflict resolution practices, and meeting structures.	• Written norms in agenda • Process observer role notes • Protocols • Team org charts

STRATEGIC TASK	GUIDELINES*¹	SOURCES OF EVIDENCE
1.2: Prepare to team effectively (*continued*)	**School leadership and other school teams** School leadership teams are formed to coordinate improvement at the school level. These teams consist of a combination of school administrators, teacher leaders, student services staff members, students and families, and representatives from populations most impacted by the initiative.	• School team agendas • Surveys • Professional learning calendars
1.3: Take stock to inform scope	**Coherence of activities** Improvement initiatives (programs) are coordinated and coherent, according to the strategic plan. The number of instructional initiatives is limited to encourage focus and efficient use of time and energy. Leaders communicate the priorities, how they are connected, and what the organization can stop doing.	• Strategic plan • Leader communications • Professional learning calendars • Board meeting agendas
	Accessibility of evidence Guiding team ensures that accurate and reliable student performance data, instructional practice evidence, and information on school and system leadership efforts relating to key strategic areas are available to teacher, school, and system teams in a format that is accessible to those who need it. Data are available at the student level and can be both aggregated and disaggregated. There are consistent practices for regular classroom observation, sharing of practice, and feedback from students, peers, and leaders.	• System-level data dashboard • Student data and surveys • School-level instructional data inventory • Common walkthrough or observation instruments • Policies and communications about observation

*These criteria are adapted from the work of Koru Strategy Group, LLC, and used with permission.

Big Ideas of Data Literacy

Drawing useful inferences based upon evidence requires attending to both what the evidence suggests and the process in which it was collected. The data literate leader collects good data, engages in thoughtful analysis and develops a compassionate understanding.* Below are three concepts Data literate leaders use to improve the quality of evidence and their inferences.

What do we want to know and who will we ask?

Is this a smaller group taken from a larger possible group (of people, assessment items, etc.)?

SAMPLING
describes a choice about what to measure

Tips
- Decide if you need a representative sample to reflect a larger population or a targeted sample to focus on a specific group
- Consider who is and is not included in the sample and how it affects your inferences
- Decide what content to measure (the domain) and how much of the domain you will measure

How will we measure it?

How can we increase the integrity of our evidence?

QUANTITATIVE DATA
when the thing you want to measure can be counted, summarized, or tallied using numbers

QUALITATIVE DATA
when you want to understand someone's experiences or opinions in their own words or through observations of their behavior

Tips*
- Consider whether there is potential for participants to misunderstand questions
- Consider whether your measure requires knowledge outside the domain
- Pay attention to the context -- the "who, when, and where"-- of data collection and how that might affect responses

*With quantitative data, paying attention to these tips will increase the reliability of your measure and guard against measurement error

What do we make of the results?

Does the evidence convince me that my inferences are well-supported?

VALIDITY
describes an inference

Tips
- Triangulate with multiple and different types of evidence
- Use measures such as assessments for their intended purposes
- Pay attention to repeated themes as well as notable outliers

*See Ivory A. Toldson, *No BS (Bad Stats)* (Leiden; Boston: Brill Sense, 2019).

✳ EVIDENCE CULTURE ASSESSMENT

Purpose

Culture is often difficult to describe because it is normalized and considered "the way we do things." By explicitly describing the culture most supportive of your goals, your team can make conscious decisions aligned with focused, shared values. This tool supports teams in setting intentions for their collective work by acknowledging the values that inform beliefs and action steps.

Goals

* Reconnect with the organization's core values

* Select System Wise values that resonate and deepen understanding of shifting priorities

* Create agreement

How to Use This Tool

Before starting, provide a copy of the organization's core value statements and encourage members of the team to review the ACE Habits of Mind sections in the introduction and immediately following the case study presented in each chapter of *System Wise*.

Fill out the tool using a "community building circle" method of sharing to encourage open and honest participation. Give all team members the same prompt and go around the circle to give each person airtime to share their perspectives, experiences, and wisdom. This method is particularly helpful when the team determines evidence to support how each value is enacted across the system.

Table A.4

Evidence Culture Assessment			
CURRENT CORE VALUES	**EVIDENCE**	**SYSTEM WISE VALUES**	**EVIDENCE**
Identify 3–5 core value statements, one per row	**Collect examples of documents, practices, rituals, and routines where each value is practiced**	**Review the ACE Habits of Mind and identify 3–5 core values, one per row**	**Collect examples of documents, practices, rituals, and routines where each value is practiced**

PLANNING COMMUNICATING A VISION OF WILD SUCCESS PROTOCOL

Timing

Thirty to forty-five minutes

Purpose

To consider a storytelling strategy that would best engage members of the organization in the team's vision for wild success.

Facilitation Guidance

In preparation, gather notes and summaries from empathetic listening and consider potential barriers to understanding and engagement. Decide whether you first need to model what you mean by storytelling or if your team can get right to working through the steps.

Relevant Information

Before using this planning tool, clearly identify your audience. You may need to structure your message to meet a diverse audience or create variations of your message for specific audiences. Once you have written out your vision of wild success, consider the variety of mediums and frequency of delivery needed to ensure understanding.

Steps

1. Review story-framing types and how they support the listener
2. Review your goal
3. Determine which story frame best addresses your goal
4. Craft a story using this frame as well as traditional story elements including setting, characters, rising action, climax, and conclusion
5. Solicit feedback from others to understand the impact of the story before sharing it broadly

Table A.5

Planning Communicating a Vision of Wild Success		
STORY FRAMING	**PURPOSE**	**STRATEGY**
Analogies and metaphors	Inquiry	Make an unlikely comparison to spark curiosity and encourage the process of seeking new connections
Personification	Reorientation	Humanize ideals with negative connotations to unveil complexity and possibility
The plot twist	Renewed hope	Use what-if statements to change the narrative of the status quo
The unassuming hero	Faith	Identify an actual member of the organization and tell their heroic story as it aligns with the ACE Habits of Mind, core values, and/or vision of wild success

SENSEMAKING CIRCLE PROTOCOL

Timing

Seventy-five minutes

Purpose

To create a radically inclusive sensemaking space for reviewing evidence.

Facilitation Guidance

* Select participants from a wide range of roles, social identities, and background experiences.

* Give participants time to review evidence collected for Step 4 prior to this meeting.

* Review your core beliefs, shared norms, and other community agreements in your invitation to participate.

* Create a private physical space and place chairs in a circle. We recommend that you remove any tables.

Relevant Information

The circle protocol has several elements: welcome, mindfulness moment, opening quote, question rounds, and closing quote. These elements can be adjusted for your specific context. For example, you may have an established organizational quote that you used to unify members of your community and would support them in quickly understanding the purpose of this space.

Facilitators are participants and should answer each question posed, but they should also ensure ideas are captured and may take notes or assign a notetaker.

We highly recommend that facilitators research the origins of the practice and even participate in training to understand the full benefits.[4]

Steps

Use the following script to facilitate a circle. Adjust the prompts for your participants and time allotment.

WELCOME: The purpose of this circle is to collectively make sense of the evidence gathered. Circle is a sacred practice that honors all voices as equal and necessary. When you have the talking piece, you are invited to speak your truth, and when you do not, you are invited to listen deeply. We pass the talking piece around the circle, but you are always welcome to decline. I will facilitate our circle by prompting everyone to answer the same question. We need to find the balance between taking up space and offering space to others, so that everyone can have their speaking and listening needs met.

MINDFUL MOMENT: Close your eyes or simply look down and take three deep breaths. The goal is to fill your belly with the joys of life, taking in as much as you possibly can. Then exhale intentionally and even longer, giving of yourself knowing that what you have to offer has value.

OPENING QUOTE (SAY OUT LOUD): "A human being is a part of the whole, called by us 'universe,' a part limited in time and space. He experiences himself, his thoughts and feelings as something separated from the rest, a kind of optical delusion of his consciousness. This delusion is a kind of prison for us, restricting us to our personal desires and to affection for a few persons nearest to us. Our task must be to free ourselves from this prison by widening our circle of compassion to embrace all living creatures and the whole of nature and its beauty." —Albert Einstein[5]

ROUND 1: Please share your name, your role, and why you joined us for this time.

ROUND 2: After reviewing the evidence provided, what stood out to you the most? What did you notice? And can you explain why that item stood out to you? What lens or experience draws you to this focus?

ROUND 3: What have you heard that surprises you? What questions are you developing?

ROUND 4: What are the strengths that we can build on?

ROUND 5: What do you see as the problem that we can solve together? Why is this important to you?

ROUND 6: How was this experience for you?

CLOSING:

People in a circle
Share stories, values, dreams
Create unity
Of life ongoing
Universal wisdom
Wedded with hope
Of a world renewed
And no one left out

—Williams Tweed Kennedy[6]

MANAGING COMPLEX CHANGE THROUGH EMOTIONS PROTOCOL

Timing

About seventy-five minutes

Purpose

This protocol is for teams that are seeking to strengthen their problem of practice by examining emotional evidence from previous improvement actions. The purpose is to engage participants in the analysis of emotional insights to better understand where they may have gaps in leadership. It also helps participants cultivate the habit of mind of maintaining a relentless focus on evidence.

Goals

* Participants identify and summarize emotional evidence in order to find patterns and trends.

* Participants leverage emotional evidence in order to better understand their leadership and to build more coherent change efforts.

Facilitation Guidance

This protocol is designed for facilitators who are comfortable engaging in conversations about emotions in professional settings. It will be most effective with teams who have sufficient relational trust. Many facilitators use this protocol when the team they are working with is struggling or they have found previous improvement cycles to be ineffective.

The most difficult part of the protocol for participants tends to be Step 4, when they are required to adjust leadership action. A strong facilitator can prepare for this by building a menu of options for ways in which the team might adjust how it approaches vision setting, skill development, incentives, resources, or action planning.

Relevant Information

Participants need to be familiar with Lippitt's framework for managing complex change, which is summarized in Figure A.2.[7]

Figure A.2

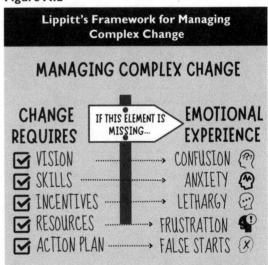

Source: Inspired by the version published in Richard Villa and Jacqueline Thousand, *Restructuring for Caring and Effective Education: Piecing the Puzzle Together* (Baltimore, MD: Paul H. Brookes, 2000).

This image summarizes the idea that the emotional experiences that people undergoing change have provided insights into the leadership supports they need. For example, if people are feeling confused, they likely need support with understanding and making sense of the vision for the change. If they are skeptical and talking about false starts, they likely need a more specific and measurable action plan.

Steps

1. **TEN MINUTES:** Review the Manage Complex Change figure (figure A.2) as a group. Discuss what you notice about the image. *Optional:* have participants discuss a time when they tried to implement change and make a connection between that change and the emotions that surfaced using the image.

2. **TWENTY MINUTES:** Reflect on previous improvement efforts within the organizations that were unsuccessful or evidence of your current improvement effort to date. Gather and examine evidence of the emotions that surfaced during those change efforts. Consider survey data from professional learning, public comment at board meetings, feedback during one-on-one conversations and town halls, and other places where people share emotional insights. Capture that evidence in the evidence column in table A.6 Evidence of Emotion Template.

Table A.6

Analyzing Emotional Experiences of Change		
EMOTIONAL EXPERIENCE	EVIDENCE	IMPLICATIONS FOR YOUR SYMMETRIC PROBLEM OF PRACTICE
Confusion (lack of vision)		
Anxiety (lack of skills)		
Lethargy at gradual change (lack of incentives)		
Frustration (lack of resources)		
Skepticism/feeling of "we've already done this"; false starts (lack of action planning)		
Confidence in sustainable change		

3. **FIFTEEN MINUTES:** Review the evidence collected in the evidence column and consider which emotions are prevalent and discuss which elements (vision, skills, etc.) might need more attention in your symmetric problem of practice. Capture your conversation in the implications symmetric problem of practice column.

4. **TEN MINUTES:** Review your symmetric learning-centered problem (see chapter 4) and review the student and teacher aspects you captured. In what ways might you need to adjust your symmetric problem of practice based on this emotional evidence? Are there additional actions that teachers need to take?

5. **TWENTY MINUTES:** Discuss the leadership aspects that surfaced in Step 3. Describe how these aspects are connected to the desired shifts in teachers and students. Write down in the left column in table A.7 what leadership moves are required by your problem of practice and the analysis of emotions for change described.

Table A.7

Planning for Symmetry at Multiple Altitudes		
What do leaders need to do differently to create the change in teacher behavior in the column to the right?	What do teachers need to do differently to create the change in student behavior in the column to the right?	What do students need to do differently in the classroom? Describe changes in task, interactions, and actions.

✳ PUSH WITH PEERS PROTOCOL

Timing

Fifteen to thirty minutes depending on how much time you have for depth.

Purpose

To predict challenges in action plan steps in order to strengthen the action plan before implementation.

Facilitation Guidance

The protocol version shared in this book includes the shortest time allocations that teams can use and still make useful adjustments to their action plans. If you are able to allocate additional time, we recommend first adding time to the probe section and then the drill section. Consider the time recommendations to be ratio guidance for how much time you have available to spend in each section. This protocol is best used when working with another team that can provide feedback and push. However, teams have also successfully used the protocol on themselves by having one team member wear the hat of presenter and the other team members role-play as various stakeholder groups. (See figure A.3.)

Figure A.3

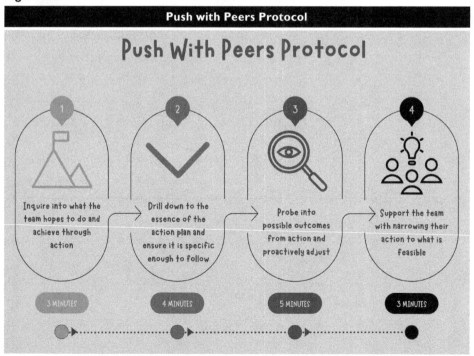

Steps

1. **ZERO MINUTES:** Ensure all participants have reviewed the team's action plan.

2. **THREE MINUTES:** Inquire.

    The presenter shares the team's problem of practice, strategy, and its action plan by answering the following prompts:

    a. What is the goal of this action plan?

    b. What concerns or challenges do we have?

    c. What actions do we plan to take? Be specific.

    d. What specific tasks do we need to complete in order to implement the actions?

3. **FOUR MINUTES:** Drill.

    The listeners ask questions in order to help identify places where the plan may be vague or relying on assumptions using prompts such as:

    a. What are some how-to steps you can take for this action?

    b. How do you . . . ?

    c. What else . . . ?

    These questions help the team ensure the plan is as detailed as needed.

4. **FIVE MINUTES:** Probe.

    The listeners then ask questions to help push on the plan to identify potential pitfalls. The following prompts can help participants ask effective questions:

    a. What barriers do you anticipate? What will you do to address these barriers?

    b. Why have ideas like this failed in the past? What can you do to mitigate?

    c. What resources or tools do you need to identify or develop to support your action?

    d. What artifacts could you bring to our next meeting to demonstrate implementation?

    e. What level of implementation depth and impact can those artifacts show?

5.   **THREE MINUTES:** Support.

    After some quiet reflection time, each listener should offer the presenter one piece of advice. While typically lots of good thinking emerges, the purpose of this step is to support prioritization as groups can rarely do everything that is raised during the protocol. Listeners can use the following prompts to provide their recommendations:

    a.   One suggestion I have is . . .

    b.   I wonder what would happen if . . .

    c.   One approach that has worked well for me is . . .

✳ IDENTIFYING IMPACT EVIDENCE PROTOCOL

Timing

Twenty minutes for each impact measure area

Purpose

To identify impact measures that are feasible and that the group feels provides insight into the effectiveness of its scaling efforts.

Facilitation Guidance

Some groups will know exactly how they want to measure an aspect of impact, and it is OK to just list those measures. This protocol is for when teams are struggling to identify a measure or have several measures that they need to decide between.

Steps:

1. **THREE MINUTES:** The facilitator selects an aspect of impact the team will focus on and asks each team member to independently write on separate sticky notes the measures they would use to understand impact in that area.

2. **SEVEN MINUTES:** The facilitator creates a graph on which the x-axis is labeled "how accurate is the evidence" and the y-axis is labeled "how difficult the evidence is to collect and analyze." See Figure A.4 for an example. The facilitator selects one measurement tool option and asks team members to show, using their fingers, how *accurate* a picture of the aspect of impact this measure would provide, with zero fingers representing not at all and five fingers representing extremely accurate. The facilitator notes the average response and then asks team members to consider how *easy* the evidence is to collect, with zero fingers representing hard and five fingers representing "we always have access to this measure, almost instantaneously." The facilitator then puts the sticky note in the place on the graph based on the team's average responses.

3. Repeat for each measurement option.

4. **FIVE MINUTES:** The team reviews the graph and confirms the placement of each sticky note. The team discusses the options in order to select the measurement source that is their best option when considering the criteria of the team's assessment of the ease and accuracy of each measure. The team writes its selection in the appropriate row of the chart in table A.8.

5. **FIVE MINUTES:** The team discusses and determines a performance level on the measure that would indicate success in that measure of program implementation. The team writes the definition of success in the chart in table A.8.

6. Repeat the protocol for additional measures of program implementation as needed.

Figure A.4

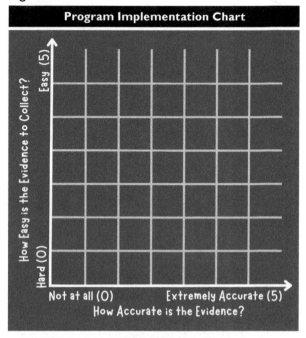

Table A.8

Impact Goals Planning Template			
IMPACT GOALS			
	WHO IS BEING IMPACTED?		
WHAT IS BEING IMPACTED?	**Learners directly served by our action plan**	**Learners indirectly served by our action plan**	**Our organization itself**
Experience (how do people feel?)			
Behavior (what do people now know or what are people doing differently?)			

✳ GROWS TO EVALUATE ACTION PROTOCOL

Timing
This protocol takes forty-five minutes to complete per group.

Purpose
This protocol is for teams that completed a round of actions and are ready to assess their progress. The purpose is to capture learning from past actions in order to facilitate the development of future actions. It also helps provide a structure for enacting the habit of mind of *acting, assessing, and adjusting.*

Benefits
* Align the group around a common story about their work

* Build collective efficacy and an evidence base that shows how effort leads to improvement

* Help the group learn what its capacity for action is

Goals
* Participants capture learning from past action in relation to the criteria for success they have identified.

* Participants select future actions based on their learning.

* Participants make transparent requests for support where appropriate.

Facilitation Guidance
This protocol is designed for teams to use as a routine each time they implement an action plan. Its value lies in repetition; that is what builds the habit of reflection.

Relevant Information
Participants need to bring their rolling action plan template and evidence of implementation to the meeting. After the first round, it can be more time efficient for team members to complete an initial draft of the "what happened" and "what we learned" columns of the rolling action plan in advance of the meeting.

Steps

1. **FIVE MINUTES:** If needed, take some independent time to review the action plan and evidence. If done in advance, read the reflections in the action plan on "what happened" and "what we learned" columns. Ask any clarifying questions about the artifacts that are available.

2. **FIVE MINUTES:** Discuss and confirm the *goals* you had for your action plan. Use the following prompts if helpful.

   — What impact did we hope to have on our problem of practice and learning-centered problem?

   — How would we describe the expected changes using our vision of wild success?

   — What "look fors" or criteria for success would be the best evidence that change occurred?

3. **TEN MINUTES:** Discuss and confirm the *reality* of what actually happened since creating the action plan. Use the following prompts if helpful.

   — What specific actions have you taken since the last meeting?

   — What artifacts from your action steps do you have to share?

   — Where did you encounter success? Where did you encounter difficulty? Why do you think that is?

   — What did you learn?

4. **FIFTEEN MINUTES:** Discuss and decide your recommendations for moving forward. Clarify what you will start, stop, or adjust within your action steps. Identify where you are stuck and where further conversation with the team might help surface *options* for how you can adjust. Use the following prompts if helpful.

   — What are some possible modifications you could make to address obstacles?

   — What actions can you take to move your practice to deeper levels of implementation and complexity?

   — What aspects of this action will you keep doing, revise, and stop doing?

5. **FIVE MINUTES:** Narrow your possible adjustments from the previous discussion to a couple that would be most impactful and are a feasible *way forward* within the next four to eight weeks. If the team struggles to narrow the adjustments, ask the other team members for advice. Team members can respond using the following prompts.

   — One suggestion I have is . . .

   — I wonder what would happen if . . .

   — Something I've tried with success is . . .

6. **FIVE MINUTES:** Discuss what *support* you will need to successfully implement the actions and from whom you need the support. Make a request for support.

If completing with other teams as a network, repeat until all teams have presented their work through the protocol.

NOTES

Introduction

1. The Data Wise Project at the Harvard Graduate School of Education offers courses and materials that support educators in collaborating so each student thrives (for more information, see www.gse.harvard.edu/datawise).

2. Michael Fullan and Joanne Quinn, *Coherence: The Right Drivers in Action for Schools, Districts, and Systems* (Thousand Oaks, CA: Corwin Press, 2015); Michelle L. Forman, Elizabeth Leisy Stosich, and Candice Bocala, *The Internal Coherence Framework: Creating the Conditions for Continuous Improvement in Schools* (Cambridge, MA: Harvard Education Press, 2017).

3. Jal Mehta and Sarah Fine, *In Search of Deeper Learning: The Quest to Remake the American High School* (Cambridge, MA: Harvard University Press, 2019); Richard Elmore, "Accountability and Capacity," in *The New Accountability: High Schools and High-Stakes Testing* (Oxfordshire, England: Routledge, 2003), 195–209.

4. Carmen Williams, "The Power of Symmetrical Structures: Cultivating Growth and Transformation to Advance System Coherence" (EdLD diss., Harvard University, 2022).

5. Ronald Heifetz and Marty Linsky, *Leadership on the Line: Staying alive through the dangers of change* (Boston: Harvard Business Press, 2017).

6. Williams, "The Power of Symmetrical Structures."

7. Peter M. Senge et al., *Schools That Learn: A Fifth Discipline Fieldbook for Educators, Parents, and Everyone Who Cares about Education* (New York: Doubleday/Currency, 2012).

8. Central office leaders in Prince George's County, Maryland, and Boston, Massachusetts, first identified this need. Meghan Lockwood, Mary Dillman, and Kathryn Parker Boudett, "Using Data Wisely at the System Level," *Phi Delta Kappan* 99, no. 1 (2017): 25–30. The Data Wise Project announced the movement to a more universally applicable process in fall 2023.

9. Elizabeth A. City et al., *Instructional Rounds in Education* (Cambridge, MA: Harvard Education Press, 2009); David K. Cohen and Deborah Loewenberg Ball, "Instruction, Capacity, and Improvement," CPRE Research Report Series RR-43, 1999.

10. In conversations with the authors July 2022, Elizabeth A. City and Adonius Lewis replace the term "learner" for "student" and "facilitator" for "teacher" in the "instructional core" to make the concept more universally applicable.

11. Thomas R. Guskey, "Gauge Impact with 5 Levels of Data," *SMEC2016 Organizing Committee* 6 (2016).

12. Cynthia E. Coburn, "Rethinking Scale: Moving Beyond Numbers to Deep and Lasting Change," *Educational Researcher* 32, no. 6 (2003): 3–12; Chris Dede, "Scaling Up: Evolving Innovations Beyond Ideal Settings to Challenging Contexts of Practice," in *Cambridge Handbook of the Learning Sciences*, ed. R. K. Sawyer (Cambridge, England: Cambridge University Press, 2006).

13. Jules Verne, *Around the World in Eighty Days* (New York: Oxford Paperbacks, 1999).

14. This framework was developed by Krysten Wendell and Adam Parrott-Sheffer in partnership with several school systems that worked with the New Teacher Center from 2017 to 2019 to build school leader networks supported with funding from the Bill & Melinda Gates Foundation.

15. The National Equity Project uses the metaphor of a lens to describe how we can begin to see our context in a different or enlightened way. A single lens or way of interpreting information will likely limit our understanding and ability to make sound judgments and decisions. System Wise teams use an equity lens when looking at data at the system level to better understand how current structures are perpetuating inequitable outcomes for students. See more on the lens of systemic oppression at https://www.nationalequityproject.org/frameworks/lens-of-systemic-oppression.

16. Edward T. Hall, *Beyond Culture* (New York: Anchor Books, 1976).

Chapter 1

1. Richard W. Scott, *Institutions and Organizations: Ideas, Interests, and Identities* (Thousand Oaks, CA: Sage Publications, 2013).

2. The concept of symmetry advances the wisdom of Jal Mehta and Sarah Fine, *In Search of Deeper Learning: The Quest to Remake the American High School* (Cambridge, MA: Harvard University Press, 2019); Richard Elmore, "Accountability and Capacity," in *The New Accountability: High Schools and High-Stakes Testing* (Oxfordshire, England: Routledge, 2003): 195–209.

3. When we refer to systems and structures, we are considering all system elements that have an impact on learning. One model we use to name these components more comprehensively is the PELP Coherence Framework. Read more about the PELP Coherence Framework at https://pelp.fas.harvard.edu/coherence-framework.

4. For guidance about setting norms, see Kathryn Parker Boudett and Elizabeth A. City, *Meeting Wise: Making the Most of Collaborative Time for Educators* (Cambridge, MA: Harvard Education Press, 2014), 73–75.

5. Simon Sinek, *Start with Why: How great leaders inspire everyone to take action* (New York: Penguin, 2011) is great, but feel free to check out the TEDx Talk to hear Simon Sinek speak directly to these ideas: https://www.youtube.com/watch?v=u4ZoJKF_VuA.

6. Boudett and City, *Meeting Wise*.

7. We typically use the Compass Points Protocol from National School Reform Faculty to identify and discuss work-style preferences. This tool can be found at National School Reform Faculty https://www.nsrfharmony.org/wp-content/uploads/2017/10/Compass Points-N_0.pdf.

8. Access the Stoplight protocol and directions at https://datawise.gse.harvard.edu/courses -and-materials.

9. Adam Parrott-Sheffer, "Intractable Conflict, Adaptable Teams" (EdLD diss., Harvard University, Cambridge, MA, 2020); Dan S. Cohen, *The Heart of Change Field Guide: Tools and Tactics for Leading Change in Your Organization* (Boston: Harvard Business Press, 2005).

10. In the launch of the guiding team, we recommend creating meeting space to identify the skills needed. A good place to start is to review the readiness guidelines in the appendix and the skills required to enact those. Teams will likely add to their list of skills as the focus of their inquiry becomes clearer. They will adjust team composition accordingly.

11. Ranjay Gulati, "Silo Busting: How to Execute on the Promise of Customer Focus," *Harvard Business Review* 85, no. 5 (2007): 98–108.

12. Ronald A. Heifetz and Marty Linsky, *Leadership on the Line, with a New Preface: Staying Alive through the Dangers of Change* (Boston: Harvard Business Press, 2017); Ronald A. Heifetz, *Leadership Without Easy Answers* (Cambridge, MA: Harvard University Press, 1994).

13. Elisabeth Kübler-Ross and David Kessler, *On Grief and Grieving: Finding the Meaning of Grief through the Five Stages of Loss* (New York: Simon and Schuster, 2005).

14. This process for attending to conflict is adapted from the negotiation expertise of Roger Fisher, William Ury, and Bruse Patton, *Getting to Yes: Negotiating Agreement without Giving In* (New York: Penguin, 2011) and repurposed as a tool for team conflict resolution.

15. Amy C. Edmondson, *The Fearless Organization: Creating Psychological Safety in the Workplace for Learning, Innovation, and Growth* (Hoboken, NJ: John Wiley & Sons, 2018).

16. A version of this protocol can be accessed at https://datawise.gse.harvard.edu/.

17. This protocol builds on work initially designed for new leaders during their entry process and expands the practice for all leaders. See Jennifer Perry Cheatham, Rodney Thomas, and Adam Parrott-Sheffer, *Entry Planning for Equity-Focused Leaders: Empowering Schools and Communities* (Cambridge, MA: Harvard Education Press, 2022) for the original version.

18. Robert Peterkin et al., *Every Child, Every Classroom, Every Day: School Leaders Who Are Making Equity a Reality* (Hoboken, NJ: John Wiley & Sons, 2011); Dr. Deborah Jewell Sherman in discussion with the authors, May 2022.

19. Beverly Daniel Tatum, *Why Are All the Black Kids Sitting Together in the Cafeteria?: And Other Conversations About Race* (New York: Penguin, 2021).

20. While we have tailored this text to focus on instructional improvement, we have seen many systems use Step 1 to organize all parts of their school systems, including operations, academics, and legal divisions.

Chapter 2

1. Chimamanda N. Adichie, "Danger of a Single Story," TED, https://www.ted.com/talks/chimamanda_ngozi_adichie_the_danger_of_a_single_story?language=en.

2. Theodore R. Sizer, *Horace's Compromise: The Dilemma of the American High School* (Boston: Houghton Mifflin, 1984).

3. Shane Safir and Jamila Dugan, *Street Data: A Next-Generation Model for Equity, Pedagogy, and School Transformation* (Thousand Oaks, CA: Corwin Press, 2021).

4. For more on the instructional core, see also, Elizabeth A. City et al., *Instructional Rounds in Education* (Cambridge, MA: Harvard Education Press, 2009) and David K. Cohen and Deborah Loewenberg Ball, *Instruction, Capacity, and Improvement* (Philadelphia: Consortium for Policy Research in Education, 1999). When speaking to system leaders, the late Dr. Richard Elmore was fond of reminding them that "if you do not see your work in the instructional core, it does not exist."

5. Inspired by author discussions with Elizabeth. A. City and Adonis Lewis, who replace the term "learner" for "student" and "facilitator" for "teacher" in the "instructional core" to make the concept more universally applicable. See also Michelle L. Forman, Tracy Fray-Oliver, and Doug Knecht, "Becoming a System of Professional Learning: Conceptualizing Improvement as a Throughline of Learning" (New York: Bank Street College of Education, 2020), https://educate.bankstreet.edu/bsec/3.

6. See chapter 2 in Kathryn Parker Boudett, Elizabeth A. City, and Richard J. Murnane, eds., *Data Wise, Revised and Expanded Edition: A Step-by-Step Guide to Using Assessment Results to Improve Teaching and Learning* (Cambridge, MA: Harvard Education Press, 2013); Daniel M. Koretz, *Measuring Up: What Educational Testing Really Tells Us* (Cambridge, MA: Harvard University Press, 2008) also has extensive information about how to interpret student assessments.

7. Organizational culture is sometimes difficult to describe because we are so entrenched in it. Zaretta Hammond describes deep culture as the mental models, core values, and belief systems of the community. Zaretta Hammond, *Culturally Responsive Teaching and the Brain: Promoting Authentic Engagement and Rigor Among Culturally and Linguistically Diverse Students* (Thousand Oaks, CA: Corwin Press, 2014).

8. David N. Perkins, "When Change Has Legs," *Educational Leadership* 71, no. 8 (2014): 42–47.

9. Multi-Tiered System of Supports (MTSS) is an intervention model that tiers supports for learners at three levels including universal, intervention and intensive intervention. Please see https://mtss4success.org/to learn more.

10. New Teacher Center, "Effective Schools Framework," NTC 2019, https://newteach-ercenter.org/resources/effective-schools-framework; "PELP Coherence Framework," Public Education Leadership Project at Harvard, 2011, https://pelp.fas.harvard.edu/coherence-framework.

11. This protocol comes from Henri Lipmanowicz and Keith McCandless, *The Surprising Power of Liberating Structures: Simple rules to unleash a culture of innovation* (Seattle, WA: Liberating Structures Press, 2013), https://www.liberatingstructures.com/24-what-i-need-from-you-winfy/.

12. Mindtools Content Team, "The Johari Window," https://www.mindtools.com/au7v71d/the-johari-window.

Chapter 3

1. The ladder of inference was developed by organizational learning scholars Chris Argyris and Peter Senge. The Ted-ED YouTube video provides a succinct and somewhat humorous explanation. Trevor Maber, "Rethinking Thinking," Ted-Ed 2013, https://www.youtube.com/watch?v=KJLqOclPqis.

2. For more support on Data Display design, see Cole Nussbaumer Knaflic, *Storytelling with Data: A Data Visualization Guide for Business Professionals* (Hoboken, NJ: John Wiley & Sons, 2015) ; Stephen Few, *Show Me the Numbers: Designing Tables and Graphs to Enlighten* (Berkeley, CA: Analytics Press, 2012).

3. Shane Safir and Jamila Dugan, *Street Data: A Next-Generation Model for Equity, Pedagogy, and School Transformation* (Thousand Oaks, CA: Corwin, 2021).

4. The first three criteria come from System Wise and our partner systems and the final criterion is adapted from Dan S. Cohen, *The Heart of Change Field Guide: Tools and Tactics for Leading Change in Your Organization* (Boston: Harvard Business Press, 2005).

5. Shane Safir, *The Listening Leader: Creating the Conditions for Equitable School Transformation* (Hoboken, NJ: John Wiley & Sons, 2017).

6. David Rock, "Managing with the Brain in Mind," *strategy+ business*, August 27, 2009.

7. Mary Northup, "Multicultural Cinderella Stories" ALA, May 2000, https://www.ala.org/aboutala/offices/publishing/booklist/booklinks/resources/multicultural.

8. Malala Yousafzai and Patricia McCormick, *I Am Malala: The Girl Who Stood Up for Education and Changed the World* (New York: Little, Brown Books for Young Readers, 2016).

9. john a. powell, Stephen Menendian, and Wendy Ake, *Targeted Universalism: Policy & Practice* (Berkeley, CA: Haas Institute for a Fair and Inclusive Society, 2019).

Chapter 4

1. Anthony S. Bryk et al., *Learning to Improve: How America's Schools Can Get Better at Getting Better* (Cambridge, MA: Harvard Education Press, 2015).
2. National School Reform Faculty, 2014, https://www.nsrfharmony.org/wp-content /uploads/2017/10/AffinityMapping-N_0.pdf.
3. For additional tools and ways to attend to altitudes within the system, see Center for Educational Leadership, "Central Office Transformation Toolkit," University of Washington Center for Educational Leadership, 2013.
4. Ronald Heifetz and Marty Linsky, *Leadership on the Line, with a new preface: Staying alive through the dangers of change* (Boston: Harvard Business Press, 2017).
5. *Undercover Boss*, CBS, 2010–2020.
6. Personal correspondence, Data Wise Leadership Institute, 2006.
7. Michelle L. Forman, Tracy Fray-Oliver, and Doug Knecht, *Becoming a System of Professional Learning: Conceptualizing Improvement as a Throughline of Learning* (New York: Bank Street College of Education, 2020), https://educate.bankstreet.edu/bsec/3.
8. Lyn Sharratt and Beate Planche, *Leading Collaborative Learning: Empowering Excellence* (Thousand Oaks, CA: Corwin Press, 2016).
9. Edward M. Kennedy Institute, "Shirley Chisholm," A Seat at the Table, https://www .bringyourownchair.org/about-shirley-chisholm/.

Chapter 5

1. Amy C. Edmondson, *Teaming: How Organizations Learn, Innovate, and Compete in the Knowledge Economy* (Hoboken, NJ: John Wiley & Sons, 2012).
2. Kathryn Parker Boudett, Elizabeth A. City, and Marcia K. Russell, "Key Elements of Observing Practice: A Data Wise DVD and Facilitator's Guide" (Cambridge, MA: Harvard Education Press, 2010) provides detailed guidance about how to be descriptive and specific when talking about practice.
3. National School Reform Faculty, 2014, https://www.nsrfharmony.org/wp-content /uploads/2017/10/AffinityMapping-N_0.pdf.
4. Laura Numeroff, *If You Give a Mouse a Cookie* (New York: Harper Collins, 2015).
5. Meredith I. Honig, "From Tinkering to Transformation: Strengthening school district central office performance," *American Enterprise Institute for Public Policy Research* 4 (2013): 1–10.
6. Dr. Mary Lippitt, D. Ambrose, and Enterprise Management Ltd., 1987.
7. A protocol similar to what Carmen designed is available in Elena Aguilar, *The Art of Coaching: Effective strategies for school transformation* (Hoboken, NJ: John Wiley & Sons, 2013).

Chapter 6

1. The rolling action plan is reminiscent of the Meeting Wise rolling agenda template that you may be familiar with. When items are completed, team members move them down to the gray section of the template so that that hard work is preserved while making space for new actions at the top of the document.
2. Richard H. Thaler and Cass R. Sunstein, *Nudge: Improving Decisions about Health, Wealth, and Happiness* (New York: Penguin, 2009).
3. Dwight D. Eisenhower, *Public papers of the presidents of the United States, Dwight D. Eisenhower, 1957, containing the public messages, speeches, and statements of the President, remarks at the National Defense Executive Reserve Conference, November 14, 1957* (Federal Register Division, National Archives and Records Service, General Services Administration, Washington, DC, 1958).
4. Early versions of this protocol were designed and developed by the School Leader Network and refined by Mariah Cone.
5. William Shakespeare, *Henry IV, part 2* (New York: Oxford University Press, 1998).
6. Robert Kegan and Lisa Laskow Lahey, *An Everyone Culture: Becoming a Deliberately Developmental Organization* (Boston: Harvard Business Review Press, 2016).

Chapter 7

1. David A. Garvin, Amy C. Edmondson, and Francesca Gino, "Is Yours a Learning Organization?," *Harvard Business Review* 86, no. 3 (2008): 109.
2. The goal in Step 7 is to decide what to change, using what measurement tool, and what performance level would demonstrate that the learning-centered problem has been substantially addressed. While it may take several cycles to reach that absolute performance level and progress on the way should be celebrated, the impact goal should describe what is needed to realize the vision of wild success, not what is needed to move the needle on learning a modest amount. Many education agencies require or recommend growth goals as part of their improvement processes. There are times when a growth goal can be framed as an absolute performance target. For example, if a system identified that its highest-performing students were not making growth targets on a particular assessment, the team could set an impact goal of 85% of high-performing students meeting growth goals on that assessment. This could show that a learning-centered problem about the learning needs of high-performing students is resolved.

Chapter 8

1. The literal translation of *sankofa* is "go back and get."
2. This model is based on similar models that have been used in coaching since the 1980s; this version revises those concepts in order to look backward at past practice instead of centering future forward practice.

3. Susie Wise, *Design for Belonging: How to Build Inclusion and Collaboration in Your Communities* (Berkeley, CA: Ten Speed Press, 2022).

4. Rachel E. Curtis and Elizabeth A. City, *Strategy in Action: How School Systems Can Support Powerful Learning and Teaching* (Cambridge, MA: Harvard Education Press, 2009).

Conclusion

1. If you are interested in joining the Data Wise community, there are many ways to connect. Sign up for our free MOOC at https://www.edx.org/course/introduction-to-data-wise-a-collaborative-process. Access our in-person and virtual courses through Harvard's Programs in Professional Education here: https://www.gse.harvard.edu/professional-education/k-12-programs/data-wise-portfolio. Finally, read more about Data Wise via our Harvard Education Press publications at https://www.hepg.org/.

2. Translation: *Yes, Data Wise can happen here.* If you want to expand access to these ideas in communities connected through other languages, let us know.

3. Shane Safir and Jamila Dugan, *Street Data: A Next-Generation Model for Equity, Pedagogy, and School Transformation* (Thousand Oaks, CA: Corwin, 2021); Tracey A. Benson and Sarah E. Fiarman, *Unconscious Bias in Schools: A Developmental Approach to Exploring Race and Racism* (Cambridge, MA: Harvard Education Press, 2020).

4. Learn more about Dr. Darnisa Amante-Jackson's work at https://digdeepforequity.org/.

Appendix

1. The Data Wise Project is grateful to Dr. Darnisa Amante for teaching us that sharing a *why* story and developing a shared version are essential first steps in building a team's capacity to work for equity.

2. Meira Levinson, Tatiana Geron, and Harry Brighouse, "Conceptions of Educational Equity," *AERA Open* 8 (2022).

3. When done on its own, this first step in the process is known in other Data Wise publications as the Equity Reflection Protocol.

4. Carolyn Boyes-Watson and Kay Pranis, *Circle Forward: Building a Restorative School Community*, rev. ed. (St. Paul, MN: Living Justice Press, 2020).

5. Walter Sullivan, "The Einstein Papers. A Man of Many Parts," *New York Times*, March 29, 1972, https://www.nytimes.com/1972/03/29/archives/the-einstein-papers-a-man-of-many-parts-the-einstein-papers-man-of.html.

6. Carolyn Boyes-Watson and Kaye Pranis, *Circle Forward*.

7. Dr. Mary Lippitt, D. Ambrose, and Enterprise Management Ltd., 1987.

ACKNOWLEDGMENTS

A t the end of our final writing retreat, the four of us gathered around Kathy's dining room table and reflected on our collaboration. An important theme of our conversation was how humbled we feel by three realizations. The first is the knowledge that the ideas we include in this book are based on what we've learned from educators around the world. Without their valiant efforts over the past twenty years to integrate Data Wise practices at the system level, we would have had nothing to write about.

The second realization is that, given the depth and breadth of the Data Wise Coach Network, there are literally hundreds of permutations of four authors who could have come together to write this book. In these alternate universes, the writing is still grounded in the ACE Habits of Mind and inspired by a shared *why* of supporting *educators collaborating so each learner thrives.* But the names on the cover are completely different. How cool is that?

The third realization is that this is by no means the final word about what it means to be System Wise. After the global Data Wise community members have had an opportunity to explore these ideas and make them their own, there will be new insights that need to be shared and new stories that must be told. Onward! Let the learning continue.

* * *

T his work would not have been possible without the *foundational leadership* of Dick Murnane and Liz City, coeditors of *Data Wise*; the *ongoing Data Wise leadership and insightful manuscript feedback* from Director of Data Wise Research Candice Bocala; the *innumerable contributions from members of the Data Wise Coach Network,* including especially Darnisa Amante-Jackson, Kentaro Iwasaki, Penny Jayne, Deirdra Joyner, Anthony King, Jae Lee, Meg Lockwood, William Marroquin, Eva Mejia, André Morgan, JJ Muñoz, Jorge Peña, Rob Wessman, and Max Yurkofsky; the *system thinking Data Wise in Action coaches* Kris Comeforo, Lisa Kingsley, JoJo Longbottom, and Anyeli Matos who were some of the first leaders to try out the ideas of this book and make them better; the *"ACE" big-picture thinking and inspired program delivery* from Cate Gardner, Jamie Ruggiero, Grace Woodward, Nathan Finch, and Dylan Marshall; the *generous and candid testimony* of the twenty-four System Wise leaders who allowed us to share their stories in this book; the *expert graphic design* by Zion Williams, the *deftly executed videography* by JJ Munoz, and the *enthusiastic support* for this book from the Data Wise Advisory Board, and the *enthusiastic support* for this book from the Data Wise Advisory Board and our colleagues at Harvard Education Publishing Group, including Jayne Fargnoli, Jessica Fiorillo, and Molly Grab.

We are also deeply grateful to *school systems,* including Boston Public Schools and Prince George's County Public Schools, for courageously pioneering Data Wise at the system level and for leading the way on developing the "Universal Swoosh," and also systems that have taught us to continue the work in new ways, including Andover Public Schools, Bedford Public Schools, Christina School District, Hartford Public Schools, Lawrence Public Schools, Logan Memorial Educational Campus, New York City Department of Education, Pennsylvania Department of Education, Mukilteo School District, and Rochester City School District. We are also grateful to *partners,* including Koru Strategy Group, Global Educational Equity Alliance, and Instituto DEEP Nexus for showing us what sustained engagements with system teams can look like, and Pursue Excellence, whose groundbreaking work launched Data Wise at the system level. We appreciate the *researchers, system toolkit developers*, and *scaling for impact faculty,* for documenting what system-level impact looks like and supporting development of the Data Wise Project's scaling strategy and to *Harvard Graduate School of Education colleagues,* including Dean Bridget Terry Long and Associate Dean Julie Vultaggio, for understanding the power of reinvesting in Data Wise research and development.

* * *

And each of us individually share our deep appreciation of these mentors, family, and friends:

- *Adam* thanks Mariah Cone, David Herrera, Colleen Oliver, Krysten Wendell, and Marishka Winters who first taught him what could be possible at scale with the right team; Deborah Jewell Sherman and Jen Cheatham for being the blueprint; Koru leaders including Monique Davis, Karen Pavlik Shoelson, Katie Skalka, Michael Stokes, and Berenice

Rodriguez for walking the walk every day; Chelsey, Nathan, and Nicky for embodying the joy that comes from learning and collaborating toward justice; Chuck Parrott, Thom and Joan Parrott-Sheffer, and Brandon Stepanek for preparing this child for the path.

- *Carmen* thanks the Jefferson Intermediate Traditional School faculty and staff for implementing Data Wise and inspiring her to continue the journey. To Kathy Boudett, Deborah Jewell Sherman, Jen Cheatham, and Monica Higgins for mentorship and opportunities to stretch as a leader. A special thank-you to her husband and children, Herschell, Zion, and Jonathan Isaiah, for unwavering support and encouragement. And to her first teachers, Pamela Harris, Allene McMorris, Pat Bailey, and Luann Bridges, for building a family legacy on strong values and faith.

- *David* thanks Marcia Edge, Sammye Wheeler-Clouse, Danette Parsley, Mike Sibersma, Liz City, and Michele Shannon, for the deep thinking, support, and encouragement they've offered personally and professionally as he became a leader in the field. He also salutes the Office of Continuous Systemic Improvement. This team dared to try something that hadn't been done before and built an incredible foundation for others to study. The years of rigorous debate, professional challenge, evidence-based reflection on practice, and real commitment to excellence modeled by each of you and the collective team is something he'll be extremely proud of forever. Felice DeSouza, Donna Drakeford, Rotunda Floyd-Cooper, Brian Galbraith, Tasheka Green, Paula Harris, Rhonda Hawkins, Trina Hayes, Niki' Newman-Brown, Elizabeth Saunders, Ebony Shields, Anthony Sims, and Jennifer Williams, know that your work continues to live, evolve, and influence. David especially thanks his nuclear family and daily support—Errol, Indigo, and Pope.

- *Kathy* thanks Liz City and Dick Murnane for launching the Data Wise family in 2002 and Ann and Gene Parker for launching the Parker Beach Club all the way back in 1964, two continually growing families, both steeped in joy.

ABOUT THE AUTHORS

Words are great (we did capture a whole bunch of them here) but we would love to connect with you and share our why via video. You can watch it at: https://bit.ly/SystemWiseWhy

ADAM PARROTT-SHEFFER, EdLD, is the strategy adviser for the Data Wise Project and cochair of the Data Wise in Action Program. He works with school, district, nonprofit, and business leaders globally to improve learning through data, to design leadership pathways with special attention to entry, and to execute strategy successfully. He teaches university and professional education courses focused on anti-racist coaching, entry for equity leaders, and change management. After teaching middle school literacy and early childhood as a special education teacher, he spent fifteen years as an award-winning principal, district administrator, school and district leader coach, and a senior adviser responsible for system leadership and impact strategy. He is a coauthor of *Entry Planning for Equity-Focused Leaders: Empowering Schools and Communities* (2022). Adam champions joyful learning, youth agency, and collaborative change as a board member of Playworks Illinois and Harvard's Data Wise Project. His most meaningful work in education is serving as a volunteer at the neighborhood school in Chicago that his children attend.

CARMEN WILLIAMS, EdLD, currently serves as the Assistant Superintendent of Instruction and Innovation in a Massachusetts public school district and the cochair of the Data Wise in Action Program. Leading with her core values of empathy, equity, and community, Carmen has supported schools and districts nationally and internationally in developing communities of practice for continuous improvement and equitable student outcomes. Carmen brings over twenty years of experience to this work as an elementary teacher, building principal, central office leader, and university instructor. She successfully led her award-winning school by implementing Data Wise and welcomes the opportunity to share and scale research-based, data usage practices that empower educators and deliver desired student outcomes. As an instructor in teacher and educational leader preparation programs, she brings restorative practices, culturally responsive teaching, and adult development together to create experiential learning spaces centered in healing, enabling collaborative work to advance academic and social goals. Carmen believes that quality education for each student is an act of justice and has committed to providing educators with structures and tools that advance equity.

DAVID REASE, JR., EdLD, currently serves as the Director Equity, Diversity, and Belonging in the Prince George's County Public Schools. Formerly, he was the Director of Continuous Systemic Improvement in the same system. In this role he led a team that built coherence in how central offices and 208 schools teams approached continuous improvement via the Data Wise Improvement Process. After teaching high school social studies for seven years, he held a series of roles that deepened his knowledge of improving instruction at scale: he credits his early-career consulting role at McREL International for igniting his passion for this work. While he has held several roles and titles, David most identifies professionally as a teacher. It is the most significant role he's held, and he brings those skills to his daily work with adult learners.

KATHRYN PARKER BOUDETT, PhD, is senior lecturer on education and director of the Data Wise Project. Her passion lies in supporting educators in collaborating so each learner thrives. She teaches degree-program courses that focus on coaching with equity in mind and using evidence and collaborative time well. She oversees the Data Wise portfolio of professional learning, which includes a massive open online course (MOOC) that has enrolled over 150,000 people from around the world, the Data Wise Leadership Institute and Data Wise in Action program, and a coach development program that has certified coaches over 150 coaches on four continents. Kathy is coeditor of *Data Wise: A Step-By-Step Guide to Using Assessment Results to Improve Teaching and Learning* (2013 in English, 2020 in Portuguese); *Data Wise in Action: Stories of Schools Using Data to Improve Teaching and Learning* (2007); *Key Elements of Observing Practice: A Data Wise Facilitator's Guide and DVD* (2010), and *Meeting Wise: Making the Most of Collaborative Time for Educators* (2014).

INDEX